What others are saying about this b

"Ms. Frank's testimony, educational programs, and her books ha
victims and policymakers alike. With this new edition of *From Victim. ... A Step-By-Step Guide for Ending the Nightmare of Identity Theft*, Second Edition with CD, Mari once again provides an excellent guide to help victims of identity theft regain their good name and peace of mind."

— **United States Senator Dianne Feinstein**

"Technological innovation has helped to form today's global marketplace where consumers can shop across the street or around the world. With these new choices, however, more consumers face the risk of privacy breaches that can make them a victim of identity theft. This condition is only exacerbated by the speed and low cost of the Internet. Attorney, Mari Frank has created an important guide to help victims avoid or mend the destructive damage of identity fraud. Her new edition of *From Victim to Victor: A Step By Step Guide to Ending the Nightmare of Identity Theft*, with CD (including steps, attorney-composed letters, logs and resources), gives consumers the critical tools and education needed to overcome the identity crises."

— **Mozelle W. Thompson, Commissioner, U.S. Federal Trade Commission**

"Identity Theft is sort of like the weather, everyone talks about it but no one knows what to do about it — Until now. Mari Frank's advice is just what all of us need to make sure we are prepared for living in this 'brave new world' of personal information and identity theft."

— **Greg Sherwood, Television Host, KQED Public Television, San Francisco, California**

"As a former victim of identity theft, I know that getting accurate information is key to victim recovery. This book contains many valuable tools that are not just time-savers but help to assert your legal rights and get your life back!"

— **Linda Foley, Co-Executive Director, Identity Theft Resource Center, San Diego, California**

"I highly recommend Mari Frank's new edition of *From Victim to Victor: A Step By Step Guide for Ending the Nightmare of Identity Theft* from a Police perspective, because there is very important information a victim needs to know to assist the Police in the apprehension, investigation and prosecution of the perpetrator. As a former Identity Theft victim myself, I recommend reading this book and using the CD with the attorney written letters because it not only contains the information and tools you need to know in order to restore your good name and your life, it tells you what you need to know to protect yourself from becoming a victim or becoming re-victimized!"

— **Clark E. Galliher, Master Police Officer, Former Economic Crimes Detective and former Identity Theft Victim, Orange County, California**

"Mari Frank's *From Victim to Victor* is a 'must have guide' for victims, investigators, and crime prevention presenters. Easy reading and educational, I've used the forms and step by step guides as an investigator, and the overall work, as an outline for community and neighborhood watch presentations in Beverly Hills. Both endeavors met with great success!"

— **Franklin F. Naumann, retired Los Angeles Police Dept. Major Frauds investigator, Los Angeles City Attorney Criminal Prosecutor, Beverly Hills Police Dept. Crime Prevention Specialist, Private Investigator and Consultant**

"No victim of identity fraud should venture near the quagmire of redemption without this book."

— **Robert Ellis Smith, Publisher, *Privacy Journal*, Providence, Rhode Island**

"For victims of identity theft who have been through an Orwellian nightmare, the book *From Victim to Victor, (Second Edition* with CD) offers a roadmap for justice, peace of mind, and restitution. You'll learn that you are not alone, and find out how to fight back."

— **Ed Mierzwinski, Consumer Program Director, United States Public Interest Research Group, Washington, DC**

"The best life saver anyone can have! A must-have for victims. Attorney Mari Frank has written the most complete, authoritative, and easy-to-follow book on identity theft. *From Victim to Victor* covers it all: where to start, how to proceed, and just the right touch of support for persons who have suffered the terror of having their identity stolen. Like a first-aid kit in your medicine chest, every person should own this mini-encyclopedia in preparedness for the probability that they, too, may fall victim to the fastest growing crime today!"

— **M. Harmon, Attorney, Chicago, Illinois**

"This book is fantastic for aiding the victim of the credit fraud nightmare. This helps them to clear up credit problems that result from a daily dreading of opening mail and receiving phone calls from collection agencies. It also greatly assists the victim in coping with the mind-numbing realization of how easily a company will believe the impersonator and how difficult this same business becomes when dealing with the identity fraud victim."

— **Detective Judd A. Levensen, Fraud Investigator, Springfield, New Jersey Police Department**

"With *From Victim to Victor* (Second Edition), victims now have an opportunity to put their lives back together. This is a giant step forward in the fight against fraud."

— **Jane Y. Kusic, President, White-Collar Crime 101, Morgantown, West Virginia**

"Spooky stuff this identity theft. Ms. Frank's book *From Victim to Victor* and its CD lead you from nightmares to memories, from sleepless nights to peaceful slumber. It takes you step by step beyond the horror of ID Theft, leaving you with eyes wide open, not with horror, but with understanding and empowerment. Packed full of information, tips, contacts and emotional support; it is vital for the victim, an absolute must for those who want to protect themselves."

— **Jerry C. McNeal, President, LB Consumer Credit Services, Hershey, Pennsylvania**

"Attorney, Mari Frank, has given us the best available information on protecting our identity from risk and harm. She guides us through the steps that take us from 'Victim to Victor.' She teaches us how to protect ourselves from identity thieves, and how to fight back should someone steal our credit or identity. This is without any doubt the most useful and valuable information of its kind anywhere."

— **Jeff Levy, Host of syndicated talk radio program *Jeff Levy On Computers*, Los Angeles, California**

"*From Victim to Victor* has useful sample letters to write to everyone from Experian and TransUnion to banks, the U.S. Passport office and the Department of Motor Vehicles. It gives an effective step-by-step guide of what to do and how to safeguard yourself."

— ***Los Angeles Daily Journal*, Los Angeles, California**

"It saved my life and sanity!!! If you are a victim of identity theft, suspect identity theft, or want to be proactive in protecting yourself against this crime wave of the millenium, this book MUST have a spot close to your local emergency numbers!!!"

— **Edwin Walters, Identity Theft Victim, San Francisco, California**

"Ms. Frank has produced a valuable, informative guide book which outlines what steps should be taken by the victim of identity theft to get their credit and identity back in line."

— **Thomas L. Burke, Retired Senior Investigator, Ventura, California Police Department**

"Ms. Frank's book *From Victim to Victor* is the next best thing to having your own expert coach guiding you through the steps to financial recovery."

— **Beth Givens, Director of the Privacy Rights Clearinghouse, Author of *The Privacy Rights Handbook***

What victims are saying:

"When my attaché case was stolen, Mari Frank came to my rescue. With her advice, those telephone calls and letters established firewalls at my bank, with credit card companies, with the credit reporting agencies, etc. She saved my identity, credit rating, reputation, and 'life.' This fascinating book is *highly* recommended."

— **Dan Poynter, author of *The Self-Publishing Manual***

"Thank you so much for authoring this book, the form letters are invaluable, a truly wonderful resource. When frustration, anger and panic set in, it's very difficult to set down your needs in a logical, businesslike letter."
   — **CR, Chico**

"I've been blundering through this identity theft mess for over two months and have made a few mistakes due to a lack of guidance. Your book has helped in so many ways, it's so comforting to have an outline and a logical way to proceed. I feel armed to take the action needed now. I also want to thank you for all the time you gave me to re-assure me and lend your expertise."
   — **BB, New York**

"I am so grateful to you for going through this pain to pass on your experience. I am a victim and your letters and steps have been a life saver. I hope people will appreciate what you are doing and trying to achieve. If I was Pope, I definitely would have recommended you for 'sainthood'; if I was king of England I would have recommended you for 'knighthood'; since I am none of them and an ordinary human being all I can say is, 'Thank you for enlightening, educating, and helping us."
   —**J.J., Virginia**

"I have been really aided by your publication and the letters...gives me a sense of empowerment. Oops almost sound like Oprah! Since I used your letters many companies have been easy to deal with!"
   — **S.S., Florida**

"After 400+ letters and 4 years I still had 5 delinquent accounts, originally there were over 40. Every time one would get deleted a previous one would be put back on. Those credit reporting agencies will drive you NUTS!!! Within TWO weeks after receiving this book and using the letters modified only slightly, my reports are clean and all my credit scores are 720+ again. Thank God for this book!!!!"
   —**Nemolaw, San Jose, California**

"If you are a victim of identity theft, suspect identity theft, or want to be pro-active in protecting yourself against this crime wave of the millennium, this book MUST have a spot close to your local emergency numbers!!! As a 15 month victim of identity theft ranging from fraudulent bank accounts, fraudulent credit card accounts to receiving government documents in my name and finally, gaining access to my own personal accounts and destroying my financial health, this book has pulled me from the mire of phone calls, letter writing, government and corporate mazes. Four months ago I had lost all hope of ever regaining my credit, life, and sanity, but this book has taken me step-by- step through the process of clean-up and given me the hope and spirit to make it through this. This may just save your life too!"
   — **George J., Phoenix, Arizona**

FROM VICTIM TO VICTOR

A Step-by-Step Guide for Ending the Nightmare of Identity Theft

CD Enclosed with Attorney-Composed Letters and Forms

Second Edition

By Mari J. Frank, Esq.

PORPOISE PRESS, INC.

Laguna Niguel, California

FROM VICTIM TO VICTOR
A Step-by-Step Guide for Ending the Nightmare of Identity Theft
Second Edition with CD
By Mari J. Frank, Esq.

PORPOISE PRESS, INC.
28202 Cabot Road, Suite 300
Laguna Niguel, CA 92677 U.S.A.
Phone: (800) 725-0807
Fax: (949) 363-7561
Website: www.identitytheft.org
Copyright © 2004, 2005 by Mari J. Frank, Esq

Publisher's Cataloging-in-Publication

Frank, Mari J.
    From victim to victor: a step-by-step guide for ending the nightmare of identity theft / by Mari J. Frank. - 2nd Edition —Laguna Niguel, CA : Porpoise Press, 2005.
        p. cm.
    CD (PC or Mac) includes forms, resources and attorney-written letters for filing to various agencies when your identity has been stolen.

ISBN: 1-892126-04-4 (book)
        1-892126-05-2 (CD)

1. Identity theft—United States.   2. Imposters and imposture—United States.   3. False personation—United States.   4. Consumer protection—United States.   5. Victims of crimes—United States.   I. Title.

HV6759.F73 2005   364.16/3—dc22 0410   2004097049

Printed in the USA

2 4 6 8 9 7 5 3

Precautions and Disclaimer

Identity theft is a complex problem. Government agencies, credit firms, and law enforcement personnel are desperately trying to stay abreast of the creative, devious criminals who commit this fraud. This book and CD-ROM contain information that was up-to-date at the time of printing. We welcome any new information and will make that available through our web site at www.identitytheft.org. If you learn of new information that might be helpful to others, contact the author at Contact@IdentityTheft.org.

The purpose of this book, CD, and supporting materials is to provide you with "self-help" and educational materials so you can regain your credit, financial reputation, identity, and good name. Although Mari Frank, the author, is a licensed attorney, this book is not meant as legal advice but rather legal and consumer *information*. Because this book cannot address all the possible factual situations, you should consult with an attorney for advice about your specific circumstances and legal recommendations. In our resources section at the back of this book, we suggest you call your local county bar association or state bar to find a specialist in consumer law and the Fair Credit Reporting Act. *I've* provided a list of attorneys who claim to be familiar with this area of the law in our resources, and *I* recommend that you carefully interview any attorney during a customary free consultation to see if that person can help you. Any resource that *I* provide is *not to be considered* an endorsement.

We have made every effort to make this book and accompanying materials as accurate as possible. However, there may be typographical or content errors. There will be changes in policies and laws that may affect our information. For example, the Fair and Accurate Credit Transactions Act of 2003 (FACTA) was signed into law in December 2003; however, many of its provisions are still being implemented in 2005 and 2006. Also, the statute requires that the Federal Trade Commission and other government entities develop rules and regulations to implement this law; so many other changes are expected. Additionally, your state's laws will affect how you will proceed with your case. New bank and credit reporting agency policies will also affect how cases should be handled. Therefore, use this book as a *support guide*. To stay up-to-date with information pertaining to identity theft, check the web sites of the Federal Trade Commission (www.consumer.gov/idtheft); your state's attorney general, the CRAs, and other such organizations listed on our resource pages in the back of this book.

The author of this book supports your efforts. However, the author of this book and the publisher, Porpoise Press, Inc., shall not have liability or responsibility to any person or entity with respect to any loss or damage caused, or alleged to be caused, directly or indirectly by the information contained in this book or accompanying materials. Though *I* offer you ideas and general suggestions, you ultimately must make your own choices and protect your interests in a responsible manner. Do not rely on the contents of this book for legal advice; contact a qualified lawyer to evaluate your unique factual circumstances. If you do not wish to be bound by the above disclaimer, you may return this book and CD-ROM immediately for a full refund. *I* wish you the very best.

Table of Contents

Appendixes

Foreword

United States Senator
Dianne Feinstein

According to the FBI, identity theft is the fastest growing crime in America. Mari Frank, the author of this book, experienced that nightmare firsthand when she had her own identity stolen in 1996.

Like millions of other identity theft victims, Mari spent almost a year trying to restore her good name, her credit rating, and her finances. Back then, however, few people knew what identity theft was, and victims had no idea what steps to take to restore their identity. After Mari spent hundreds of hours working to get her own life back, she resolved to help create new laws and guides to assist other victims in navigating the system so that they wouldn't have to go through the same hardships that she had faced.

Mari developed the Identity Theft Survival Kit and testified before Congress several times. I first met Mari when she testified as a witness at the hearing that Senator Jon Kyl (R-Ariz.) and I co-chaired regarding the Identity Theft and Assumption Deterrence Act of 1998. This law made identity theft a federal crime so that consumer victims could get help from federal law enforcement. It also designated the Federal Trade Commission as a central agency to act as a clearinghouse for complaints, referrals, and assistance for victims of identity theft. Mari also testified at a Senate Judiciary Committee field hearing I chaired in August 2000. She was a passionate advocate at the hearing, describing the threats from identity theft, the steps victims need to take when their identities are stolen, and the legislation needed to assist victims and protect our citizens.

Mari's saga, and the stories she shared about other victims she had helped, opened my eyes to the growing financial and human costs of identity theft. I learned that it takes the average victim roughly two years to recover from this crime, and thousands of dollars of out-of-pocket costs. That's why I pledged to work with Mari and other consumer advocates to fight identity theft. This ultimately led to new laws and privacy protections to help victims restore their identity. These include:

- Giving every American consumer access to at least one free credit report a year from each of the three major credit bureaus.

- Requiring merchants to redact all but the last five credit card numbers on customer receipts so that discarded receipts are no longer a source of fraud.

- Allowing victims to put up barriers against the issuance of new credit in their name by requiring credit bureaus and credit issuers to adhere to "fraud alerts" on the consumer's file.

- Increasing criminal penalties with the passage of The Identity Theft Penalty Enhancement Act, which created the new crime of "aggravated identity theft", and added to penalties for those committing identity theft as part of a more serious crime like terrorism or murder.

But with almost 10 million new identity theft victims every year, there is clearly more that we need to do. In this era of the Internet and vast information databases, American consumers face an overwhelming task in controlling how their personal information is used and secured. That's why I continue to push for legislation to set higher standards for how an individual's personal information is protected, and to prohibit the public display of Social Security numbers.

With support from consumer representatives and privacy professionals like Mari Frank, I am confident we will ultimately turn back the tide of identity theft crimes. Mari knows firsthand as an attorney, sheriff reserve, and former victim, what it takes to protect your personal information, and how to successfully restore your identity if it is stolen. Her testimony, educational programs, and her books have been invaluable to victims and policymakers alike. With this new edition of *From Victim to Victor: A Step-by-Step Guide for Ending the Nightmare of Identity Theft (with CD)*, Mari once again provides an excellent guide to help victims of identity theft regain their good name and peace of mind.

U.S. Senator Dianne Feinstein

Acknowledgements

As you know by now, support is the name of the game in overcoming identity theft. And the older I get, the more I realize that support is key in every aspect of our lives. Someone may steal your name, your financial identity, your profession, and your good reputation, but they cannot take the essence of who you are, and they can't take away the support from your loved ones and friends. Be thankful for your wonderful friends, family, and for kind strangers that you meet along the path of regaining your identity. It is during those times of distress that you recognize what's really most important in life; the endearing relationships and genuine connections that you make with other people are what truly matters.

When I experienced my own nightmare of identity theft, I was grateful for the fantastic relationships I had that sustained me through my identity loss. Although few people understood the depth of the experience that I was enduring, they were sympathetic and encouraging. I felt fortunate to have met Beth Givens, the director of the Privacy Rights Clearinghouse, who had pioneered work on identity theft and provided great insights into the reality of identity fraud issues. I was also lucky to have contacted the Ventura Police Fraud Department Watch Commander, David Inglis, who himself had been an identity theft victim. He was empathetic and legitimized my concerns. He and Detective Tom Burke (now retired) took the time and effort to investigate and follow through to help prosecute my impostor.

Today, years later, as I am finishing my new educational materials and Second Edition of *From Victim to Victor*, I am very appreciative for the fabulous support I am now receiving. Many terrific people have helped me develop this new edition of *From Victim to Victor, A Step-By-Step Guide for Ending the Nightmare of Identity Theft* and the CD that goes with it, and I feel privileged to express my gratitude.

First, I am honored and humbled to thank Senator Dianne Feinstein, who wrote the Foreword to this book. I'm proud to say that Senator Feinstein effectively represents my home state of California in the United States Senate. She has built a reputation as an independent voice working with both Democrats and Republicans collaboratively to find solutions to the myriad problems facing our nation. As ranking member of the Terrorism Technology and Homeland Security Subcommittee, Senator Feinstein has introduced numerous bills addressing the epidemic of identity theft. I was privileged to first testify for her committee in the U.S. Senate in 1998, when she and Senator Jon Kyl (R-Arizona) co-chaired a hearing in Washington, D.C. concerning the impending passage of the Identity Theft and Assumption Deterrence Act. That was the first legislation making identity theft a federal crime, so that consumer victims could be recognized as the true victims — allowing them to obtain a police report. Throughout the years, Senator Feinstein has continued to support identity theft victims and consumers by introducing criminal and privacy legislation concerning identity theft, and I have testified several more times for her and other senate committees. In 2003, Senator Feinstein introduced legislation known as the Privacy Act. The Privacy Act protects the most sensitive personal information such as our Social Security numbers, and financial and health data. She stated:

"A person should be able to have control over how his or her most sensitive personal information is being used. But our right to privacy only will remain vital, if we take strong action to protect it."

Senator Feinstein also supported legislation to allow all consumers to choose not to allow companies to share their data with affiliates, and to require companies to obtain the express consent of consumers before sharing their personal data with other companies. Although this was not passed at the federal level, she promoted the legislation, which did pass in California, providing more protection than federal law for California citizens. In July of 2004, President Bush signed the Identity Theft Penalty Enhancement Act, which was originally authored by U.S. Senator Dianne Feinstein. This imposed tougher penalties on identity thieves and made it easier for prosecutors to target those identity thieves who steal for the purpose of committing the most serious crimes, including terrorism.

I am grateful to Senator Feinstein for authoring the Foreword of this book. It is because of the determination of Senator Feinstein and her colleagues to help fraud victims, and to protect the sensitive information of all citizens, that our laws have improved. With the passage of new statutes addressing identity theft, I can now coach you with more effective strategies to overcome the challenges of identity theft. I also wish to thank Senator Feinstein's aide, Scott Gerber, who coordinated with the Senator to accommodate her busy schedule.

I am also gratified to be able to thank the fabulous individuals who supported me in this update of *From Victim to Victor, A Step-By-Step Guide for Ending the Nightmare of Identity Theft.*

Much appreciation and many hugs go to:

Ellen Felton, my terrific long-time executive assistant and dear friend, who is always in good humor; Lori Rodriguez, for her wonderful enthusiasm and patience in learning to read my scribbles, and for her great concern for victims of identity theft; Vicki Gibbs, my talented, efficient, and inspiring editor who provided tremendous support and education; Cynthia Frank, my wise publishing manager and her terrific organizing team for their guidance; Chuck Hathaway, my graphic artist, whose joyful perseverance made the collaborative creative process fun; Tony Tiano, the CEO of Santa Fe Productions, for his mentoring, insight, and for asking me to host the PBS special *Identity Theft: Protecting Yourself in the Information Age.* This book, along with *Safeguard Your Identity (Porpoise Press, Inc., 2005),* served as gift items for the PBS television special when audience members pledged donations to support public television; The Privacy Rights Clearinghouse for all the work that they have done to protect privacy for American citizens, and their efforts in assisting victims and promoting better laws; Linda Foley and Jay Foley, the co-executive directors of the Identity Theft Resource Center, for all of the great work they do for victims, and their incredible empathy and persistence in pressing for more protection for victims. I appreciate their friendship and collaboration, as well.

The United States Public Interest Research Group and Director Ed Mierzwinski, for the important lobbying they do on behalf of consumers; Joanne McNabb, director of the California Office of Privacy Protection, for her leadership in guiding consumers and helping businesses create best practices with regard to privacy, data protection, and identity theft avoidance; Joanna Crane of the Federal Trade Commission's Identity Theft Program, for the wonderful resources, research studies, hearings, and the suggestions they present to the legislature to improve laws and consumer protection; the many dedicated law enforcement personnel across the country, including the local police, the FBI, the Secret Service, the Postal Inspectors, Social Security Administration investigators, the ID Theft Task Forces, and the prosecutors and judges who take this crime seriously — I applaud their valiant efforts; the many reputable companies and their fraud investigators who truly care about their customers and go out of their way to help those victimized by fraudsters, I appreciate their time and diligence; and to those thousands of identity theft victims who have contacted us to share their stories and concerns, I send my best wishes and gratitude for their insights.

My lovable golden retriever Raido, I appreciate the nose-nuzzling and tail-wagging that kept me positive during the sometimes-tedious authorship journey.

And to my children, Alyssa and Bryan, may my experience teach them that there will be times in their lives when they may feel victimized, but they never have to succumb to victimhood. May they believe that every life difficulty is a lesson, and, with faith, they can overcome adversity.

And to my dear husband, Lloyd Boshaw, Jr., I thank him for his love, patience, fun-loving spirit, and never-ending support.

Finally, a special thank you for God's eternal love, guidance, and support.

Mari Frank

Preface

Transformation often arrives in surprising ways. For me, the traumatic experience of being victimized by identity-theft gave me a mid-life clarity — I'd already been through a mid-life *crisis*.

In my profession as an attorney (mediator), I tell my clients that the pain of their crisis should serve as a springboard for great growth and new opportunities. I know that an optimistic attitude creates an atmosphere conducive to positive results. I also believe in using a holistic approach to challenges, focusing on what I call "solutioneering" — a process in which we turn our attention away from blame and anger, and use a creative problem-solving approach to get what we need to resolve the challenges in our lives.

However, when my own crisis of identity-theft occurred back in 1996, I realized sifting out anger and blame wasn't so easy. *I* was the innocent one being victimized, and I had to go into deep contemplation so I could stay calm. I learned that everything happens for a purpose and that sometimes life has an interesting way of teaching us new lessons. I believe I was spiritually directed to help other victims, to help foster societal changes, and to develop educational materials like this book and CD.

Actually, when I wrote the first edition of *From Victim to Victor: A Step-by-Step Guide for Ending the Nightmare of Identity Theft* and *The Identity Theft Survival Kit,* I would have preferred *not* to spend any more of my funds or re-live my nightmare by reviewing, researching, and editing my letters to write my book. I *desperately* wanted the ordeal to end so I could go on with my life. But hundreds of identity-fraud victims kept calling me with pleas for help, and my heart went out to them. They convinced me to create easy solutions for others who were victimized by this crime. The feedback from the thousands who purchased our first edition of *From Victim to Victor* and *The Identity Theft Survival Kit* was overwhelmingly positive. Those victims felt empowered by the information, and relieved by the ability to write letters *themselves* that effectively and completely resolved their complicated identity theft cases. I was encouraged to write a revised and updated edition.

As time passed, many of us who advocated for better laws and policies helped enact new statutes and positive changes — but then different problems arose for victims of identity theft. Because of the major changes resulting from the passages of the Fair and Accurate Credit Transactions Act, I too felt it was time to update, revise, and expand this book — to create critical steps and compose updated letters, incorporating new laws and the requirements expected of victims. I'm hopeful that the guidance in this book, along with the easy-to-complete letters and forms on the CD, will serve as your personal coach to enable you to protect yourself, overcome the challenges, and regain your identity.

Thank you for your efforts and know that *I* care about you. You may contact us at www.identity theft.org.

Best to you,
Mari Frank
2005

Introduction

How *My* Long Nightmare Can Shorten Yours

"You're the best victim we've ever had!"

When a fraud investigator at the Ventura, California Police Department spoke these words to me, I felt dumbfounded. This was a *compliment?* I don't like to think of myself as a victim. Although I've endured setbacks and even tragedies in my life, just as you probably have, I've always been able to survive and grow in the process. But not until I became a victim of identity theft — when someone impersonates you to commit various types of financial fraud (or worse yet, commit crimes in your name) — did I know how devastated, overwhelmed, and really frightened I could be. It was a nightmare. But I guess, as the detective suggested, I was a very good example of what to do when very bad things happen.

A lot of very bad things did happen. But I hope this book is one of the good things that has emerged from my ordeal … and I hope it assists you in getting the help you need!

One thing I learned back in 1996, when this happened to me, was that no step-by-step, "fill-in-the-blanks" guide for identity-theft victims even existed. Though I met some helpful, sympathetic folks whom I'll tell you about, I generally found a lack of hard information about what to do and *how* exactly to do it. Worse yet, I ran into a brick wall in the form of major banks and government bureaucracies. It took tremendous effort for me to overcome these obstacles and to assert my legal and financial rights. I had to prove my innocence. Today, these same challenges exist for victims of this crime; however, new laws have helped improve the situation somewhat.

If you've had the misfortune to become an identity-theft victim, the information in this book and on this CD can help shorten your nightmare. If you are not a victim, but wish to avoid becoming one, you can use this book as your *protection* guide. But before we start, just so you'll know I'm no stranger to what you're facing, let me tell you what happened to me.

On August 16, 1996, I received a telephone call from the Bank of New York, Delaware, asking why I had not paid my $11,000 credit card bill. I was shocked! I didn't have a credit card from that bank, and I certainly didn't owe $11,000. Clearly, someone claiming to be me had made the purchases — and who knows how many more accounts they had opened in my name?

I hadn't lost my wallet. I hadn't been mugged. I hadn't loaned my credit cards to anyone; in fact, I'd always taken pains to be careful with my confidential documents. So how could this have happened?

I had no idea. What's more, I had no clue what to do about it. Suddenly, I *did* feel like a victim. My life seemed out of control; my carefully woven rug of financial security had been pulled out from under me. It's not too strong to say I felt violated — "financially raped." Somewhere out there I had an "evil twin" who had cloned me!

Luckily, I had the presence of mind to insist that the Bank of New York, Delaware, send me all documents, including the original application by the fraud perpetrator, and the billing statements (at the time, there was no law requiring companies to provide documentation of the fraud, and most companies refused.) Finally, after much pleading on my part, the company told me that the card had been issued to an address in Ventura, California — four hours from my home. The bank informed me that its fraud department would handle my case, but that I should call the credit reporting agencies immediately and deal with the other false information that might have been put on my credit report.

Well, the bank *didn't* send the documents as promised. Instead of helping me with my account, the bank sold it to a collection agency. Soon, I began receiving threatening phone calls and letters from bill collectors. In fact, the bank wouldn't send the police or me any documentation until I finally was able to corral a bank vice president on the phone to say they were obstructing justice.

After receiving no assistance from my local police, the FBI, or the Secret Service, I called the Ventura Police Department, in the city where the perpetrator received the credit card. Although most victims don't get much help from police (because there are too many cases and they are labor-intensive to investigate), I was lucky, because Dave Inglis, the watch commander in the VPD's fraud unit, had himself been living in identity theft hell for over a year. I will forever be grateful to him for going beyond his duty to investigate my case. His empathy as a fellow victim was a blessing.

Within five days of my learning about the fraud, the Ventura police went to the address where the credit cards had been sent. They spoke to a woman living there who claimed to have known me. She told them that she received mail in my name because I used to live in that home.

When I told the police that I'd never lived in, or even visited, Ventura, they returned to her home. After discovering that she was on probation for shoplifting, the police got a search warrant and were able to search her home and find a variety of items in my name, including: billing statements from various creditors; letters from collection agencies; a letter from Thrifty Car Rental threatening to sue me at her address for damages to a vehicle she had rented; checks with my name on them; my own business cards snatched from my

office identifying me as an attorney; and a credit report that she had obtained from Equifax (one of the three major credit reporting agencies). They also found drugs and a .22-caliber Beretta handgun.

The suspect was arrested and released on bail. Thus, she was free to continue driving the red Mustang convertible that she had purchased using my name and credit, and to continue to apply for more fraudulent accounts using my credit. Although many months later she pleaded guilty to six counts of felony fraud, and didn't show up for her sentencing hearing, the judge leniently allowed her to participate in a work-furlough program instead of going to jail — after all this was *not* a violent crime. She didn't enter that work-furlough program until 10 months after she was first arrested. During that entire time, she was able to continue her identity theft against me, and others. After her short "punishment," she was picked up in another state for committing identity fraud on another victim.

At the same time that I was assisting the police, district attorney, and courts in prosecuting the fraud perpetrator, I was also overwhelmed by the task of cleaning up my destroyed credit. (The woman who stole my identity used over $50,000 worth of credit in my name. She obtained a $15,000 credit line that included checks with my name, and several high-limit credit cards, including a telephone card.) Straightening all this out was a true ordeal, which depleted me physically, emotionally, and financially.

I spent hours on the Internet, researching identity fraud. I tried to find out what steps I should take and who could help me to regain my financial stability and my identity. At that time, there was little help for victims. Now that we have an identity theft epidemic, there are more resources available, such as those listed by the Federal Trade Commission at www.consumer.gov/idtheft and others listed in our resources Appendix B. I spent over 500 hours on the phone, and writing 90 certified letters to firms and agencies. I dealt with crime investigators, various credit grantors, my own banks, government agencies, the State Bar of California (remember she was parading as an attorney, passing out my business cards), and even my auto insurance company. During that hectic first month, and on and off for months afterwards, I was unable to sleep, however with tenacity I did regain my identity.

How to use this book

To make your path easier, I've laid out step-by-step instructions, listed the agencies to contact for help, and provided all the legal letters you need to write. (In fact, this book and the CD include form letters to help you speed up the arduous task of letter writing. The letters are complete with the legal demands you can make in accordance with the current law; you just fill in the blanks.) I have created for you the package that I wish I would have had when I was victimized. This guide and CD will ease your anguish and expedite the process of regaining your credit, your identity, and your sanity.

First, it's critical to get organized. You must make a list of priorities, and you must document *in writing* all your conversations with the various agencies and companies. At first, I didn't — I just stuck little notes everywhere and got terribly confused. Then, I wised up (and started thinking like a lawyer again), and began keeping a detailed record so that I could hold everyone accountable to provide me with the information that I requested, and was entitled to, in a timely manner. Those records saved me many times. (In Chapter Five, I'll explain how you can set up a similar system.)

You not only need to clear up your present situation, you'll also want to protect your future financial profile and make sure you don't have a false criminal profile out there. So, you must ensure that the appropriate corrections are made on all your records, and that all fraud is completely removed. This means following up thoroughly, and that's another reason it's so important to get organized, so you don't forget about an account that will surely resurface later.

Lacking a step-by-step guide to follow, I had to make one up as I went along. Fortunately, I found the Privacy Rights Clearinghouse (www.privacyrights.org) and received a sympathetic ear from the director, Beth Givens. They developed the first strategic list of what to do if you become a victim of identity theft. Our guide in Chapter Four is similar, but greatly expanded and more detailed.

In addition to being organized and persistent, you must brace yourself for the fact that many times you're going to be treated as the "suspect." Though identity theft is a form of robbery that nets more money than the kind with guns, it's often hard to educate others to take the crime seriously. Police may not want to make a report because if they do, they will feel obligated to investigate. With their mounting workload they just don't have the resources to investigate most cases. The Department of Motor Vehicles prefers not to issue a new license because that in itself may be an invitation to fraud. And, the Social Security Administration doesn't like to give out new numbers because one is supposed to last a lifetime and, creating a new SSN can lead to confusion and abuse for the victim. In fact, a new Social Security number makes the victim look more suspicious to creditors because the prior number will show up in the credit reporting database with an alert.

In my case, the credit grantors, such as banks, and the credit reporting agencies were suspicious of me even though the real criminal had already been arrested. Further, as I say, it's still not unusual for companies and police departments to glibly state that *we,* the individuals, are not the victims. The real victims, they still contend, are the credit grantors (such as the credit card companies), who may lose thousands of dollars. It's true, federal law protects us with regard to credit card fraud. But it's a tragic misperception to think the individual is not the real victim. The credit grantors don't have to live day and night with calls from collection agencies, and learn about new accounts falsely opened in their names. The banks don't fear personal financial ruin or endure the emotional impact of not knowing what's going to happen next — whether it'll be a bankruptcy filed under your name, a new luxury car charged to you, thousands of dollars borrowed by someone claiming to be you, a criminal record for a crime you didn't commit, or the very worst, terrorism committed in your name.

After myriad hours of research, hundreds of frustrating phone conversations, and writing letters until my fingers ached and my mind reeled, I was able — after about 10 months — to regain my pristine credit rating. But the emotional toll was staggering. Ideally, victims shouldn't be burdened with this task — but that's the way it is. Even with new identity theft insurance options, the victim still has work to do. There are some companies now that offer "fraud resolution services." This is a better alternative than insurance if there is *real* help in writing letters and dealing with issues, but you as the victim still must spend many hours providing extensive information and dealing with companies to be sure everything is handled correctly.

In my own case, I was fortunate to have my legal training and my own business, so I could devote the necessary time to get my life back. Having researched all aspects of identity fraud, I became a "reluctant expert"— by necessity, not by choice! Soon, I became an active advocate for other victims. I was vocal and testified before legislative hearings, and was asked to appear on several national and local television shows, in magazines and newspaper articles. I volunteered my time to testify before federal agencies and Congress because I believe it's critical to bring this insidious crime to the forefront, and to rally consumers to become aware and to take action to protect themselves.

I spoke with hundreds of victims of identity theft who contacted me after reading about me or seeing me on television. I realized that sharing my journey and providing a proven method for restoring one's identity would be healing for me as well as for others. Millions of victims need help and coaching on how to move beyond this "identity crisis." (One in five adults will become victims according to the FBI.) The Federal Trade Commis-

sion reported 9.9 million new victims just in 2003.

Fortunately, several non-profit consumer groups *do* fight for the rights of identity-theft victims: The Identity Theft Resource Center (www.idtheft center.org), The Privacy Rights Clearinghouse (www.privacyrights.org); and U.S. Public Interest Research Group (www.uspirg.org/calpirg); are three of the best non-profit organizations helping victims. Still, there was no step-by-step survival guide written for victims that included coaching them and giving them legal letters to deal with the agencies. So, I originally created this book in 1998 with updates in 2000, which included form letters on diskette and details of what works and what doesn't. I shared information that I learned, created, and developed materials — so that your ordeal would be easier than mine.

Now, this second edition of the book *From Victim to Victor: A Step-by-Step Guide for Ending the Nightmare of Identity Theft* (with CD) will facilitate your efforts and ease your concerns. The cost of this book and CD is far less than what I would need to charge you for just one letter! Please know that I consider it a privilege to save you time and money.

I encourage you to share the advice and suggestions in this book with your friends and family, in hopes that they can avoid, or at least be better prepared for, what we've gone through. This book and CD will serve as a user-friendly coach, and allow you to be triumphant and redeem your financial security, your emotional stability, and your good reputation very soon. I've shared my story with you, and as you'll see, I also include stories of other victims.

If you're reading this, you're probably currently going through, have gone through, or are worrying about your own identity-theft ordeal. I know your fear, anger, and frustration; and I offer you this guide in hopes that you can transform yourself from "Victim to Victor" … just as many others have done.

Please visit our web site at www. identitytheft. org.

Rest assured you are not alone, and you will be victorious!

Chapter 1

Read This — Even If You Read Nothing Else!

You're sitting at home minding your own business, when a credit card company you've never heard of calls to ask why you haven't paid the $30,000 you owe them. You think it's a prank call … but it's not. Or maybe your own credit card company calls to ask if you're sure you want to apply for three more cards and have them sent to a different address?

Or, worse yet, you *don't* get a call at all. Instead, you learn you can't refinance your home mortgage because your credit report shows numerous accounts in your name, and you never applied for any of them. Perhaps you open your credit card bill one day to find $10,000 in charges springing from a week at a five-star hotel in Maui — complete with luxury rental car, daily herbal massages, and a case of the best champagne. And … you've never even *been* to Maui.

What's happening here?

More important, what can you do to stop it? What's happening is that someone is posing as you, for financial gain. And you've just joined the almost 10 million Americans who each year become victims of identity theft. It's a vicious, largely faceless crime that takes an enormous financial and emotional toll on its victims.

No one physically mugs you, robs you at gunpoint, or kidnaps you. No, this crime is hidden, insidious — most times you never meet your imposter. But you're still left feeling battered. Your self-image is beat up, your financial reputation is ruined, your sense of who you are is stolen, and your identity is, in a manner of speaking, taken hostage. It'll probably take you months, (maybe years in the scenario where someone commits crimes in your name), before you get your good name back, and before your life returns to normal. But this book is here to help you, and to speed up the resolution!

What you need to do.

This book explains about the crime, your rights, and the steps you need to take to set things right and regain your life. It also gives you many tips designed to prevent such a dilemma from happening again. It explains why it's so important to stay organized, how to surmount the hurdles you'll encounter, and gives you tools for getting your personal profile and financial life straightened out. Other important features include easy-to-use letters to complete that you must send out to businesses and agencies, and a list of other places to go for help.

I strongly urge you to read through the entire book and use the convenient CD, which includes steps, logs, letters, and resources.

You may be in a state of fear, even panic, right now. Please have hope — this coaching book will ease your concerns. This chapter is a short course in identity-theft first aid. You need to know more and do more than you'll learn from this section, and I'll repeat these steps later in greater detail. But this section will point you in the right direction and get you started. That alone will help your peace of mind.

Do the Following Immediately: For Financial Identity Theft

1. Contact the three big credit reporting agencies (hereafter CRAs) and alert them to the fraud.

Federal law requires that if you call one of the agencies below, they must contact the other two. This doesn't always happen, so *I* suggest you call all three agencies just to be certain; they are competitors and have different information and formats. You will place a fraud alert on your profile in response to voice prompts. You'll need to give them your Social Security number. They will immediately send you your credit reports at no charge.

Here's how to reach these agencies to report fraud:

Trans Union	800-680-7289
Experian	888-397-3742
Equifax	800-525-6285

Next, send them each a letter (See Letter 1-A in Appendix A at the back of this book and on CD). Make sure you send it *"Return receipt requested."*

I can't guarantee that each of the three credit reporting agencies will honor your requests. But you may get help from a recent, promising law, which I'll tell you more about in Chapter Three. This law says that CRAs must immediately block all fraudulent accounts from your credit report when they receive a police report, or "identity theft report" from a government agency, indicating that your name was fraudulently used to open accounts. The police report *must* list the phony accounts.

Once the fraudulent accounts are blocked, the credit grantors are notified by the agencies and you should notify them by phone and in writing, too. They can't put the disputed accounts back on your credit report without proving that you really owe this money. In any event, the law makes it doubly important that you obtain a detailed law enforcement report that lists all the fraudulent accounts. (See #6, below.) Then, send that police report to the three CRAs with your cover letter and request immediate blocking of the fraudulent accounts from your profile.

As you will soon learn, these calls and letters to the credit bureaus are only a start. They're not cure-alls and certainly shouldn't be reason for complacency. Criminals can get access to your credit quickly, so you'll need to act rapidly to minimize damage. Making these contacts, though, is an important, necessary first step.

The point of your calls and letters will be to alert the CRAs and creditors to the possible fraud, and to get them to "flag" your account with a fraud alert so that anyone posing as you and attempting to open more lines of credit will be subject to extra scrutiny. In fact, you should *demand* to be contacted for verification before any further credit is opened in your name. The fraud alert will state something like "...don't issue credit without calling me first at this phone number_____." (*I* suggest giving your cell phone number, so the merchant can call and speak to you right then for verification; should you, for example, apply for instant credit or wish to buy a car on Sunday.)

2. Ask each of the big three credit reporting agencies for your *free* copy of your credit report and go over it very carefully. When you call them, use the voice prompt to request that your *free* credit report be sent immediately.

When you receive the reports, look for anything out of the ordinary. You'll need to find out immediately what accounts have been opened. You might notice accounts you didn't apply for, or inquiries by creditors, landlords, employers, or others with whom you've had no dealings. (In Chapter Four, I'll go over in great detail what to look for in your report.)

3. Contact all credit grantors — department stores, utility companies, credit card issuers, etc. — with whom you believe your name may have been used fraudulently.

Again, contact them by phone and by letter. (See Letter 2-A in Appendix A.) Get replacement cards with new account numbers to replace your accounts that have been used fraudulently. Ask them to close any of your true accounts affected by fraud, and have those accounts noted as "Account Closed at Consumer's Request." New fraud accounts opened by the impersonator should be permanently removed from you profile, not just closed.

4. Report the incident to the police or sheriff in your local area and also where the crime was committed.

Talk to the fraud unit in your hometown; give officers whatever documented evidence you have (don't give them copies of your credit reports unless you black out your personal information) and ask them for a copy of whatever report they file. Tell them it's very important to list the fraudulent accounts in their report. You'll need that in the report for your further dealings with banks and credit card companies.

Be aware that you may meet resistance. Many police departments are reluctant to take reports because they don't have the time or resources to investigate; so if they balk, ask for a report "for informational purposes only." That makes it easier for police to help you without the requirement of investigating.

With police manpower being what it is and the lack of financial resources, officers may prefer not to file a report on your case, much as they no longer file reports on routine accidents that don't involve injuries. However, you've got to convince them that this isn't a fender bender. This is your life and your credit. Regardless of the extent of monetary loss, this incident could imperil your ability to buy a home or a car, use a credit card, get a job, or get to sleep at night. Police may tell you that the credit grantor who lost the money must file a report first. This is *not* the case under federal law; however, you should agree with police and demand that the credit grantors cooperate with law enforcement.

Without a police report, you're going to be severely hampered in your dealings with other agencies — so persist! Since there are state and federal laws acknowledging the consumer as the victim, you should contact the Federal Trade Commission at 1-877-IDTHEFT, to help you get a written report if the police refuse. If a friend or a member of your family commits the fraud, you may be reluctant to file a police report. That's your decision — but understand, that's a choice that will make credit cleanup much more difficult. *I'll* discuss this more in Chapter Four.

5. Start a log of all your contacts with authorities and financial institutions, including those you've already contacted in Steps 1-3. (See Sample Log in Appendix A.)

This is very important! Sad to say, you probably will be talking to a lot of different people at many different firms and agencies over the next weeks and months. It's imperative that you keep track of whom you spoke or wrote to and when. Otherwise, you'll almost certainly become hopelessly lost in the bureaucratic maze and your efforts to clear your name and credit will suffer.

In Chapter Five, I tell you how to stay organized and I suggest specific information you'll need to record in your log entries.

6. Complete the Uniform ID Theft Affidavit (Document 10 — Appendix A)

This Affidavit provides important details about the fraud you are experiencing. Fill in the blanks and attach a chronological history with bullet points of what has taken place and what you have done. Make several copies of this document to give to agencies, companies, and the police.

7. Carefully monitor your mail, credit card bills, and credit reports for evidence of new fraudulent activity.

If you find more fraud, repeat Step 3 with those additional credit grantors, and write to the CRAs again. You'll also need to update your police report and affidavit if you learn of new fraud.

There! You've gotten started.

What I've suggested here are the bare rudiments; I'll go into all of this in much more detail in Chapter Four. For now, at least, you've begun to fight back.

If you're like most identity theft victims, you've got a lot more to do. Remember, though, this is do-able, and your guide (this book) will take you by the hand and lead you through the maze. If you're not too overwhelmed, jump to Chapter Four for more details of what to do. Remember all the form letters you need are in this book and on the attached CD.

And now that you've become proactive, you've set some wheels in motion. The identity thief is probably still a couple of steps ahead of you; however, you've now caught on to his or her game, and you've begun countermeasures.

Now — keep your spirits up and keep going!

Chapter 2

What's Happening to You? And Why?

All David was expecting after dinner was dessert — but he got a great deal more, and it wasn't sweet. The Kansas businessman, dining with business associates, finished his restaurant meal and handed his credit card to the waiter. The waiter returned to the table to say the credit card company had rejected the charge.

"I thought: 'That's impossible,'" David later said. "I'd paid my (credit card) bill. There's no way this could happen."

Though shaken and embarrassed, he gave the waiter a different card, which went through. Once he got home, David called the credit card company to question the rejection and was told his card had been cancelled because of his recent bankruptcy in Los Angeles…except, he hadn't filed for bankruptcy — and he'd never been to Los Angeles.

David was just beginning a long, Kafkaesque journey that millions of Americans face each year: It starts when someone, in effect, steals your name. First, the thief links your name with some identifying code — often a Social Security or credit card number, or I've heard even a fingerprint (biometric information). And then for the thief, the sky's the limit; for you, the victim, the nightmare has begun.

Identity thieves are very imaginative in the ways they choose to use your ID. They may lease apartments, purchase homes, buy room after room of furniture, rent limousines, purchase cars and jewelry, take a holiday to Disneyland, get their teeth fixed, obtain cellular phones, or just go on shopping sprees (one spent $11,000 just at *Toys R Us*). They may print blank checks (with your account number) or use the number on your ATM card with the Visa/MasterCard logo, so they can drain your bank accounts. Sometimes they siphon the cash from mutual funds or insurance policies. They may even commit other crimes, and if they're caught, identify themselves as you (after all, they do have a fake ID with your name), thus creating an instant arrest record for you.

In some cases, innocent victims have been fired from their jobs because of crimes committed by the imposter. In one case, a businessman had his identity stolen by a notorious drug dealer. Time and again the victim, an executive who traveled a lot, was pulled over by authorities when he crossed international borders. Once, he was even awakened in his bedroom by drug agents, their guns pointed at his head. It got to the point where he had to carry with him at all times a letter from other law-enforcement officials stating that he wasn't the drug dealer who was listed in a national crime database. (Note: It's a good idea to carry the first page of your police report in your wallet in case of just such an emergency.) I'll tell you many ways to protect yourself, and I'll show you ways to find out if your evil twin has used your identity to commit crimes in your name. I'll also give you simple steps to take and attorney-composed letters to write to clear your name.

Throughout the book, I'll share various stories and examples from other victims … such as the following:

A woman contacted us to say her wallet had been stolen while she was going through a security check at the Chicago airport. The thief managed to charge $10,000 on her credit cards in just four hours. Though the victim was able to cancel all her credit cards, her credit was damaged. In addition, her personal infor-

*mation was passed on to another woman who, using the victim's name, had a baby that night in Chicago. **Talk about a mess!** The victim then had a stack of unpaid bills from the hospital's maternity ward — and, on paper at least, a child in another state who could claim to be her heir.*

Once a crook has assumed your identity, he or she may escape detection by spending as much money as he or she can in as short a time as possible before moving on to someone else's name and account information. By the time you find out about the big bills, start receiving collection letters, and notify authorities, the thief is often long gone. Then, months or years later, he or she may start up again, using your ID or passing it on to a fellow felon.

"This is the consumer rip-off of the Information Age," says Ed Mierzwinski of the US Public Interest Research Group (CALPIRG). Automation and computerization have made life more convenient for us — and more lucrative for the identity thieves.

Identity theft is "an absolute epidemic," states Robert Ellis Smith, a respected privacy author and publisher of *The Privacy Journal*. "It's certainly picked up in the last four or five years. It is nationwide. It affects everybody, and there is very little you can do to prevent it and, I think, worst of all — you can't detect it until it's probably too late."

Our Fastest Growing Crime!

Law-enforcement authorities call identity theft "the fastest growing crime across the country right now." In fact, identity theft is the most called-about subject on the Federal Trade Commission's telephone hotline. "Most victims don't even know how the perpetrators got their identity numbers," says Beth Givens of the Privacy Rights Clearinghouse, who receives thousands of calls from victims. But, generally, Givens says, "Law enforcement doesn't pay much attention to this crime — they go after robbers with guns but not robbers with paper. And credit issuers and department stores will write off the losses."

And It's Getting Worse.

For one thing, we've gotten out of the habit of really identifying people. As one police officer notes, "We have become a society of writing numbers, swiping cards, and relying on computers. No basic identification is being done whatsoever anymore."

Plus, we've become so mobile and global. It's no trick at all to rent a private post office box (or a temporary address) and order new or duplicate credit cards sent there. With communication by Internet, we have no idea where order information has really originated.

A yet bigger reason that this crime is increasing may be the burgeoning information industry. Nearly invisible to most people, companies are compiling huge information databases from public records and private industry marketers, about nearly every adult American (and kids, too). With computers and complex software, they compile nearly complete dossiers on anyone. Big companies and information brokers don't do so with fraud in mind; they're in business to sell the information to law firms, insurance investigators, loan officers, private eyes, employment background checkers, myriad marketing firms, and other companies and individuals.

But this data compilation and sale is a virtually unregulated industry. Unlike the credit reporting industry, where you have a right of access and right of corrections, you have little control or access to all the companies and information brokers who sell your information. It's easy to understand how such information falls into the wrong hands — or is used by unscrupulous employees.

In one case, for example, employees of a cellular phone company used customer data to create fraudulent accounts. The dishonest employees and their friends then used the bogus accounts to ring up thousands of dollars in calls.

For the criminal, identity theft is a relatively low-risk, high-reward endeavor. Credit card issuers don't investigate this crime very often and rarely report it to the police. Why? The firms figure it's not cost efficient. In other words, the creditors will write off the fraud — it's the cost of doing business. So, since they've already lost money, why spend money on investigating and taking more employee time to work with law enforcement? They'll rarely catch the bad guy and almost never get restitution. The human cost of fraud is yours to bear. A victim may be unable to close escrow on a house because someone impersonated him and tarnished his credit report, or he might toss sleeplessly through the night wondering where or when the identity thief will strike next. Creditors (although financial victims) don't experience the emotional trauma that the victims do.

Various factors tie the hands of local police, who also are hampered by the fact that many such crimes involve a victim in one state and a perpetrator in another state or country. Additionally, the crime is often very complex — the imposters steal information about you, but may transfer it to others who order products on the Internet. There may be numerous players in various states opening a multitude of accounts using the victim's identification for various purposes, such as renting apartments, getting a job, and establishing utility accounts. Law enforcement is hindered by the lack of resources to investigate these crimes unless they involve a crime ring or a threat to homeland security.

All the thief needs is to get some basic information. Banks and other credit grantors make the rest simple by issuing credit cards so freely.

How do thieves get such data?

Stealing wallets used to be the easiest way for someone to take on your identity ... and that still happens. But today's white-collar criminal is likely to use other techniques, ranging from the simple to the sophisticated. Here are just a few examples:

- **"Shoulder Surfing."** At ATM machines or when you're providing your credit card at a retailer, someone may look over your shoulder — or use binoculars or other devices (like a photo cell phone) — to capture your personal identification number (PIN).

- **Stealing from mailboxes.** Bank and credit card statements, pre approved credit offers, telephone calling cards, driver's license numbers, convenience checks, utility statements, or tax information all can be grist for the identify thief's mill.

- **"Dumpster Diving."** Unshredded credit card and loan applications often end up in trash bins. This can happen at your own house, or in the dumpster behind your doctor's office or your bank.

- **Impersonating you** and filing an address change with the post office. That way all the bills and new credit cards are sent to the new address where, of course, they go unpaid. Or, perhaps the **minimum** payment is made to keep the account active. To thwart this, the U.S. Postal Service has created a system that sends a postcard, for verification, to your old and new addresses — but this isn't foolproof.

- **Obtaining your credit report fraudulently.** The thief might pose as your boss, landlord, or a loan officer and order your credit profile, which includes your Social Security number and other critical information. (In my own case, the identity thief apparently posed as a private detective to get my credit report while she was working in a law office in another county.) A firm that has a legitimate subscription service to such reports may have a dishonest employee who gets access to the credit profiles of customers and sells the reports to identity thieves (this has happened in car dealerships and in the CRAs themselves).

- **Accessing computerized records.** A skilled, if malicious, person with a computer can find out a lot about almost anybody. In fact, some firms even advertise on the Internet that they can show you how you can get the most detailed information about friends, neighbors, enemies ... *anyone*.

- **Phishing.** This scam involves deception and identity theft. The imposters create bogus e-mails, pretending to be from reputable companies to trick victims into revealing personal information including Social Security numbers, credit card numbers, personal identifying numbers, and online banking passwords. The con is to gain the confidence of the victim and appear real, using authentic-looking logos and Web addresses (URLs) that look impressively similar to the real Web address for the company they are impersonating.

- **Phone Scams.** They scam you by phone, pretending to be a legitimate agency or company asking for your personal data.

An elderly gentleman from the Midwest became an identity fraud victim after providing his personal information to a woman who called him late at night pretending to inquire about his need to serve on jury duty.

- **Burglary,** to steal computers and hard copy files. A very common method is to break in and steal a company's personnel files, computers, and cabinets with sensitive information. (Even the IRS became a victim when someone stole computers from one of their offices.)

In June 2004, a computer was stolen containing the Social Security numbers, birthdates, and other personal information of 145,000 blood donors from a university hospital.

- **Technology thieves and computer hackers.** Fraudsters anywhere in the world can break into government and corporate web sites and steal computer data.

A hacker stole 300,000 credit card numbers from the Internet Retailer CD Universe and then posted 25,000 of the numbers on a web site when the retailers refused to pay a $100,000 ransom.

Some states, such as California, require that companies that experience a security breach of unencrypted files of sensitive information notify all potential victims of the breach, so that they may protect themselves with a fraud alert and take action to protect their accounts. Federal guidelines for financial institutions encourage notification to potential victims as well.

- **Internet searches** of chat rooms, e-mails, and the web sites of information brokers can provide thieves with lots of personal information about you.

In May 2004, a man was convicted of accessing information from innocent victims and sending 850 million junk e-mails through accounts he opened with stolen identities.

- **Trusted individuals with access**. Some identity thieves obtain in-home access to personal documents. They might be relatives or friends, roommates, household workers, home-healthcare providers, or spouses going through a divorce who hold a grudge.

- **Relatives who know too much.** Worse yet, in a small percentage of cases, sons and daughters do this to elderly parents, and some parents steal the identity of their children. While we hate to think of those closest to us committing identity theft, it is more common than you might think. The Federal Trade Commission's study at the end of 2003 found nine percent of identity theft derived from a family member.

Most victims of identity theft have no clue how their identifying information was obtained by the imposter. The victim rarely meets his impersonator, and in most cases, because law enforcement hasn't the resources to investigate, the crime goes unsolved. The fraudster is free to find new targets.

Faulty information handling practices

As if protecting your identity from theft wasn't already a challenge, some merchants, agencies, and banks seem to almost open the door for identity thieves to commit fraud. Merchants rarely examine the signature on your credit card. Many businesses fail to properly dispose of documents by shredding, and don't bother to lock up filing cabinets containing your personal data. The financial industry is in the best position to prevent the crime, but often, because the untrained employees are eager to issue new credit cards and loans, the proper verification doesn't take place.

Numerous financial institutions and agencies still require the last four digits of the Social Security number (SSN) as the default PIN for access. Many health and life insurance companies, and even the military, use the SSN as the key identifying number and emblazon it on each document, which must then be carried in the wallet. Medicare cards display the SSN. Countless educational institutions still use the SSN as the student ID, even posting grades by this number. In a few states the SSN is still the driver's license number. All these uses of our allegedly unique identifier put us at risk. Because of this risk, there has been new state legislation and proposed federal legislation to limit the use of the Social Security number. As a result, the trend toward authentication and verification using biometric information, such as your fingerprint, iris scan, or facial scan etc. is lauded as a panacea; however, the accuracy of that data is not wholly reliable, and if the minimum level of protection for that sensitive data is comparable to the protections now used for the SSN, victims will have far more problems proving who they are if defrauded using a unique body identifier. We must develop safeguards and accuracy standards for biometrics verification *before* it is considered the ultimate unique manner to identify us.

No respect…and no help: What happens to victims of identity theft?

Even though each identity fraud case is different, the experiences of all victims are all too similar. You may get little or no help from the agencies and companies who allowed your identifying information to be used fraudulently in the first place. Law enforcement rarely investigates. Identity theft occurs far too often for them to handle it all, al-though many police departments are expanding their financial fraud departments. Some police departments still will not issue a police report to victims, telling you that since you will not have to pay credit card bills, the bank is the true victim due its monetary loss. Federal and state law make identity theft a crime, which requires law enforcement to make an identity theft report. Plus, federal law (The Fair Credit Report Act) requires a police statement or an "identity theft report" for you to clear your name with the CRAs and the credit grantors. I'll give you the tools in Chapter Four (and in letters in Appendix A) to at least get a written description from law enforcement to clear your name.

You may have difficulty reaching the credit bureaus or fail to receive responses in writing. When you first call, you won't be able to talk with a real person, only a voice prompt requiring you to key in very sensitive information including your Social Security number. You may encounter rude treatment by some creditors, debt collectors, and government agencies. Don't lose your temper — remember … you want them to help you.

You'll spend a great deal of time regaining your identity. You may be forced to take several days off work to make the necessary phone calls, write letters, and meet with law enforcement. This all costs money as well. The Identity Theft Resource Center surveyed victims and found that they averaged 600 hours in time spent clearing their name. (www.idtheftcenter.org - see the 2003 report.) But those victims didn't have the use of this book! The steps and letters in the book and CD will greatly reduce your time, effort, and expenses! Since you have this guide in hand, you are in a much better position to regain your identity more quickly and easily than most victims.

If your imposter works under your name and/or SSN, the earnings will show up on your Social Security Administration account. If that happens, the Internal Revenue Service will investigate you for under-reporting income. Although this is a challenge, I'll give you steps and letters to correct this and settle those financial issues.

If a thief commits crimes in your name and you are arrested and/or required to stand trial for a crime you did not commit, this is a frightening and horrific scenario. But don't panic; Chapter Four and the letters in Appendix A, will show you how to tackle the problem, and deal with the various agencies and databases to get your good name back.

* * *

Essentially, the burden of responding to this crime is placed on your shoulders, and it can be quite emotional. You probably feel violated and helpless — and very angry. After all, you may be unable to obtain credit, get a mortgage, rent an apartment, or acquire a job — all because an imposter's bad credit history, or worse yet, a false criminal background is recorded in countless databases ruining your name. If your identity theft includes criminal charges or revenge, the restoration of your normal life can be demanding; but don't lose heart — this book is here to coach you one step at a time to alleviate your worries to get your life back soon!

Yes, it can happen to you!

The only requirement to become a victim is that you have an identifier like a SSN or, in the near future, your biometric information (i.e. fingerprint). Anyone can become a victim — whatever your age, occupation, or place of residence …even after you go to heaven!

*A widow began receiving collection calls and was informed of an FBI investigation of her deceased husband for actions that took place six months **after** he died.*

You, the victim, may have obtained this book because you were finding that it was overwhelming to deal with the many tasks involved in regaining your identity. The more accounts opened and the more severe the fraud, the more time it will take you to deal with the various agencies — but the system in this book will facilitate your efforts and guide you to recapturing control over your life. Although your credit record may be in chaos now, it's fixable. Your background check may come up with arrests or convictions in many jurisdictions and on innumerable databases, but the steps I've developed will show you how to clear your name quickly. Although most of the mind-numbing burden of finding out how much damage was done falls to you, I'll give you the tools to deal with the challenges.

The majority of the rest of this book will be devoted to giving you specific, effective ways to get your credit and your life back on track if you're victimized. But Chapter Seven will also address defensive steps for the future — so you won't be re-victimized. While it's impossible to ensure you'll never be a victim or that it won't happen again if you're already a victim, there is much you can do to reduce that likelihood. Once you've been targeted as a victim, and your sensitive information has been acquired, it can happen again, unless you take steps to protect yourself.

Remember David, the Kansas businessman with the cancelled credit card? He found that someone in Los Angeles had filed for bankruptcy using his name and SSN — but he learned this only after the imposter took a job, rented an apartment, bought a luxury car, and got a driver's license, *all in David's name*. He endured two years of confusion and hassles as he tracked down the problems and set the record straight.

He was lucky in that the thief didn't commit crimes that could've put David in jail. But the thief did complicate David's life for a long time, forcing him to hire a lawyer and spend many anguishing hours dealing with police, FBI, attorneys, judges, court clerks, CRAs, and others. David told us that this book and CD would have made his life much easier, since all those issues are addressed and the letters are pre-written and ready to send to the agencies, courts, and others.

Like most victims, David never did find out how the thief got his personal information. And it troubles him that the situation could easily happen again. But he says there's a moral to his story:

"Be ever vigilant. Write all letters promptly and

keep organized. That's the best thing to do. Stay on top of it. Watch for information that's being sent to you. Every time you're asked personal questions when you buy something in the future, ask where your information is going. Ask questions; don't blindly give *merchants data just because they ask for it. Ask why they want it. If they can't give you a good answer, say, 'Sorry I'm not going to give it to you.' Don't be afraid to deny unnecessary information."*

Be vigilant, be assertive, and be positive!

Chapter 3

What Are Your Rights, and Will Anybody Help You?

One of the paradoxes of identity fraud is that the victim often has to prove his or her innocence. This shocks most new identity theft victims; they naturally expect the police, the credit grantors, and the CRAs and others in high places to believe them and help them. Maybe it *should* be that way … but often it isn't.

Some examples:

- A thief stole Wanda's purse and ordered new credit cards using her identification. Wanda was outraged to learn that one major department store gave a credit card to the thief, despite the fraud alert Wanda had placed on her credit report. A second store also issued the imposter a credit card in Wanda's name, even though the imposter gave an incorrect date of birth and phone number.

- Alberto learned that somebody in another city was working under his Social Security number (SSN). Not only would that ultimately confuse his Social Security benefits and cause him more tax liability, but Alberto also feared the imposter might commit crimes and saddle him with a criminal record. He contacted the Social Security Administration, which told him it was his responsibility to contact the other employer and report the fraud. He did. But the employer wrote back saying it had a copy of its employee's birth certificate and driver's license and was not prepared to look into the matter further.

- Unfortunately, an imposter got a copy of Betty's driver's license. Doubly unfortunate, the imposter was a bad driver. As a result of this imposter's numerous accidents and citations, Betty's license was suspended. She also received a warning from her insurance company. To add insult to injury, when Betty went to the department of motor vehicles to get copies of "her" bad-driving record, she was told she needed more information to prove who she was before they could help her.

I could go on with numerous cases, including my own, where agencies and firms that might have helped were actually a hindrance. Often their practices even *facilitated* the perpetuation of the crime.

Why is getting help so difficult?

First, many firms and agencies are large, impersonal bureaucracies not geared to helping individuals as much as making a profit or maintaining the status quo. Many times their employees are not trained in verification or other precautions involved in issuing credit. There's pressure to add new customers as quickly as possible; too often, these new customers are impersonators.

Second, with regard to financial fraud, because laws protect the victim from most large out-of-pocket monetary losses — but *not* from major emotional and financial headaches — there's a tendency to let the victim "go it alone." The banks seem to believe that their only responsibility is to close fraud accounts. They often act as if they are doing you a great favor when they absorb the losses, when, if they'd been more *careful* before they issued an account to your impersonator, the fraud probably could have been prevented in the first place.

For example, Tom's credit was compromised when a credit card company issued a $10,000 credit line to an imposter who received a promotional application in the mail. The impersonator crossed out his own name and wrote in Tom's name. Similarly, he filled in Tom's Social Security number and a few weeks later the imposter received the card with Tom's name at the impersonator's address. Had the bank employees been careful? *Hardly!* Federal law requires that companies use reasonable procedures to verify the identity of the applicant, but the enforcement measures leave much to be desired. So, companies in their rush to issue credit are often careless — creating millions of new identity theft victims each year.

A third reason companies often aren't much help is that the banks and stores have already lost a lot of money. Investigating and prosecuting the fraud is going to take a great deal of employee time and resources … *and more money*. So, from a reasonable business perspective, the creditors are reluctant to assist the police or fraud victims because that would take employee time and be a further cost, which will cut into their profit. Because most impersonators are not caught — or even if they are, can't pay restitution — there's little chance banks or merchants will recoup their losses if they expend the time and effort to investigate or prosecute.

Fourth, to take the charitable view, the firms and agencies want to be careful not to commit a new error or compound an earlier one. So, when victims call the creditors to notify them of the fraud, the company may not be willing to believe them. Thus, caution — if not apathy — comes into play when you call and want help from companies who issued fraud accounts.

Fifth, the CRAs are the hub of the wheel; they are the clearinghouses for credit information. However, though our credit information is their lifeblood, you and I are not their customers — unless we sign up for their fee-based credit monitoring. The clients they most need to please are the credit grantors, mortgage lenders, and employers who spend millions of dollars to order our information from them.

Sixth, no single government agency will take action to redeem your good name. The Federal Trade Commission (FTC) is charged with providing resources and research, and setting up rules for the implementation of the Fair Credit Reporting Act. They also enforce the Fair Credit Reporting Act, which seeks to guarantee accuracy, completeness, and openness in dealing with your credit report. And the FTC is required to maintain a clearinghouse for complaints and a referral resource for victims at www.consumer.gov/idtheft and 1-877-ID Theft — but they aren't able to pursue each individual case.

The FTC cannot investigate nor bring a lawsuit against any company on your *individual* behalf. While it's required to take complaints, and the information it receives helps with its report to Congress for making recommendations for legislation, its enforcement power is limited when it comes to bringing cases in which there are myriad consumers affected by deceptive practices or violations of the law. If the agency receives a threshold number of complaints, it may begin an investigation into a company's practices. As a result of that investigation, the FTC may take legal action against a company. However, you personally wouldn't be represented in such an action. I have a great deal of respect for the educational materials on the FTC web site and for the work they do with the resources allocated. But, for victims wanting extensive help, the FTC is not equipped to take your specific case.

Other agencies, such as the Office of Consumer Affairs in your state and in Washington, D.C. may exert some influence, but they lack regulatory power. The various bank commissions usually will take no action. The state attorney general's office normally will refer you to the local police, and may assist you with criminal identity theft (when someone uses your name to commit other crimes). The Secret Service deals mostly with the criminal aspects of fraud rings and danger to the economy as a whole, they take on very few individual cases unless other major crimes are involved.

The fraud unit of the local police department where you report the fraud will only deal with the criminal aspects. As mentioned, even getting law enforcement to investigate may be a challenge. Violent crime and homeland security, of course, take precedence over identity theft — and major embezzlements or other such white-collar crimes are given priority over the relatively small amounts likely involved in individual cases.

The credit bureaus consider themselves receivers of information from the banks and merchants. If there are errors, they say it's due to the erroneous reports they receive. The CRAs won't help you clean up the credit mess, although new requirements under federal law require them to give you some written steps to take. They will request that you *prove* the fraud to them so they can investigate within the bounds of the law — you'll have to send extensive information, and comply specifically with the requirements of the law to clear your name. In this chapter, you'll see what their obligations are and what you must do. Then in Chapter Four, I'll tell you the steps you need to take and the letters you need to send, which you'll find pre-written for you in Appendix A. *I'*ll make it all understandable for you.

The creditors (banks, credit card companies, cell phone companies, computer companies, utility companies, etc.) who are the ones that issue the fraud accounts, are the least likely to spend time helping you deal with fraud that occurs with other creditors … unless you purchase their "Fraud Resolution Service." Carefully scrutinize the fraud services advertised by several banks to make sure that the help they claim you will receive really covers all of your fraud cleanup needs.

As a result of this lack of support from all areas, victims feel like they are being given the runaround. It's not necessarily that these firms and government agencies don't want to help people; it's that they have other missions. Plus, they lack the information or the authority, or they are overworked on other fronts and lack financial resources. Numerous insurance companies offer identity theft insurance (Traveler's, Chubb, AIG, etc). These usually will not resolve the issues for you, but they will provide an opportunity for you to make a claim for monetary reimbursement for your out-of-pocket costs and lost wages. This is another reason to keep accurate logs of out-of-pocket expenses with receipts, as well as time logs for lost wages. You'll find these form logs in Appendix A and on the CD.

Nonetheless, the result is that trying to regain your own identity and clean up the confusion involves the complete opposite of one-stop shopping. There are a zillion agencies, firms, and individuals to deal with. The bottom line is that you, as victim, must be the CEO of your identity theft resolution program and manage it, stay on top of it, and make sure all is resolved. *I* will give you the steps and letters in the next chapter — as promised — but first you must understand what you are entitled to under the law.

You do have rights!

In this chapter, I want to explore in non-technical terms what those rights are with regard to law enforcement issues, and your rights under the Fair Credit Reporting Act. (FCRA)

You may have other rights under the laws of your state (contact a private consumer law attorney, your state attorney general, or consumer affairs office for more details.) You can find all the state criminal laws relating to identity theft at www. consumer.gov/idtheft. Click on *Consumer Information*, then on *Laws*, to find the identity theft statutes of your own state. You can find the complete text of the FCRA, as well as helpful fact sheets about the FCRA and regulations at the Federal Trade Commission's web site (http://www.ftc. gov).

Your victim rights with regard to law enforcement:

Trying to report the crime of identity theft may create challenges for you, since, unlike other major crimes, it's rare that the victim lives where the actual fraud was committed. Many states and federal guidelines encourage the victim to make a police report in the jurisdiction where he or she lives. And you'll see later, when *I* discuss your rights under the Fair Credit Reporting Act and its new amendments, it's *critical* to obtain an "identity theft" report from law enforcement in order to resolve all the fraud issues. Even though we have identity theft statutes at the state and federal level, some police departments still refuse to write a report for several reasons:

- Some agencies still don't acknowledge that the consumer victim is truly a victim, since you don't have to pay the fraudulent bills.

- The law enforcement agency may be concerned that reporting the crimes will inflate their jurisdiction's crime statistics unfairly because the crime didn't occur in their community.

- If they actually wrote a report for all the victims who wish to make one, they would be overwhelmed with work that is labor intensive, and there wouldn't be time to investigate major crimes.

- The financial resources aren't available and neither is the man- or woman-power.

- And finally, they simply don't know what to do with identity theft victims (they may tell you it is a civil matter — when it is both criminal and civil), and many offices don't know how to investigate these types of complex cases, especially if it involves high tech theft.

In November 2000, the International Association of Chiefs of Police (IACP) adopted a resolution calling for all law enforcement agencies in the United States to take responsibility and record all incidents of identity theft in their own jurisdiction, and refer the victims to the Federal Trade Commission Hotline at 1-877-IDTHEFT. The Secret Service, the Postal Inspector, the Social Security Administration, and others endorsed this position, but there are still victims who can't get a report.

Another frustration for victims is that there exists no national *standard* identity theft report — each local agency has its own format. Some cities take an informal narrative report, some classify the report as an Identity Theft Report, some

call it fraud … even the FBI doesn't give identity theft its own classification. Victims are often told by the financial agencies that the police report they received from the victim is not adequate, so they cannot clear the record. That's why it will be your job to inform the law enforcement agency exactly why you need the identity theft report, and what must be included in that document. See Chapter Four and the letters in Appendix A to help you educate the police.

If your local police won't write a report, you have a right to *politely* demand that an informational report be written, including the documentation of the fraudulent accounts, fraudulent addresses, and other fraud. Your rights arise by virtue of your state and federal law making identity theft a crime. (Please note that if an officer doesn't believe that a crime was committed against you because he believes you just don't want to pay your bills, he/she may refuse to write a report — so you'll need to present more evidence.)

Before you call the police, locate your state penal code and print it off to have with you when you speak to an officer. (Go to www.consumer.gov/idtheft, and click on *State Laws*.) Tell the officer that you understand his department's constraints and say that, at the very least, you must have an informational report that lists what happened to you, all the fraud that's appearing on your credit reports, and any other evidence. Let them know that you understand that they are *not* required to investigate an informational report. Although you may provide oral evidence at first, follow up with written documentation of the fraud. (Use the Police Report Addendum; see Document 3-C(1) in Appendix A in this book and on the attached CD.)

Don't send the actual copies of your credit reports (unless you black out all the personal identifying information and your true financial records), since in most states this report becomes public record. Additionally, the defendant (if the perpetrator is brought to trial) is entitled to view all evidence with his defense counsel. So, to keep your private information and your finances out of the public records, only list the fraud information.

If your imposter committed crimes against you

in a jurisdiction other than your own, and your local law enforcement won't write a police report, (they will tell you they can't investigate in another state), you may contact the local office of your FBI, the Secret Service, your Postal Inspector, or the Social Security Administration Inspector's office in your local area. (See your local phone book.) Under federal law, The Identity Theft and Assumption Deterrence Act, (Relevant Code 18 USC 1028 (a)) makes identity theft against a consumer victim a *federal criminal offense*. You may *kindly* remind law enforcement that: Identity theft is committed if a person "knowingly transfers or uses, without lawful authority, a means of identification of another person with the intent to commit, or to aid or abet, any unlawful activity that constitutes a violation of federal law, or that constitutes a felony under any applicable state or local law." The Secret Service has jurisdiction over federal financial crimes, and even if they refuse to investigate, (which they will do, unless there is a very high dollar loss or it involves a crime ring or terrorism) if this crime involves crossing state lines, you should be able to get a law enforcement report from the Secret Service, or they may help you get a report from local law enforcement. If you live in a city where there is an Identity Theft Task Force, which includes local law enforcement and various federal law enforcement agencies, your Secret Service may team with local law enforcement to issue a report and possibly investigate. Please know that it is estimated that only 10 percent of the identity theft crimes reported are investigated.

You must exercise your rights and persuade law enforcement to prepare a report, and provide it to you. If you still have a problem, call and write the chief of police (see our letter in Appendix A), call the Federal Trade Commission at 1-877-IDTheft, show the police this book, or contact us at our web site at identitytheft.org for assistance.

Your rights: If you are a victim of criminal identity theft...

If a criminal uses your name and/or Social Se-

curity number when arrested, you will be saddled with a criminal record. The definition of identity theft includes the fraudulent use of your identification for *any* unlawful purpose, without your authorization; so you are entitled to obtain a police report with regard to this false impersonation.

If you learn via a background check by a potential employer that you have a criminal record, you'll have the right to get a copy of that background check. At that point, visit your local law enforcement agency and ask them to run a national criminal search for your name and Social Security number. If you find out because you are arrested for a crime you didn't commit, you will need to prove who you are, but you still have the right to make a local police report where you are arrested and where you live, and to ask them to contact the law enforcement agency where the crime occurred.

There is no federal law specifying the rights that you have with regard to clearing your name. Some states, such as California, have specific steps for victims to take to get a "Certificate of Innocence." But no matter where you live, you have a right to clear your criminal record if you are innocent, but you'll first need to get copies of all arrest records, court records, and any other documentation.

You have a right to the following:

- To file an impersonation report. The police will be suspicious of you, so you'll need to confirm your identity and prove you aren't the criminal. The police will need to take a full set of your fingerprints, your photo, and copy your identification documents such as a driver's license, passport, etc. You'll need evidence to show that it wasn't possible for you to have committed the crime (i.e. residing and working in another state, etc).

- To obtain the records regarding any criminal record in your name. Ask your local law enforcement agency to help you contact the law enforcement agency where the perpetrator was originally arrested. Explain that you are the victim. You will need to pay for copies of all documents.

- To obtain the entire booking record of the crimes that were committed. This will pull up the fingerprints and mug shot of the real criminal, so that the police can compare them with your documents to prove your innocence.

- To request that police recall any warrants and give you a "clearance letter" or certificate of release (if you were arrested). You must carry that document with you always in case you are stopped by law enforcement in the future.

- To have the district attorney's office in the jurisdiction where the crime was committed take steps to amend any complaint against you. You'll need to have the law enforcement agency assist you with this and provide all documentation.

- To direct that the law enforcement agency correct *all* records, replacing your name with that of the true imposter (*if known*). You must ask the attorney general of your state to then clear your name on the databases at the county, state, and federal level.

- To correct all court records. You have a right to have the prosecutor's office that originally prosecuted the case, or the victim assistance department of the prosecutor's office, make a motion to the court to clear your name and issue you a court determination of innocence. You shouldn't have to hire a private lawyer, but you may wish to consult with a criminal defense lawyer or ask for a public defender if you have no funds.

This process can be complex, and there is no standard procedure for the clearing of your name with the various criminal enforcement agencies and courts. However, the department of justice in your state should provide procedures. To find the attorneys general offices (DOJ) in the 50 states, visit the web site of the National Association of Attorneys General, www.naag.org. Contact your attorney general's office by phone and in writing. (See Appendix A.)

Once you've cleared your name from the records, it will be important for you to verify that the fraudulent criminal record is not appearing on the Internet in various databases; unfortunately, many victims clear their name only to find that information brokers don't update and correct their files. One of our clients cleared his name for arrest for murder, only to find that that erroneous information was resold by brokers *after* all the records were corrected. If that happens to you, you may sue the company who resold the inaccurate report. It's critical that you run your own background check — especially before you give someone else permission to do so. There are numerous online information brokers; here are a few that have been recommended to us as legitimate: www.mybackgroundcheck.com, www. ussearch. com, www.uslocate.com, www.whoishe.com. If you are concerned that an employer may use a private investigator to obtain more extensive information, you may wish to hire one yourself to be sure that you have a professional helping you to find out everything that is being revealed about you. To find private investigative services in your area, visit the web site of the National Association of Security and Investigative Regulators at www. nasir.org/licensing.htm or the National Association of Legal Investigators at www.nalionline. org.

Your rights under The Fair Credit Reporting Act

The Fair Credit Reporting Act (FCRA) (15 USC 1681 et. seq.) was enacted to provide protection for consumers with regard to the use, accuracy, and privacy of our consumer credit reports. Back in 1970, Congress originally passed this bill that allows consumers to see the information that lenders, credit card companies, insurers, and others obtain about them. The companies use this information to make decisions about extending credit, loans, and other services. Then, in 1996, new amendments were passed to improve the accuracy of our reports. At that time, there were temporary federal preemptions instituted that kept states from enacting stronger protections than federal law. Those preemptions were set to expire in 2003. So, at the end of 2003, the financial industry lobbied desperately for those preemptions to stay in effect. Understandably, they were worried that if each state were to pass its own complex laws, it would be very difficult for the financial industry, especially the CRAs, to comply with 50 different types of laws. At the same time, identity theft had become an epidemic and many states had passed identity theft legislation to protect their citizens, since the FCRA had not dealt specifically with identity theft. It was very clear in 2003 that the financial industry was not doing all it could to protect consumers from identity theft. So, the financial industry was willing to bargain for continued preemption of federal law in exchange for some protective provisions and accountability for victims of identity theft. In December 2003, President Bush signed the Fair and Accurate Credit Transactions Act, which amended the FCRA and made some improvements with regard to protecting consumers from identity theft. Unfortunately, many stringent laws enacted by states like California and Texas were preempted by the more lenient federal law, which in essence voided those greater protections. Consumer advocates were concerned that the new federal law, which on the surface looked like a tremendous improvement for victims, actually took away many state rights already established for victims. The federal law also precludes victims from suing companies who fail to act in good faith with various provisions of the FCRA. I will explain those restrictions at the end of this chapter.

Before I clarify your specific rights as victims of identity theft, you need to understand the basic rights that you and all other consumers have under the FCRA.

In its simplest form, The Fair Credit Reporting Act guarantees that:

1. **You can find out what's in your credit profile and your credit score**. If you request it, the credit bureau must give you the information in your file and a list of everyone who has requested that information recently. If you are a victim of fraud, unemployed, denied credit or insurance, or on public welfare, you are entitled to a *free* credit report. Also, in accordance with the recent amendments, every consumer is entitled to one free credit report disclosure annually from each of the three major CRAs. If you wish additional reports annually, you may be charged no more than nine dollars per report, and a reasonable additional fee to receive your credit score, which is a risk predictor used by lenders and creditors in deciding whether to issue you credit. Visit www.experian.com; www.equifax.com; and www.transunion.com for more information, or see our resources list at the end of this book.

2. **You can review your non-credit-based consumer report.** You also have the right to receive a free consumer report from the Nationwide Specialty Consumer Reporting Agencies. These are companies that provide consumer reports that don't deal with your credit information but that relate to medical records or payments, and your tenant history, your check-writing history, your employment history, your insurance claims, and other information. Go to www.ftc.gov for a list of these agencies, and the toll free number that will be instituted, to order your free annual reports.

3. **You must be told if information in your file has been used against you.** Anyone who denies you credit, or turns you down for a job or insurance or a place to live based on your consumer report, must tell you the consumer reporting agency that furnished the information. Under these circumstances, you're entitled to a free copy of that report also.

4. **You can dispute inaccurate information.** The credit bureau must investigate any

items you say are inaccurate and give you a free copy of your updated written report after its investigation. They must conduct an investigation free of charge within 30 days of receiving your dispute and within 5 days of receipt of your complaint. They must notify the creditor who originally supplied the information. If the investigation doesn't resolve the dispute to your satisfaction, you have the right to include on your credit profile a brief 100-word statement of your own, which must be sent by the credit reporting agencies (CRAs) to all companies that received your credit report in the last six months, or to employers who received it in the last two years. However, the CRA is not required to remove accurate data from your file unless it is outdated (normally more than seven years old), or cannot be verified. If your dispute results in any change to your report, the CRA cannot reinsert a disputed item into your file unless the information source verifies its accuracy and completeness. In addition, the CRA must give you a written notice telling you it has reinserted the item. The notice must include the name, address, and phone number of the entity that provided the information.

5. **Access to your file is limited (Permissible Purpose)** The credit bureau can provide information about you only to people with a need to know — such as creditors, insurers, employers (with your permission), landlords, child support agencies, the FBI for counterintelligence purposes, and others with whom you have a business relationship.

6. **You can dispute inaccurate items with the source of the information.** Creditors have a duty to furnish accurate information to the CRAs. You may dispute information that they provide to the CRA and they must reinvestigate. In addition, once you've notified the source of the error in writing, it may not continue to report the information if it is, in fact, an error.

7. **Outdated information may not be reported.** In most cases, a CRA may not report paid tax liens, civil suits or judgments, or other negative credit information that is more than seven years old — 10 years for bankruptcies.

8. **Your written consent is required for reports that are provided to employers.** A CRA may not give out information about you to your employer, or prospective employer, without your written consent. Medical information in your report must be coded to hide the healthcare provider and the nature of your medical services, and credit grantors may not use medical information in their credit decisions.

9. **You may choose to exclude your name from CRA lists for unsolicited credit and insurance offers.** Creditors and insurers may use file information compiled by the CRAs as the basis for sending you unsolicited offers of credit or insurance. Such offers must include a toll-free phone number for you to call if you want your name and address removed from future lists (1-888-5 OPT OUT.) If you call, you must be kept off the lists for five years. Request, complete, and return the CRA form provided for this purpose in writing and you may be taken off the lists indefinitely.

10. **You have a right to notice of risk-based pricing.** You have a right to receive a notice whenever credit is extended on terms "materially less favorable than the most favorable terms available to a substantial portion of the consumers" from that creditor. A bank creditor must give you written notice that the terms offered you are based on information in your credit report and that you are entitled to request a free credit report.

11. **You have a right to complain to the Federal Trade Commission.** You have a right to make complaints to the Federal Trade Commission with regard to any violations of

the Fair Credit Reporting Act. If you complain about a *CRA*, the Federal Trade Commission is required to transmit each complaint to the *CRA* involved.

Next, the agency must review each complaint, determine whether they've met their legal obligations, provide a report back to the FTC regarding the action that it has taken, and record the disposition of each complaint to show that they've been in compliance. Annually, the FTC will report to Congress regarding the complaints and make recommendations for changes in the law.

12. You may seek damages from violators — but there are many limitations. If a CRA, a user (e.g., a credit grantor), or, in some cases, a provider of CRA data, violates the FCRA by committing willful or certain negligent acts, you may, as an individual, sue them in state or federal court. There are many provisions in the amendments to the FCRA, which I will list at the end of this chapter, in which you may *not* sue as an individual. Also, the FCRA sets time limits as to bringing an action. You must file an action within two years of the discovery of a violation of the act, but no later than five years from the date of the violation. Many times victims are unaware of identity theft until years after the violation, but the CRAs needed protection from unlimited legal exposure. So, Congress limited the statute of limitations to five years. For that reason, it is very important to review your credit reports at least twice a year after the fraud is resolved.

Your rights as a victim of identity theft with regard to The Fair Credit Reporting Act (FCRA) as of Dec. 1, 2004:

1. Initial phone fraud alert notification

You have a legal right to add a Fraud Alert to your credit profile with each of the CRAs: Equifax, Experian, and TransUnion. If you call the fraud number for one agency (see resources — Appendix B), that bureau must notify the other two agencies and place the alert in their files as well. This alert must notify all prospective users (potential creditors) that the victim does not authorize any company to establish any new credit plan or extension of credit without calling the consumer to verify his identity and permission before extending credit. This means that a potential creditor can't issue new credit, additional cards, or extend a higher limit unless the victim is called or other reasonable steps are taken to verify that the victim authorized it. If creditors abide by the fraud alert, you will get a call before a fraudster is issued credit in your name.

Once you place an Initial Fraud Alert by phone, you'll be able to request a free copy of your credit report, which must be sent to you within three (3) business days after your request. (*I* suggest you provide your cell phone number if you have one so you may apply for instant credit and can be reached when you are not home.) The Fraud Alert will be placed on your file and will stay active for not less than 90 days from your request, unless you write a letter asking for an extended fraud alert (see Letter 1-A and Letter 1-B**).** You can only receive this by writing the letter and asking specifically for the Extended Fraud Alert for seven years.

2. Extended Fraud Alert — Additional Rights

To request that an extended fraud alert remain on your file for up to seven (7) years, you must include with your letter an "Identity Theft Report," which must include:

- Allegations of the identity theft- affidavit

- An official, valid report filed by you with a federal, state, or local law enforcement agency, and

- Your proof of identity. (See Letters 1-A and 1-B in Appendix A.) To avoid consumer fraud, you are subject to criminal penalties for providing any false information.

The CRAs must notify you of your right to receive two credit reports over the subsequent 12 months from when you first requested the fraud alert. You also have the right to be excluded from the pre-screening (it will stop "pre-approved offers" for up to five [5] years).

3. Credit bureaus must block fraudulent information

Once you identify in writing, fraudulent information in your credit reports for the three CRAs, each agency must block the fraudulent information from showing up on your credit report (not later than four [4] days after they receive your letter — so make sure you send it *return receipt requested*.) They must notify the furnisher of that information that you are claiming to be a victim of fraud. Then, the creditor must both investigate the information and take steps to prevent it from being re-submitted to any of the three CRAs. Under the FCRA, those companies that report fraudulent information must establish reasonable procedures to respond to the notices by the CRAs that your information was blocked due to identity theft. Once a creditor receives an Identity Theft Report from the victim, and appropriate documentation, that creditor is required to stop furnishing that information to the credit bureaus. Once you send your letter, with your Identity Theft Report attached, to the credit grantor who has issued fraud accounts, they must re-investigate the underlying information and they may *not* transfer that debt to another company or to a collection company once they are notified that the debt is a result of fraud. In Chapter Four you will see what steps you must take to comply with this law.

4. Identity theft victims' access to fraudulent transaction information

You, as the victim, are entitled to request from any business entity that instituted a fraud account to an identity thief all documentation about the transactions by the thief. You may also request that copies of the documentation be sent to a law enforcement agency as well.

You must make a written request for the information and include any relevant information that you know about the transactions. You must provide proof of your identification, the government-issued ID, personal identifying information, (more than the thief was required to give), or the same type of information that the business usually requests from new applicants. You must also send your Identity Theft Report from a law enforcement agency and your completed Federal Trade Commission Identity Theft Affidavit. Then, once you send this, *return receipt requested*, to the business, you should be provided copies of the application and all the business transactions within 30 days of receipt of your letter … at no cost to you. Now, here is the challenging part:

The business can refuse to give you access to such records even if you do all the things that you are supposed to do under the law, if the business determines "in the exercise of good faith" that any of the following exceptions exist:

- The business does not have a high degree of confidence in knowing the true identity of the victim who is requesting the information, even though the victim has satisfied the Identity Verification Requirements;

- The request is based on a misrepresentation of fact; or

- The information requested is "Internet navigational data or similar information."

Another problem with this provision is that you have no right to enforce this business transaction, meaning you have no right to sue the company if they fail to provide you with the information, and your own state attorney general is precluded from suing on your behalf. Worse yet, the states are preempted from making strict laws to protect you. This is especially disappointing for residents of California, whose previous law allowed a victim to get all of the documentation upon presentation of the verifying information, the police report, and the other requirements, and get that information within 10 days at no cost. If the company refused to provide the information, then the victim had a right to sue. So, the benefit of this provision is going to be effective only if the business is willing to comply with the requirements. The only agencies that have the right to sue are the Federal Trade Commission or other federal agencies. So, if a company refuses to provide you this information (which *I* believe will happen in many cases), you should lodge a complaint with the Federal Trade Commission, and also notify the U.S. Public Interest Research Group and the various consumer, nonprofit agencies to let them know that this is happening. *I* believe that if you let your state and federal legislators know, and let the media know, then perhaps some "teeth" will be put into this provision.

It is critical for you to get documentation of the crime, and for the law enforcement agency to get documentation of the crime, so that they can pursue the perpetrator. Many companies are reluctant to send you this information, since it will evidence their negligence. But you must explain to the company that in order for there to be prosecution and conviction, you need to find the thief, and you must have evidence to do so. And if the thief is prosecuted and convicted, then, of course, you are entitled to ask for restitution for your out-of-pocket expenses and your losses. So, it's critical for you to get fraud data, and you should demand it. Please contact us if you continue to have problems getting the evidence.

5. Debt collectors must provide information to victims

You have the right to notify any collection agency that the debt is fraudulent or resulted from identity theft. The debt collector must notify the original creditor and provide you with the information required under the debt validation of the Fair Debt Collection Practices Act. That allows you to demand written notice of the amount of the debt, the name of the creditor who's claiming that the debt is owed, and a statement that you have the right to dispute the validity within 30 days, (otherwise the debt collector will assume that it's

valid). You must dispute the fraud debt in writing, (*I* have letters for this in Appendix A). The collector must provide you documentation of the verification of that debt, and the name and address of the original creditor. Then you may follow through with requesting access to the Thief's Transaction Information as above. A creditor who has been notified of a fraudulent debt must not sell it to a collection agency. So, be sure to write your letters and document any violation.

6. Agency responsibilities to block all fraud

You have the right to have all fraudulent information on your credit profile blocked (that means that it will be deleted from the view of any potential creditor and will not appear on your consumer reports unless they prove it is not fraud). You must provide the credit bureaus with the following information:

- Proof of your identity

- A copy of your Identity Theft Report

- Your identification of the fraudulent information, and

- Your statement that the information does not relate to any transaction that you've made. (See Letters 1-A and 1-B in Appendix A)

Once the credit bureau receives this information from you (*return receipt requested* to verify the date), they must block the items within four (4) business days; so the information in your file should be restored to what it was without the fraud. This is especially important if you're trying to buy a house or car, or get a job because the fraudulent information will be blocked immediately, and your score will be re-adjusted. But you must do this in writing!

7. Credit bureau must notify furnisher

When you write your letter to request a block of all the fraudulent information on your credit report, you should include not only fraudulent accounts, but also fraudulent bankruptcies, fraudulent tax liens, fraudulent addresses, fraudulent names, etc. (There may be many errors besides just accounts and fraud inquiries.) Once you notify the three major credit bureaus (in writing) that you're requesting that the information be blocked from your credit reports, each of the agencies has the duty to notify the entity or companies that furnished the information that was blocked due to your Identity Theft Report. They must notify the furnisher of the *date* of the block, and all other information pertaining to the fraud — so you must include all of the fraud information in your notification.

8. Resellers of credit reports

There are hundreds of resellers of consumer information that sell to mortgage companies, law offices, real estate brokers, car dealerships, etc. If you see a copy of your credit bureau report from a reseller, you have the right to inform the reseller of the fraud. The reseller must block the report and notify you of the name, address, and telephone number of the major consumer reporting agency that provided the original information. Then you, as the victim, have the right to enforce the block with that major credit agency, in the manner described for dealing with the CRAs.

Your rights with regard to the creditor or furnisher of information

The creditor who furnished the information must institute procedures to prevent the re-reporting of that information to anyone, not just the credit bureaus. The creditor who issued the fraud account is required to purge their file of your fraud. You must submit your Identity Theft Report and letter directly to the furnisher or the creditor, and *I* have provided you letters in Appendix A to do this. Although this is extra work, take advantage of that right under the law. Once you submit your report and tell the creditor that the information was based on identity theft and the creditor stops reporting that information to the credit bureau, they can only re-report that information if they

subsequently research and find out and "know" that that information is truly correct and not fraud. Again, the problem here is if a creditor re-reports the information improperly, you have no right to sue them. Also, your state attorney general is precluded from suing them, and the states are preempted from regulating this by creating more stringent laws. One possible help to victims is that when a CRA provides the creditor with notice that there's been a block of your fraudulent information, the creditor is under a duty not to furnish information that they "know or have reason to believe is inaccurate." So, if the creditor does report this information, depending on the facts, you may have a right to bring action against the creditor.

1. **Creditors may not sell fraud accounts to collection companies**.

   Once a creditor is notified that the information that they've reported to the CRAs was fraudulent as evidenced in an Identity Theft Report, the creditor may not sell, transfer, or place the debt for collection. This is a major improvement for victims who in the past would report the fraud to the original creditor, and then the creditor would sell the account to a collection agency that would then sell it to another collection agency. Some victims would clean up their credit reports only to find new collection agencies would appear on their reports.

2. **Check verification companies and your rights under the Fair Credit Reporting Act**

   Check services companies (which issue authorizations for the purpose of approving or processing checks, electronic fund transfers, or similar payments) are exempt from the blocking guidelines of fraud information to retailers and others who use their information. So, this is still a challenge for victims. However, once you notify a checks services company that you are a victim of identity theft with regard to check fraud, the checks services companies that you notify must no longer report fraudulent information resulting from your identity theft. That information won't appear on your credit report; however, you may still have problems with various retailers who have your name in databases as one who writes fraudulent checks. You'll need to deal directly with the check verification companies to clear your name to be able to write checks at retail establishments. *I* strongly suggest you use credit cards at retailers.

3. Unblocking of your fraud

If a consumer credit bureau "reasonably believes that you misrepresented this fraudulent information or that, indeed, you received goods or that there was an error, then the agency has a right to rescind the block." Any genuine debts would not be blocked. (The furnishers of the information may provide information back to the CRA, which verifies that it is your debt —incorrectly, or in bad faith). Unfortunately, the agencies and creditors make mistakes. So if the agency decides to unblock your fraudulent information, they must notify you of the rescission and the specific reason for the rescission within five (5) business days, which is similar to what they must do to notify a consumer if they're reinserting formerly deleted information. Therefore, if an agency tells you they unblocked the fraud and it will reappear on your consumer report, you have the right to dispute this and reassert the fraud. To protect your rights, you must document timelines and actions that the credit bureaus take. If the action is deemed willful, you may sue!

Preventing theft of your identification

There are some new provisions in the Fair Credit Reporting Act that attempt to protect your sensitive information and decrease your vulnerability to identity theft.

1. Protection of active duty military consumers — Active duty alert

I've heard from hundreds of victims of identity theft who have served or were serving in the military. Unfortunately, the military ID number is the Social Security number, and if military personnel are out of the country, they become a vulnerable target for identity thieves. Under the FCRA, if a person is assigned away from his usual home, the military consumer may place *an active duty alert* on his credit profile for *at least 12 months*. That person will also automatically be removed from the "pre-approved" offers of credit for *two years*. The consumer may ask that no credit be extended without verification of such authorization by calling the military consumer at the number provided by him/her. Then the potential credit grantor is required to call the military consumer for verification before extending credit.

2. Truncation of credit card numbers

Retailers, service providers, and other companies that accept credit cards are now required to truncate (black out all but last five numbers on credit and debit cards on electronically printed receipts). This provision will be phased in and effective for all *receipt-printing machines* by December 4, 2006. (Most companies are complying now.)

3. Redact Social Security numbers

You can ask that the CRA withhold all but the last five digits of your Social Security number on your credit report.

4. Address verification

Credit bureaus that receive a request for a consumer report from a creditor for the purpose of issuing a new credit card, credit line, or a loan will include an address of the consumer. If that address is substantially different from the address that's on your credit application, a CRA must notify that creditor of the discrepancy when they provide a copy of the credit report. Then the creditor is required to take reasonable steps to verify the correct address. (Those reasonable steps won't be clarified by federal agencies until after the printing of this book.)

5. Proper disposal of credit report information

Credit card companies, and others who have access to and acquire consumer information through credit reports, now have a duty to properly dispose of that consumer information when they discard it. They're not required to immediately dispose of it, but when they do discard it, they must dispose of that information in a way that protects the data (shred, completely destroy). The Federal Trade Commission will decide on new regulations with regard to what is proper disposal. Dumpster diving is a very easy way for potential impersonators to get your private information; this provision may help reduce that risk.

6. Creditor guidelines for red flag alerts

The FCRA also calls for the FTC and various banking agencies to issue regulations that will require creditors and financial institutions to establish "reasonable policies and procedures for implementing red flag guidelines regarding identity theft." For example, if a bank or credit card company receives a request for an additional replacement card on an existing account within 30 days of receiving a change of address notice, before the company issues a new credit card, they must do one of the following:

- Notify the cardholder of the request, using the former address.

- Notify the cardholder of the request by other agreed upon means, i.e. telephone, or

- Validate the change of address in accordance with regulations. (At the time of this printing, not all these regulations have been finalized.) You may find them clarified at www.ftc.gov.

7. Information accuracy and integrity

Those who furnish information to CRAs (banks, credit card companies, collection agencies, insurers), have a responsibility to report accurate information. Recent changes to the Fair Credit Reporting Act include an obligation to:

- Cease furnishing blocked identity theft-related information.

- Follow new accuracy and integrity guidelines, which will be developed by the Federal Trade Commission. (Go to www.ftc.gov.)

- Notify you, the customer, that the institution (bank, lender, etc.) is furnishing negative information about you to a consumer reporting agency. You have a right to dispute that negative information to that creditor. The hope is that this will let you know about fraud data as well (if they don't send the notice to the fraud address!).

If a financial institution notifies you that they're reporting negative information to the credit bureau, it should alert you to any inaccurate information or fraudulent information. So, if you receive information from a creditor that they're going to provide information to the credit bureau that's inaccurate, you must write to them *immediately*, because you are not entitled to any further notices when additional negative information is reported about that same account. Therefore, upon the very first notice, you must deal with that institution within *(30)* days of their reporting that information. Also, the financial institution must give you notice within 30 days of reporting that negative information to the credit bureaus. You must dispute it in writing *yourself*, meaning you can't have a credit repair organization or someone else dispute it for you or it won't be valid. In fact, you probably would have a problem having a lawyer dispute it for you. So, it is best that you use our form letters to dispute it yourself.

Once you send a dispute or letter of fraud, the company that furnished the information, must investigate the dispute and report back to you within 30 days, and they must correct the information with each CRA they furnished with that information. But you have no right to sue that creditor if they don't follow this provision. There's no enforcement except for the FTC or other federal agencies to sue, and they won't sue on your individual behalf. You must rely on the good faith of the companies. My suggestion, again, as to the enforcement of those rights would be to complain to the Federal Trade Commission, contact the various agencies listed in our resources section, including our office, and consider speaking to your federal legislators and the media.

8. Verification and authentication — biometrics study

The Fair and Accurate Credit Transactions Act of 2003 recognized that the Social Security number has not been properly protected, and that for an identity thief your SSN is the key to the kingdom for financial gain, as well as for avoiding prosecution for crimes. The Fair and Accurate Transaction Act required a government study of the use of biometric technology to combat identity theft. Biometrics is a technology that uses a unique body characteristic such as your fingerprint, your iris scan, facial scan, hand scan, or retina scan to identity you. The purpose of studying this technology is to reduce the incidence and the cost to society of identity theft by providing evidence of who actually performed a given financial transaction. Presently, the accuracy of biometric information is still in doubt. There are many false-positives and false-negatives with regard to the biometrics. The hope is that this study will set forth specific guidelines and safeguards that need to be implemented in order for us to insure the accuracy of the biometric information and safeguard it from corruption, sale, and transfer, which would subject us to high tech thievery of our identity.

Limitations on your right to enforce your rights

Now that I have shared with you many of your rights as a consumer and victim under the newest provisions of the Fair Credit Reporting Act, I must also share with you the limitation of enforcement of those rights. Following is a list of new obligations by creditors and furnishers of information that are protected from private lawsuits. These are also protected from state lawsuits by your attorney general and may only be enforced by certain federal agencies including the Federal Trade Commission. These agencies may not represent individuals. Class actions are not permitted and you do not have a right to sue creditors and furnishers of credit information as an individual under the following provisions:

1. You can't sue creditors and furnishers of information due to fraud for failure to abide by a fraud alert. Nor may you sue when a company resubmits fraudulent information to your credit report after it has been deleted.

2. You can't sue a financial institution for failure to notify you that they're furnishing negative information to the CRAs about you, even though they are required to do so.

3. You can't sue a creditor or furnisher of information to the credit bureaus for failure to reinvestigate a dispute or an allegation of fraud, nor for its failure to investigate within a designated period of time.

4. You can't sue a creditor for failing to notify each CRA that the information that they provided to the bureau was inaccurate.

5. You also can't sue persons or entities in the business of providing medical services, products, or devices for failure to inform agencies of their status as a medical information furnisher, which means that if your medical information is placed on your credit report and used by creditors, you can't sue that medical provider who violated that provision of the law.

6. You cannot sue businesses that issued fraud accounts to your imposter.

7. You can't sue a business for failure to provide you documentation of the correspondence from the impersonator and other evidence of the fraud.

8. You also cannot sue potential creditors for failure to abide by the obligations to provide you risk-based price notices. You are to be given prior notice if credit is offered to you on less advantageous terms because of your credit report.

9. You cannot sue federal banking agencies, the National Credit Union Administration, or the Federal Trade Commission for failure to establish adequate accuracy and integrity guidelines for creditors and other furnishers. Nor can you sue the federal agencies for failure to prescribe effective regulations requiring the creditors to establish reasonable policies and procedures for implementing those guidelines.

10. You may not enforce the obligation of credit grantors to issue red flag guidelines and regulations with regard to verification of change of address for credit cards.

You can, however, pursue private actions in accordance with the Fair Credit Reporting Act's Willful and Negligent Liability Provisions; but in order to do this, you will need to review your individual case with an attorney who is experienced with the Fair Credit Reporting Act.

From reading all the above, you can see that recent amendments to the Fair Credit Reporting Act have enacted many new obligations on the part of creditors and furnishers of your credit-reporting information and the CRAs. However, the implementation of these positive changes will be dependent upon the goodwill of the various companies. In my experience dealing with the CRAs and the credit grantors in the past, I am concerned that many of these rights that you have been granted through these federal laws may not be implemented by some agencies, and that will increase your frustration.

After several times testifying at the state and federal level, I learned that when new legislation is passed, it imposes challenging obligations on big companies. It takes time for them to incorporate those new procedures. If there is a failure to comply, hundreds or thousands of victims complain to the various agencies, and the media; then legislators get the message, and the laws are reviewed and improved. So, now that you aware of your legal rights, if they are not satisfied by the various agencies, you must speak up, write your complaint to the federal agencies, to your state and federal legislators, and to the various consumer lobbyists. (See the back of this book for our resources section.) With your voice, these rights granted under federal law will become enforceable. We will collaboratively exert pressure to make sure that those companies that are in violation step up to the plate to comply with their duties to protect you and help you regain your good name.

Now that you understand the laws meant to help you, you'll need to set forth your strategy to ask for what you are entitled to receive in order to regain your identity. In the next chapter, I'll give you a detailed list of things to do that will speed up your efforts and make them less burdensome, plus, some specific steps to take, and the corresponding letters to write, to exercise your rights and clear up your blemished good name.

I'll help you get through this...you're not alone!

Chapter Four

The Steps You Must Take Now

Like a snowflake — or more apropos, like a fingerprint — each case of identity theft is unique. As you've already learned, it's your job to figure out how (if possible), and to what extent you've been victimized, then to take action. What you discover may upset you, making you feel angry and frightened. Such feelings are normal. You *will* be able to resolve the problems if you prioritize, get organized, and follow the simple steps I give you. You *will* get your life and identity back, and this guide will help you.

Following these steps will put you on the road to what I call the 3Cs:

- Clean up the credit mess

- Clear up your name and reputation

- Control your life

You do need to deal — and *soon* — with the details of your case. That's because, for one thing, the identity thief may be continuing his or her crime spree even as you read this. Further, by delaying action, you could complicate the case, or look negligent yourself for not dealing with the issues. A new credit card established in your name, for example, may change hands, making the trail harder to follow. The perpetrator may travel to a distant state or country, adding to the jurisdictional hurdles even as he or she orders new cards and gets more instant credit or commits other crimes. Further, some legal remedies can expire if you don't act within a certain time period.

Generally speaking, federal law says the victim of credit card fraud is liable for only the first $50 of losses *if* they notify financial institutions immediately upon learning of the loss, and luckily many financial institutions will waive even that amount. For other types of financial fraud (loan, mortgage, insurance) you will probably be able to avoid all liability, once you *prove* you are innocent, if you notify the companies as soon as you learn of the fraud.

Please remember that you should *not* pay an imposter's bills in your name, you could be left with a bad credit report and months, if not years, of trying to restore your financial health. You also may be hassled by bill collectors, banks, merchants, and others. You'll need to convince them that an imposter — *not you* — made the purchases, filed the bankruptcy, rented the apartment, or committed the crime.

It often won't be a case of these creditors needing to prove your guilt as much as you being forced to establish yourself as a victim of crime. The critical step will be to get an "Identity Theft Report." For many victims who don't have a coach, it's a long, tiring, costly battle. However, if you persevere and follow the next steps, it *will* end in a timely manner with less effort.

Don't expect much help from authorities in your quest to set matters straight. They are overwhelmed themselves. To ease your burden, I've put together a list of 20 steps you need to take as soon as possible. (Not all 20 steps apply to every victim, so you'll need to pick and choose. If, for example, your case doesn't involve a civil judgment against you, you will skip the step about dealing with the civil court.) If new problems arise at a later date, you will have this guide to consult. Also, you'll have the pre-written letters in Appendix A and on the CD, to help you clear up the problems quickly and effectively.

Taking on the challenge.

No one can really take on this challenge for you entirely, not even a lawyer! *You're* the only one who knows your credit, your personal data, and your financial picture, such as which are the fraudulent accounts and which are the legitimate accounts. Only you know your background, so it's up to *you* to act quickly and assertively to minimize the damage.

Equally important, in all dealings with the authorities and with financial institutions, remember to:

- Keep a clipboard with a log of every conversation, including dates, names, and phone numbers. Otherwise, you're sure to get confused as to who said what and when. You can use the logs on the CD that comes with this book. Make several copies and keep them up-to-date.

- Log all time and expenses, too. You'll need such information if you eventually seek reimbursement for damages in settlement or legal actions against companies who may have acted inappropriately. You'll also need this to give to a judge if your impostor is caught and restitution is ordered. Also, your fraud losses and out-of-pocket costs may be tax deductible under the United States IRS Code 165e. You can show these logs to a lawyer, accountant, or judge, depending on the circumstances, to help you with these financial issues.

- Get the name of the supervisor of the fraud department when you call any agency. Also ask for his/her direct phone line, fax number, and e-mail address. Don't waste time telling your story to someone with no authority to take action. Even if the supervisor isn't available to speak to you, ask for a return phone call — this saves tremendous time and aggravation in follow-up. Take copious notes with the date, names, and facts.

- Confirm all phone conversations in writing.

(Employees you speak to may leave, be transferred, or be negligent in follow-up.) Use the letters already prepared on the CD to save time.

- Always send correspondence by certified mail (*return receipt requested*) as stated in our letters. This is important to show notification and to document that correspondence was received. You'll need to mark in your log the date this was received since it may be a legal issue later (i.e. timelines and statute of limitations issues). A company may have liability for not responding in a timely manner.

- Keep copies of all letters and documents in organized files (alphabetical order, by category) in banker boxes, in a safe place, clearly labeled (i.e. Social Security, Equifax.) Also, keep copies of your letters on a separate CD filed in a locked cabinet. Remember, you have personal data in those letters!

- Complete the **Uniform Affidavit** (of the facts of your situation) developed by the Federal Trade Commission. You'll find it in the Appendix A section at the end of this book (also on the CD). Update it regularly with new information you learn about your case. Make sure you complete a bullet point chronological history (with dates) of your case and keep it up-to-date. This will be a great help for law enforcement. Also, if at some point you need an attorney, it will make it easier for her or him to understand your case.

Twenty Steps You Must Take Now!

As your coach, I'm telling you that the best way to restore your finances and regain your good name is to begin following these 20 steps as soon as possible. The list may look daunting at first, but taking these actions will ultimately save you time and empower you. And for your own sake, you *must* do a thorough job. The identity you save will be your own. So, have no fear, your coach is here!

Step No. 1: Contact the credit bureaus.

Immediately call the fraud units of the three major credit-reporting firms: TransUnion, Equifax, and Experian. You'll need information from all three bureaus because each may have a different version of your credit report. Recent federal law states that to place a fraud alert, you need to call only *one* bureau, and that agency will contact the other two; but it's *safer* to call all three to make sure you have protected your rights, and to get your free reports.

You'll get an automated voice recording prompt which will allow you to add a fraud alert and receive a *free* credit report. You'll need to punch in your Social Security number; it's required. Be sure to listen to all of the choices, as it can be very confusing. If your situation involves an imposter who's opening up new accounts in your name, your follow-up letter to the credit bureaus will state your identity has been used to obtain credit that you haven't applied for. Request that a fraud alert be placed in your report immediately and remain on for at least seven (7) years. When you call, they will automatically place a fraud alert for 90 days. To extend the fraud alert protection, your request must be in writing.

Call these numbers:

• **Equifax**

To report fraud: (800) 525-6285
P.O. Box 740241
Atlanta, GA 30374-0241

To order copy of report: (800) 685-1111
P.O. Box 740241
Atlanta, GA 30374-0241
Website: www.equifax.com

To opt out of pre-approved offers of credit:
(888) 5 OPTOUT [(888) 567-8688]

• **Experian (formerly TRW)**

To report fraud: (888) 397-3742
Experian Consumer Fraud Assistance
P.O. Box 9532
Allen, TX 75013

To order copy of report: (888) 397-3742
P.O. Box 9532
Allen, TX 75013
Website: www.experian.com

To opt out of pre-approved offers of credit:
(888) 5 OPTOUT [(888) 567-8688]

• **TransUnion**

To report fraud: (800) 680-7289
Fraud Victim Assistance Division
P.O. Box 6790
Fullerton, CA 92634

To order copy of report: (800) 888-4213
P.O. Box 6790
Fullerton, CA 92634
Website: www.transunion.com

To opt out of pre-approved offers of credit:
(888) 5 OPTOUT [(888) 567-8688]

Remember, if you're a victim of identity fraud or if you have been denied credit, insurance, or employment because of something on your credit report, you're entitled to a *free* credit report. It's the law. (You're also entitled to a free credit report if you're unemployed or receiving welfare.) Federal law that began at the end of 2004, allows everyone to get a free credit report once a year. As of this printing, the final regulations have not been established. The agencies must establish a toll-free number for non-victims, which you will find on their web sites.

Other points to make in your follow-up letter to the credit bureaus:

• Ask that your account be flagged as one on which fraud is suspected. Make sure to extend the fraud alert as long as possible. The fraud alert should be kept on there for at least seven years (see Letters 1-A and 1-B to the CRAs at the end of this book). The fraud alert allows you to state, "Don't issue credit without calling me first at this number." *I* suggest you provide your cell phone number so that if you want to buy something on instant credit (i.e. a car on a Sunday), you'll have your phone with you when they call to verify its really you!

- Depending on your state law, you may be entitled to a security freeze. Some states like California, Texas, Louisiana, and others are passing laws that would entitle you to take your credit profile offline so a fraudster cannot get credit (and neither can you), without providing a PIN to allow your credit report to be reviewed by a creditor. With a "freeze," you may place a security freeze on your credit reports. This essentially prevents anyone from accessing your credit file for any reason, until and unless you instruct the credit bureaus to unfreeze or "thaw" your report with a password. A freeze provides much more protection than a fraud alert. (*I know of many cases where the fraudster got new credit from careless creditors even with a fraud alert on file.*) If creditors ignore the fraud alerts and the thief continues to get credit in your name, and if you live in a state that allows this, you should strongly consider using the security freeze to curtail access to your credit file unless you are applying for credit yourself immediately. In California the security freeze is free to victims of identity theft; non-victims who wish to use the freeze for prevention purposes must pay a fee to activate it. Not all states permitting freezes will allow non-victims to freeze their reports. Check out your state's laws at www.consumer.gov/idtheft. Call your state attorney general and legislators to ask them to implement this effective option.

- Add a "victim's statement" to your report, up to 100 words. (Something like: "An imposter has opened the following accounts in my name and has worked using my Social Security number xxx-xx-xxxx. My police report is # xxxxxxxx. Please contact fraud investigator _____ at _____ Police Department, phone number _____.) This will increase your credibility with creditors regarding the fraud, and reputable companies will call you before issuing credit.

- Ask the credit bureaus in writing (see Letter 1-A) to provide you with free copies of your credit report. (Federal law allows *two free* reports for a victim in one year.) They must also provide you a free report with the corrections made after you report the fraudulent information.

- Ask for immediate access to the names, addresses, and phone numbers of credit card companies and other credit grantors with whom fraudulent accounts have been opened, and for the inquiries that were made from companies without your permission.

- Request that the credit bureaus remove all inquiries (lists of names of companies that received a copy of your credit report for the purpose of issuing you credit) that have been generated due to the fraudster's request. Get the names, addresses, and phone numbers of all companies who made any inquiries listed on your credit report. These fraudulent inquiries must be removed because they can negatively affect your credit rating. Creditors who received your credit report must be notified of the fraud so they don't issue credit to the impersonator!

- Ask the credit bureaus to contact any company or agency that received your credit report in the last year (two years for employers) and alert them to the fraud information. You want them to know that you are a victim of fraud. Remember, a creditor may offer credit up to a year after receiving your information. So, you must be proactive and stop the fraud before it is extended.

- Ask to be removed from pre-screening (pre-approved offers) for at least five years.

Send a letter *immediately* to the credit agencies summarizing your requests. (See Letters 1-A and 1-B.) Be aware, though, that these measures may not entirely stop an imposter from opening new fraudulent accounts. That's because some credit grantors offering instant credit do not carefully screen your report for fraud alerts. Although recent federal law requires that creditors honor your alert, there are still companies who are less than cautious.

When your credit report arrives, carefully read the instructions that accompany it. There's a wealth of information on the report, and close study will give you clues to the nature and extent of the fraud as well as possible cures. Scrutinize each report line by line.

What specifically to look for on your report

- Verify that your Social Security number is exactly correct and that your name is not misspelled. See if there is a similar name on your profile. This is a red flag! Inform the agencies of each and every fraud/error, or it will be reported to credit grantors incorrectly.

- Verify your address to make sure it has not been changed to a fraudulent one. Check to see if former addresses are correct. Insist that any incorrect address(es) be removed from your credit report promptly and completely. Otherwise, pre-approved cards may be sent to the impersonator at an alternate address.

- Find the date of the opening of the first fraudulent account. You'll also need to look at the inquiries to see when that company first accessed your credit report. The first company that issued the fraud account is the most careless. That account will be used to open other new accounts.

- Then look for other inquiries, which appear as unfamiliar accounts (i.e., which bank, credit card company, or mortgage firm received your report before the opening of the fraudulent accounts). Ask each such company (where fraud occurred) in writing for a copy of the original application with the forged signature used to obtain credit in your name. Ask for all information and documentation they have for the fraud account. This may lead you to the impersonator. Under federal law, the companies must send you a corrected file and the information, free of charge. (See Letters 3-A, 3-B, and 3-C).

- Demand that credit bureaus notify all those companies who received your credit report in the last year that you are a victim of fraud. This will alert those merchants to the fraud, and, hopefully prevent them from issuing credit. The credit bureaus must also notify those who've made inquiries so new accounts are not issued. Request copies of each of those notifications for your records also, to make sure it gets done.

- Request a list of phone numbers and addresses of every creditor who received your history from the CRAs in the last year. You should notify these institutions of the fraud and ask them not to issue credit to the impersonator. Remember, some of your legitimate creditors also received credit reports in the last year.

Step No. 2: Alert your creditors and fraud creditors

Immediately call, and follow up in writing, your creditors — especially those with whom you believe your name has been used fraudulently. (See Letters 2-A, 2-B and 2-C.)

Make sure to request:

- Cancellation of the fraud accounts and removal of all fraudulent information on your credit reports, including the inquiries made by the company. These negative accounts pave the way for more fraud accounts to be opened, which lowers your credit score.

If the fraudster was able to use your credit card or have a duplicate card issued, cancel the card and get a replacement card with a new account number. Only cancel your accounts that were used *fraudulently*. Ask that each of your true closed accounts be labeled as *"account closed at consumer's request."* (That's better than saying, *"card lost or stolen,"* because that wording, when reported to credit bureaus, might imply that you're to blame for the loss, and may affect your credit score).

- All documentation of the account, including:

   √ Initial application with forged signature.

   √ All billing statements.

   √ Address and phone number where the cards were sent.

   √ All correspondence between the fraudster and the creditor.

   √ Any other electronic or hard copy information relative to the case.

   √ Any video or audio evidence.

Make sure you also request:

- Copies of transmittals from creditor to CRAs and collection agencies documenting removal of the fraud from your credit report profile.

- Placement of fraud alerts on all of your true bank accounts, investment accounts, retirement accounts, and credit cards or lines of credit. Put a new password on all such accounts. Do *not* use your mother's maiden name if that is what you used before, since it is on your birth certificate, which is public record and can be accessed on the Internet. (Create a new password for each true account.)

Federal law allows the victim, upon presenting proper identification, a law enforcement report, and a completed Federal Trade Commission Affidavit, to obtain the above information free of charge within 30 days of the written request. The victim may also designate a law enforcement agency to receive evidence of the fraud as well. (See Letters 2-A and 2-B.)

Remember: Don't cancel any of your valid accounts unless fraud has been committed on that account. This will only look more suspicious in the future and may make it more difficult for you to get credit later. *So, don't cancel your good cards!* If you must cancel a card due to fraud, loss, or theft, order a new card (new account number) with the company *immediately*. Bear in mind that it may be tough to get new credit during this ordeal if you don't do this now. Make sure you have at least two valid credit cards to show credit-worthiness.

Banks and creditors may ask you to fill out and notarize many fraud affidavits, a process that can become expensive. The law does not require a notarized affidavit, and a written statement and supporting documentation should be sufficient. Use the affidavit at the end of this book and on the CD. Notarize only once and make a dozen copies; then, unless the creditor offers to pay for the notary for their "special," stick with the copy of your affidavit. If they balk, offer your bank's guaranteed signature. Use the Uniform Affidavit sanctioned by the Federal Trade Commission (in the back of this book and on the CD — also available at http://www.consumer.gov/idtheft).

Overly burdensome requirements by creditors should be reported to the Federal Trade Commission. If you need help in determining which agency to contact, call the Federal Trade Commission at 1-877-IDTHEFT and check our resource pages at the back of this book.

Step No. 3: Report the crime to police or the Secret Service, and the U.S. Postal Inspector by phone and in writing.

Within 24 hours of learning of the fraud, after calling the credit bureaus, report the crime to the fraud units of your local police or sheriff department's "white collar" or economic crime unit. You may also contact law enforcement in the area where the fraud occurred. Often the police in another county or state may not want to help you or even *take* a report, so you must call your local law enforcement. Give them as much documented evidence as possible, and in turn, make sure you get a copy of all police reports they file. Ask your local law enforcement agency to contact the law enforcement agency where the fraud occurred. If it crosses state lines, they may contact a federal law enforcement agency. Since there is a federal identity theft law (18 USC 1028), the Secret Service (or the FBI, Social Security Inspector, or the U.S. Postal Inspector) may investigate (if there is a high dollar value, evidence of a fraud ring, or if the crime crosses state lines.). If police in other states (where the fraud took place) won't help, contact your local office of the Secret Service, which has jurisdiction when the crime is inter-state. There are many cities that have Identity Theft Task Forces made up of local law enforcement, the Secret Service, the postal inspector, the Inspector General of the Social Security Administration, the FBI, and other agencies. Remember, even if your case is small and they can't investigate, your local law enforcement has a duty to provide you at least an informative report under most state laws. You must have an identity theft report to use with the *CRAs* to get the fraud deleted from your profile. Also, the creditors will ask for the report. The police report must list in detail all the fraud information.

In dealing with law enforcement, make sure you:

- Are very polite, no matter how frustrated you feel! Please understand they have limited resources.

- Tell them the address where the credit cards (or credit lines) were sent. You will have learned this from the creditors or *CRAs*.

- Provide them with copies of *all evidence* you have gathered in your case. (Don't give them originals.) Include copies of all forged signatures, applications, addresses, and telephone numbers given for the fraudulent cards. Keep a copy of *everything* for yourself. Do not give them copies of your credit report unless you block out your real account information. Your police report becomes public record, so give police a list of the fraud accounts on a separate page to protect your privacy and finances. (Also, by now I hope you have written the creditors and asked them to send evidence of the fraud to a specific investigator designated by you. See Letters 3-A, 3-B, and 3-C) (See Police Report Addendum Document 3-C(1))

- Provide them with the names and telephone numbers of all defrauded creditors so that the investigators can ask for records to aid the investigation. The report needs to list each fraud account so you can use it to get the *CRAs* to delete the fraud. (See the Letters 3-A, 3-B, 3-C and Document 3-C(1) to Law Enforcement).

- Kindly insist that police file a report, even if it's only an *informational* report as opposed to an actual *crime* report. Some police departments are reluctant to write reports on such crimes, because if they write an actual report it requires them to investigate. You must understand that these cases are labor-intensive and most law enforcement agencies don't have the personnel or the financial resources to investigate and catch the imposters. So be persistent! You *will* need a report whether or not they investigate. Let them know that you are sensitive to the fact that they may not be able to investigate, but you must have a written report. *CRAs*, credit card companies, and banks will require you to show an identity theft report in order to verify the fraud and clear your name. *CRAs* are required to remove the fraud when they have it documented in a police report or report from the Secret Service. (Federal law requires the *CRAs* to block the fraud information if a police report documents the fraud accounts.) This will clear your credit report, then the creditors are notified of the fraud by the *CRAs*. But you must also notify the creditors yourself.

In fact, many creditors will *not* close the fraud

account or remove fraudulent information from your file unless you file a police report and provide them the name of the fraud investigator and a copy of the police report, or at least the number of the report. Make sure the report lists *all* the fraud accounts. You must file an addendum to the report if you learn of new fraud accounts. (See Document 3-C(1))

So, don't let the police (or other law enforcement agencies or at least your Department of Motor Vehicles Fraud Division) turn you away without a report! Help them understand that the report is essential for you to get your life back. Inform them of the federal law (18 USC 1028) and your own state laws (find those at www.consumer.gov/idtheft). If you need to, call or write to your chief of police, a city councilperson, the district attorney's office, or your local victim assistance office. You may even need to call a state legislator or attorney general's office, or even your governor's office, if they refuse to give you a report. Do whatever is required to get that police report, because others to whom you're reporting the crime will need to see that report before they'll take you seriously. (See Letter 3-B to the chief of police demanding a report.)

Understand also that because you placed fraud alerts on all your accounts, you may be the subject of suspicion by banks and merchants that don't know you. To avoid delay and embarrassment, it's a good idea to carry a copy of the first page of your Police Report in your wallet at all times so you can prove you're not the imposter. Also, keep the phone number of the police fraud investigator handy and give it to creditors and others who require verification of your case.

You should also insist that the credit card companies, banks, department stores, collection companies, and other commercial "victims" who lost money call the police, cooperate with any investigation, and report the theft as well. They often are unwilling to help the police since it is very time-consuming and they have already lost money, and don't wish to waste time on a case that will prob-

ably not provide restitution. It's an economic decision by the company.

If a family member has impersonated you, and you choose not to file a police report, you'll be making the credit cleanup more difficult. It's still possible, though, to clear your name if you follow all the other steps. You may be able to file a report with the Department of Motor Vehicles or another agency such as the Postal Inspector. (Mail fraud is usually part of these cases.) If a family member has done this to you, and they won't take responsibility, it's our opinion that they should suffer the consequences. The reality is, even if you file a police report, often law enforcement will not bother to investigate if they know it's a family member. They consider it a civil matter, which isn't the case. You should consider having the relative admit the fraud (in writing), and offer to pay the fraud bills to the creditors. In some cases, the creditor will transfer the account to the impostor's name if they believe they will be paid. (Go to www.idtheftcenter.org for fact sheets on dealing with family members and fraud.)

Other necessary follow-up with police:

- Once a report is filed, and if an investigation begins, demand copies of any evidence collected by the police fraud investigators that has your name on it. The police may say you have no right to that information because of the privacy of the accused. However, you *do* have a right to anything with *your* name on it. (*Ironic isn't it? What about your privacy?*) You will need this evidence in order to correct errors and fraud.

- Don't contact the impersonator *yourself*. Let the police handle it. Most impersonators are not violent, but it is wise not to confront these people. One victim, for instance, contacted her impersonator by phone, and subsequently this person stalked her with numerous phone calls.

- Agree to cooperate if the district attorney or a federal prosecutor files a case. If there's enough evidence, the identity thief may agree to a plea bargain, which will eliminate your need to testify. Don't panic; ask the DA to provide you with a contact in the victim assistance program.

- If there is a plea bargain or conviction, you should write a letter (Victim Impact Statement) to the judge regarding the sentencing and to request monetary restitution as a victim. (See Letter 8-B writing to a judge)

- If you find you are a victim of criminal identity theft where someone uses your name and personal information while committing other crimes, you will need to clear your criminal record. Contact your local law enforcement agency. Have them run a background check, and allow them to take your picture and fingerprints. Then they can compare those prints with those of the real perpetrator. You'll also need to have your information sent to the law enforcement agency where the arrest was made. You'll need to clear the local and federal records with the help of your local law enforcement and the attorney general's office of your state. If the case went to trial, you'll need to write to the prosecutor and perhaps hire a criminal defense attorney. (See Letter 8-B to deal with criminal identity theft.)

Step No. 4: Write a description of your situation and complete the Uniform Affidavit.

As soon as you've figured out the basics of what's happened to you, complete the Uniform Affidavit explaining *who, what, where, when,* and *how* (if you know). Give pertinent information about yourself and attach a utility bill (which may be required to prove your address), a government issued identification, and the police report — once you receive it. Having this completed affidavit handy will save time because you won't need to repeat your story or re-write it to all the agencies that will need to hear it. Make numerous copies and put them in a file to send with letters. Keep the affidavit on a CD as well. Then update with a chronological history and save again on a CD. You don't want your sensitive information stored on your hard drive. (See the **Uniform Affidavit** in Appendix A and on the CD.)

Step No. 5: Re-assert control of your bank accounts.

If you had checks stolen or bank accounts set up fraudulently, first report this to your bank, and then to the check-verification or check-guarantee companies. You'll find the verification companies listed below and in our resources section.

When you pay for a purchase by check, merchants often use one or the other of these kinds of firms to learn about your check-writing habits. A *check-verification company* provides an electronic database of people who've written bad checks or had their bank accounts closed because of bad checks. A *check-guarantee company* does the same, and also promises to reimburse the retailer if the check bounces.

Not all of these companies will have a record of bad checks written in your name, and not all allow proactive fraud alerts. So it's important to contact each of these companies and explain your situation. They each have different requirements to follow to clear your name. When you call, you will hear voice prompts, so be patient.

- Certegy Check Services, Inc. (800) 437-5120
- ChexSystems (800) 428-9623
- Cross Check (800) 843-0760
- Global Payments, Inc. (800) 766-2748
- SCAN (877) 382-7226
- TeleCheck (800) 710-9898

The databases of the check guarantee/verification services sometimes contain errors. You might, for example, be listed as a bad-check writer by mistake; or someone could be using your driver's license number or checking account number to pass bad checks. In either case, you have a right to have the error corrected.

If you write a check and have it declined by the merchant, ask for the name, phone number, and address of the check guarantee or verification service that rejected your check, and call to obtain copies of the fraudulent checks. (You'll also need to follow up in writing.) Ask what information about you is in their files and, if necessary, how to correct erroneous information.

If you suspect fraudulent use of your own checks, you'll also need to:

• Put stop-payments on any outstanding checks that you're unsure of. If your checks are stolen, you should not only report that to the check-verification companies, but also immediately contact your bank, stop payment on all the checks, and close the account. When you open your new accounts, put your initials and last name only on your checks. Do not pre-print your Social Security number, driver's license, or phone number on the check. If you live in a state that uses the Social Security number for your driver's license number, change the number. *I* suggest that you use checks as little as possible because your checks have the bank routing number listed on them, and it's easy for thieves to purchase blank checks at an office supply store and create checks with your checking account information. Instead, use a credit card everywhere you can — at the grocery store, gas station, retail stores, etc. You are safer using a credit card since you are protected from fraud.

• Put a new password (not your mother's maiden name) and a fraud alert on any old or new accounts. Open new accounts only if the current accounts have been affected by the fraud.

• Cancel those checking and savings accounts that have been affected by fraud. Obtain new account numbers and give the bank a secret password for these new accounts. (Never use your mother's maiden name because that's on your birth certificate, which is an easily available public record. Also avoid using children's names or a dog's name because those may be well known to other people.) Also, some banks will allow an extra security code; don't use your Social Security number.

• Tell the bank that your password is *required* for use before any action can be taken on the account — withdrawals, name change, address change, billing information, and so on (follow this up in writing).

• Call and write to your own *non-fraudulent* accounts and notify them of the fraud situation and place a fraud alert. Also, for accounts that haven't been fraudulently invaded, change your password and add a security code. (See Letter 2-D in the back of this book and on the CD.)

Step No. 6: Don't pay fraudulent bills.

Don't pay any credit card bills or merchant invoices that are not yours, even if you think it's going to make your life easier. When you acquiesce, it's as if you're admitting that the bill is yours — *Don't do it!*

Similarly, never cover any fraudulent checks. Never file bankruptcy due to fraud! If collection companies continue to harass you after you have written letters, inform them that they're violating the law and keep documentation so you may take legal action if they persist. If a family member or ex-spouse took your identity, don't pay the bills. You are a victim. Some companies will threaten you if a child, parent, or cousin has used your identity telling you that you are a conspirator. If you are innocent, you must *not* give in!

Step No. 7: Get a new ATM card *without* the Visa or MasterCard logo.

If your ATM or debit card has been stolen or compromised, close that account and open a new one with a different account number and a new password. Then get a new ATM card without the Visa/MasterCard logo. Do *not* continue to use your old password.

When creating a PIN for your new card, don't use common numbers like your address, the last four digits of your Social Security number, or your birth date. Again, those are too obvious. Use a mixture of numbers and letters, at least eight digits long.

Ask for a debit card that does *not* have the Visa or MasterCard logo. ATM cards with credit card logos are *dangerous*. Charges incurred are removed directly from your checking account (without your prior review), and federal law does not protect you in the same way that it does when you use a regular credit card. With a debit card, you cannot dispute disbursements *before* payment, like you can with a credit card. With the ATM Visa or MasterCard you must *prove* fraud, and it may take months to get your money back, if you *ever* do! With a regular ATM card, you can still obtain cash or make a deposit at an ATM and use it as a check guarantee card. Use your regular credit card for purchases, so if fraud occurs you can dispute the charges before they are paid. (Use Letter 2-C.)

Step No. 8: Straighten out your mail.

Mail theft is a felony. Notify the local U.S. Postal Inspector if you suspect an identity thief has filed a change of address form in your name with the post office, or has stolen your mail or used the mail system to commit any type of fraud.

Call and write to the postal authority where you live and in the city where the fraud was committed (e.g., the address to which fraudulent credit cards were sent), and ask for a criminal investigation. Your local postmaster can give you names, addresses, and telephone numbers of postal authorities where the fraud occurred. Ask for a fraud complaint form to complete to make sure no mail with your name on it continues to be sent to the fraudster's address.

In fact, tell the post office not to deliver any mail with your name on it to that fraud location – not even "junk mail." All mail should be forwarded to your true address. This is *not* a change of address — it is the *correct* address. Remind them that the fraud address was *never* correct.

Get the name and phone number of the postal carrier who delivers mail to the fraud address(es). Inform him or her of the problem and ask the carrier not to deliver any mail to the fraud address in your name. Seek to make friends with the carrier, so he or she will be inclined to help you. (One impersonator obtained new fraud accounts because the carrier kept delivering pre-approved offers to the fraudster for a whole year!) (Use Letter 4 in the back of this book and on the CD.)

Step No. 9: Alert your public utilities.

Call your telephone, electrical, gas, trash, and water utilities and ask for a password. Warn them of the possibility that someone may attempt to open new service using your identification. Give them a password that will be required before any account changes will be made. If the impersonator has opened accounts in your name, cancel the accounts due to fraud, and place a fraud alert. You should write to any utility company in which fraud occurred and ask that documentation of the fraud be delivered to you and to law enforcement. (Use Letter 2-E.)

Step No. 10: Contact the Secret Service or FBI if the fraud occurs out of state.

The Secret Service has jurisdiction over financial fraud, but it usually doesn't investigate individual cases unless the dollar amount is very high or you are among the victims of a fraud ring. The Secret Service is more concerned with organized criminals and terrorists that may be committing identity theft. That's especially true if such thefts extend across county, state, or country boundaries and, thus, are beyond the reach of the local authorities.

So, just keep in mind that the Secret Service and the FBI are mainly interested in seeing if the information you report fits into a larger picture. The agencies are probably not going to investigate your impostor's crime unless you can show them evidence that links the crime to a bigger scheme.

However, to further interest the Secret Service in your case, you may want to ask the fraud department of the credit card companies and/or banks, as well as the police fraud investigator, to notify the particular Secret Service agent they normally work with and possibly the local Identity Theft Task Force. Your case may be similar to those of other victims, and if they discover a pattern, the federal authorities may investigate. (You may use Letter 3-A if the crime crosses state lines.)

Step No. 11: Notify Social Security and taxing authorities.

Call or write the Social Security Administration to report fraudulent use of your Social Security number. Don't expect much help here, though; there's little the Social Security Administration can do. The Social Security Inspector General's Office will collaborate with the Secret Service and Identity Theft Task Forces on large cases of mail fraud, computer hacking, terrorism, etc. (See our resources at the back of this book.)

Even though the identity thief may have used your Social Security number, *don't change it*! That will only make you look more suspicious to future creditors. Your new number will be linked with the old numbers and will appear in databases such as those at the *CRAs*, and background checks. In fact you will appear to be a suspicious person and it will cause delays in obtaining new credit.

Getting a new SSN will also cause confusion with all earlier records, such as those pertaining to your health, education, legal status, and finances. Thus, canceling your old number and requesting a new one may be a "cure" that's worse than the "disease"! The only time *I* suggest a person obtain a new Social Security number is if a child's identity is stolen. If a person under 16 has been victimized, it may be more efficient to get a new Social Security number. You'll have to make a special request to the Social Security Administration.

Request your Personal Earnings and Benefit Estimate Statement (PEBES) from the Social Security Administration to make sure that the impersonator hasn't been using your Social Security number for his or her earnings. The IRS could tax you for earnings that aren't yours. Order your Personal Earnings and Benefit Estimate Statement by calling: (800) 772-1213. You may write to them as well. (See the address in the back of this book, and the letters referred to below.)

Be proactive. If you write to Social Security to report the fraud, copy the Internal Revenue Service (with a cover letter) and copy the letter to inform your state tax board as well. (See Letters 5-A and 5-B in Appendix A and on the CD.)

Step No. 12: Check on your passport.

If you have a passport, notify the passport office in writing to be on the lookout for anyone ordering a new passport under your name. There have been cases of impersonators committing crimes in other countries with fraudulently obtained passports. Terrorists use fraudulent passports, as well.

Tell the passport office not to issue a new passport with a change of name or address without verification in writing from you. Ask them to place a fraud alert on your file. Along with your correspondence, send a copy of the key pages of your current passport.

If you don't have a passport, you may wish to apply for one to establish a further form of identification, and to block your impostor from getting one in your name. Check the government pages of your phone book for the number of your nearest passport office or go to your local post office for information (www.travelstate.gov/passport-services.html).

The new passports will include biometric information including a fingerprint, and facial scan. *I* are hopeful that this will reduce passport fraud, but there is the possibility that someone will use your name and SSN with their own biometric information to commit fraud.

Another good number to know: Federal Government Information Center: (800) 688-9889 for help in obtaining government agency phone numbers. (See Letter 7 to write to the passport agency, and see our resources pages.)

Step No. 13: Protect your phone card and cell phone.

If your long-distance calling card or cell phone has been stolen or you discover fraudulent charges on your bill, cancel the account and open a new one with a fraud flag on the account. Provide a password, which must be used whenever the account is changed. You are entitled to request all evidence of the fraud from these companies as well. (See Letter 2-D.)

Step No. 14: Change your driver's license number if used by fraudster.

If someone is using your driver's license as identification on bad checks, you'll need to go to the local office of the state Department of Motor Vehicles (DMV) to request a new number.

If an impersonator is using your driver's license number, and he/she has many violations or an accident, you should get a new license and cancel the old one. Don't cancel your driver's license number until the DMV verifies that a new card with your name and number was issued to an imposter at a different address. Remember that fraudsters often obtain false driver's licenses on the street. Under those circumstances, it may look real to merchants, but the Department of Motor Vehicles cannot help you.

You should also:

- Call your state department of motor vehicles fraud office to see if another license was issued in your name.

- Put a fraud alert on your license.

- Fill out the department of motor vehicles complaint form to begin a fraud investigation. Send supporting documents with the completed form to the nearest department of motor vehicles investigation office.

- Tell the department of motor vehicles in writing *not* to issue a new driver's license without your verification of a change of address or name. (See Letter 6-A in Appendix A.)

- Be aware that the impersonator can easily purchase a fake driver's license for a small fee from another criminal. The department of motor vehicles has *no* jurisdiction over such a fraudulently manufactured license. If you suspect that such a license was produced with your name and the impersonator's picture, let the department of motor vehicles know. Also let your auto insurance carrier know this.

- Get a copy of your driving record to see if there have been any traffic violations or accidents involving the impersonator. If there have, write to the department of motor vehicles and request that they be removed from your record. Get a copy of any court records and police reports, and get the records corrected, and send them to your auto insurance carrier.

- Find out if a picture or a fingerprint was taken of the imposter if he or she went to the office of the department of motor vehicles. If so, get copies of any such documents and give them to the police, or ask law enforcement to get the evidence. (Use Letter 6-A.)

Step No. 15: Contact your auto, health, life, or business insurer, if necessary.

If your driver's license is misused, you'll also need to notify your auto insurance company that someone may be using your name while driving a car. This will help protect you if the impersonator has an accident or commits a moving violation. Sometimes an imposter will use your health insurance or business insurance, or even buy a life insurance policy in your name making himself (the impostor) the beneficiary and using his real name! Remember, any insurance you can buy, your impersonator can also purchase using your credit. (See Letter 6-B.)

If someone used your name for your professional license, you must notify the agency to protect yourself. (See Letter 9.)

Step No. 16: Clear your name in the courts, civil and criminal.

Sometimes identity-theft victims become the object of civil actions brought on by the impersonator. Even worse, victims sometimes are wrongfully accused of crimes committed by the imposter.

James was an investment manager of $100 million in client accounts for one of the nation's largest and most respected mutual fund companies. When his Pennsylvania insurance license came up for renewal, the company, doing a routine background check, discovered a shocking revelation: James was a convicted felon who had pleaded guilty to loan and credit card fraud. So the company immediately fired him. James insisted that he had never been arrested, much less convicted of any crime. But the company forced him to leave the building immediately, without returning to his office to gather his belongings. The truth was the real James was truly innocent.

Here's what to do in the event you have a civil or criminal action against you:

Civil Judgments:

If you are served with a civil lawsuit (i.e., involving a legal action by a credit card company, a bankruptcy, a landlord, etc.) because of something done by the imposter, contact the court where the suit was filed and get the name, phone number, and address of the attorney who filed the case against you. Call the attorney for the company (Plaintiff in the lawsuit) and clarify that you are a victim of identity theft. Write a letter to the attorney and judge in the matter. Then find out what you need to do to get the case dismissed to clear your name. (See Letter 8-A.)

You may discover civil *judgments* on your credit report or you may learn that there have been attempts to attach your bank accounts or put a lien on your property. For civil judgments, also call the court in which the civil judgment was filed and find out how to get a copy of the entire court file. Write and request that the file be sent to you.

(There will be a fee for those copies.) Call the attorney(s) involved in the case. (Their names will be in the file.) You will need to provide a background letter and your completed affidavit explaining your situation to the judge of that court and to the attorneys involved in the case so they may help you to rid yourself of the judgment. (Use Letter 8-A.)

Criminal Prosecutions:

You could be wrongfully named in a criminal complaint. That could happen if the government charges the imposter with a crime he committed while using your name … or worse yet, the government could charge you for a crime he committed *in* your name. In either case, it's serious business, and you'll need to clear your name.

Contact your local police and provide all documentation of the fraud. Have them help you contact the police in the jurisdiction where the perpetrator was arrested and/or convicted. You should also contact the attorney general of your state to find out the specific record. Some states, such as California and Ohio, have set up a system for a victim to go to court to get a certificate of Identity Theft, (or a Certificate of Innocence) and you may register your name with the Department of Justice to protect you. In some courts, you may need help from the prosecutor in the case or a criminal defense attorney who is familiar with identity theft. Ask the local bar association for a referral. If you do not have the funds, ask the court to provide you a public defender, or assign the prosecutor to help you clear your name. If your files are complete and organized with evidence (and you write Letter 3-C) you can expedite the clearing of your name.

Remember, a false criminal charge against you is potentially a very serious problem, perhaps a worst-case scenario of identity theft. In addition to getting a lawyer, you will need to contact the Federal Department of Justice, or the FBI to assist you in clearing your name from the National Criminal Databases.

If you find civil judgments on your credit reports

or you learn of criminal records with your name, conduct a background check on yourself to check on other civil actions or criminal records against you. Do this when you learn of the identity theft, then again about three months after you believe you have cleared your name.

It's quite expensive to hire a private investigator, so first contact your local law enforcement office and request that they run a criminal background check on you to see if anything appears on your record. Some law enforcement offices will do this as part of their investigation. If they find anything negative, they should help you by contacting the agency where the fraud occurred. (Use Letter 3-D.)

If law enforcement won't do a background check, you must do your own. There are web sites that do this for a fee, such as www.knowx.com, www.docusearch.com, www.ussearch.com, www.mybackgroundcheck.com, and others. You may wish to look for a certified private investigator in your area or ask for a referral from your local law enforcement.

Step No. 17: Consider getting legal help to restore your credit or take legal action against negligent agencies.

As I've said, the burden is on *you* — and there's a limit to what an attorney can do that you can't do yourself in terms of cleaning up the financial mess. However, you will need legal representation if you intend to file a suit to seek damages for your losses against companies that were violating laws, which caused your loss.

If yours is a complex case involving very large amounts of money and/or you run into difficulty clearing up your credit history, you should consult a consumer-law attorney. A lawyer could help you decide whether to sue creditors and/or credit bureaus if they're not cooperating in removing fraudulent entries from your credit report, or if you think their negligence led to your problem. Make sure you consult with an attorney who is familiar with the Fair Credit Reporting Act, identity theft, your state laws, and other federal pri-

vacy laws. (Chapter Three gave you information about your rights.)

There are strict time guidelines as to when you must bring action for negligence in your state. There are also deadlines (statute of limitations) under the Fair Credit Reporting Act. Federal law now says a victim must bring an action within two years from the date of discovery, but no later than five years from the violation of law (regardless of the discovery date.) So, carefully review the inquiry section of all three of your credit reports. Look for the companies that may have inquired about your credit as a result of an impersonator's request for credit. Find the dates of that first fraudulent inquiry. If your credit mess isn't cleared after sending the letters in this book with the appropriate attachments, seek out an attorney to review your case *immediately*. Write the date you first learned of the fraud. Also determine the date of the first violation. It must be within the last five (5) years. Bring copies of your letters and correspondence with your affidavit and chronological history to the lawyer. Keep copies for yourself.

Unfortunately, many victims do not even discover the fraud for over a year or more. Get legal advice for yourself based on your situation as *quickly* as possible.

I am not encouraging you to sue. But in fact, I encourage you to negotiate a settlement if possible to keep your personal information out of the public record. I am telling you to get legal advice and find out the legal options available for your specific case. You should have the opportunity to decide if you wish to take legal action before you lose your right to do so. There are several different timelines (statutes of limitations) affecting your case. So make sure you get legal counseling from a qualified consumer-law attorney in your own state. The information you receive may give you leverage to negotiate a fair settlement yourself even without a lawsuit. If your case is especially egregious, and the companies refuse to help you, you may consider speaking to your federal legislators and the media to get an investigation and quick action.

Before you make an appointment to see a lawyer, make sure that your expense logs and correspondence are in order and that you have copies of everything. (Please see our resources section for a list of attorney-referral organizations and attorneys who claim to be familiar with the identity theft issues.)

Step No. 18: Get a handle on the stress.

Know, for starters, that you are not alone. Many others have gone through this, or are going through it now. The Federal Trade Commission's study found that there are about 10 million new victims each year. Many victims find psychological counseling helpful in dealing with the stress and anxiety.

Try to use your anger and emotional response effectively. Don't get hostile and yell at customer service representatives, advocates, or government workers. Even when frustrated, try to stay calm and polite so you win the person's sympathy and assistance, and then you will get the kind of help that you need.

Remember: Even if a company facilitated the fraud or the government agency is being balky, the person you're talking to is not personally at fault. You're angry at the situation, not the people whose help you need to resolve it. So try to separate the person from the problem. This is *critical*! (However, if someone is rude to you, ask to speak to his or her supervisor immediately. Make notes of the conversations, which you may document in a letter. This will save time and be easier on your emotions.)

In any event, don't think you're going crazy. It's common to have strong emotional reactions, such as crying and feeling despondent, angry or agitated. Many people victimized by this crime experience emotional and physical distress, and even Post Traumatic Stress Disorder. Go to www.idtheftcenter.org and look at their fact sheets on dealing with the emotional issues. There, you may join a support group, or even start your own identity theft group in your area.

For identity theft and privacy issues, sign up for the mailing list or the electronic newsletter of the Privacy Rights Clearinghouse (www.privacyrights.org) and the Electronic Privacy Information Center (www.epic.org).

Step No. 19: Seek changes in the law.

Use the energy that stems from your frustration to motivate you to help solve the problem. Your experience will almost certainly have made you sensitive to the fact that there are few effective laws to prevent identity theft. The United States Public Interest Research Group (www.uspirg.org) lobbies to promote your rights as identity theft victims. Consider joining them.

When you have your own situation under control, begin to broaden your concern into the privacy and identity plights of others. Join in demanding policy changes in the institutions that make the crime of identity theft so easy!

Write to your state and federal legislators. Write letters to the editor of your local newspaper. (It's easy to do this by e-mail.) Demand stronger privacy protection and fraud assistance by creditors and credit bureaus.

Make complaints to The Federal Trade Commission (877) IDTHEFT, or visit the FTC Identity Theft Complaint Center at www.consumer.gov/idtheft.

Step No. 20: Don't give in, don't give up!

Perhaps, most important, *persist*. Don't lose heart! Be prepared for a long-distance run, not a sprint. In short, if you're like most identity fraud victims, you've already experienced fear and exhaustion, but this book will make your job much easier, so don't give up.

The most important thing to remember is that phone calls are not enough — a company can say they have no record of your call — so always confirm all conversations in writing … *return receipt requested*. Use the CD attached to this book to complete your organized letters and keep copies in organized files. If you write all the necessary letters and still have a problem, you may wish to write us for a referral or consult with an attorney in your area to review your legal rights and possible violations relating to your situation. In our resource section, you'll find a list of attorneys who practice this type of law. *I* encourage you to interview any lawyer you're considering retaining. You shouldn't need an attorney to write the letters for you, since they are included with this book and CD. You'll need a lawyer if you have written the letters and the companies refuse to rectify the situation. Most of the time if you have a case, it will be against a negligent creditor or against the credit-reporting bureaus for failing to follow the law and correct your reports.

Fair credit-reporting and identity theft cases are very complex, expensive to litigate, and invasive. You will experience stress. You will be required to relive the ordeal, over and over, participate in depositions and other discovery, and appear in court. Much of your private life will become public and open to cross-examination by the defendant's attorney. It's time-consuming and may take many months or years to settle or to even get a trial.

This area of law takes special skills and experience. The firm/attorney should have prior experience with identity theft, the Fair Credit Reporting Act, the Fair Debt Collection Practices Act, and related areas of the law. *I* recommend interviewing several attorneys prior to hiring one, and make sure that you feel comfortable. You must be completely honest at all times so that they may adequately assess your case. Be prepared!

Here are some questions you might want to ask:

- What is your experience with ID theft cases?

- How many other cases involving the Fair Credit Reporting Act (FCRA) or Fair Debt Collection Practices Act (FDCPA) has the firm handled? What were the results of those cases?

- Do you have testimonials from some clients or may I speak to other victims who your firm represented?

- Who will handle the case?

- Would the firm/attorney take this case on a contingency basis (they take a percentage of the final settlement or award) or would I need to pay on an hourly basis?

- How long does it normally take for the office to return phone calls?

Ask to see a copy of the attorney's retainer agreement. Read it and then if you feel comfortable with the lawyer, clarify any terms of the agreement that you don't understand. If you wish to find out more about the attorney, you may call your state bar, or visit its web site and check out information about the lawyer.

Keep these thoughts in mind:

Use the form letters in this book, but keep in mind that one letter may not suffice. You may need to write one or more follow-up letters because, for instance, some companies will send you some of what you requested but not all … or a *CRA* may take a few errors off your report but leave on — or even *add* — other inaccuracies. You may re-use the letters and amend as necessary.

You may also find you need to write letters to other agencies that aren't provided for in our forms. If you need help, e-mail me (contact@ identitytheft.org), and I'll advise you of options. Or you can adapt the letters to your special needs. (A reminder: Make sure you keep a hard copy as well as an electronic copy of all your letters, and have a file folder in hard copy in a locked file and on a CD.)

You may get weary of merchants and collection agencies dogging you about debts run up in your name by the imposter. As I cautioned earlier, resist the temptation to pay any bill or a portion of any bill, which resulted from identity theft. If any merchant, financial institution, or collection agency threatens you, simply restate your willingness to cooperate. However, don't allow yourself to be coerced into paying any fraudulent bills. If you do, it looks like proof of guilt, when you are really innocent.

Keep up your letter writing…keep up your

records of whom you've talked to and what was said…keep up your efforts…keep centered…and keep up your spirits! Remain firm. It's not you who's done anything wrong.

Do all that… and your credit rating and your reputation should not be permanently affected, and no legal action should be taken against you.

You'll emerge as a victor, not a victim!

Chapter 5

Why It's Important to Get Organized — and How to Stay Organized

You say your garage looks like Berlin after World War II? Your fridge contains so many old bottles and half-eaten cheese sandwiches that bacteria might choose it as a convention site? One peek at your clothes closet might make a brave man tremble?

That's O.K. Maybe there's even joy in such sloppiness because you're making a personal statement. However, once you start fighting identity theft, such lack of organization will cost you — *big-time*. Take my word on this: If you don't get organized — and *stay* organized — in your attempt to restore your name and your credit, you will soon feel totally overwhelmed, powerless, and confused. You'll lose critical papers, and you'll forget what you've done and what you still have to do. Plus, not only will you feel foolish and awkward when dealing with authorities and agencies, you'll hurt your chances for success.

As a result, your identity-fraud problem will get worse, not better. If you don't deal with this crisis immediately *and systematically*, your credit could be ruined, collection agencies will attack, and creditors could obtain court judgments leading to liens on your property. This might even cause you to want to file bankruptcy. (*Don't do it!*) Worse, if someone used your identity to commit crimes, you could end up in jail.

This chapter is meant to help you gain credibility with companies and agencies so you'll have the data you need when you need it! You'll have the records on which to base your request for reimbursement of out-of-pocket costs for restitution. If companies are negligent and you feel you have

a case, your attorney will need to see organized files and documented evidence — and you'll be prepared!

When you are organized, you'll feel empowered and you won't be perceived as *the fraud perpetrator*! You'll no longer feel like a victim if you are organized and have a plan.

So, again, please take it from me (and others who've been through this): If you've never been organized before, get organized *now*. The stakes are high.

Why am I so adamant about this? Because being organized and prepared will help you to:

- **Appear more professional**. Thus, companies, agencies, lawyers, and law enforcement will treat you with more respect.

- **Gain peace of mind and confidence**. You'll feel empowered when you have access to the information you need when it's requested.

- **Answer questions effectively and clearly explain what's transpired**. When you have all documents arranged in an orderly fashion, your thoughts will be clearer, you'll be more articulate, and you will be able to speed up the repair of your credit.

- **Prove possible violations of the law**. A documented paper trail can show continued negligence, and an attorney will want such documentation before he or she can analyze your case and advise you. Without proper written backup, an attorney will not be willing to take your case ... especially on contingency (which means you pay fees only when you win). Detailed records proving damages and out-of-pocket costs are critical for negotiating a settlement on your own or winning your case in a lawsuit. Out-of-pocket costs are reimbursable through restitution by a court if the perpetrator is brought to trial (accepts a plea bargain). Also, out-of-pocket costs may be deductible from your taxes under 165e of the U.S. Tax Code for fraud losses. You'll need to be organized to show documentation to an accountant.

- **Hang onto your sanity.** If you can't keep track of what you've done, what you're doing, and what you need to do, you'll make the ordeal — and its emotional impact — twice as hard as it already is. Often, so many incidents are happening at once it's easy to forget or get confused. If you don't document what's happening, you're more likely to misspeak, and then you'll look suspicious. It's crazy-making.

Ten Easy Steps to Help You!

Follow these simple steps to get organized and become proactive in your effort to regain your personal power, your financial security, and your upstanding reputation:

1. Get the proper supplies.

These include:

- file folders
- file storage boxes or filing cabinets
- colored labels (example: red for *CRAs*, green for credit grantors, blue for government agencies, etc.)
- legal pads
- carbon phone log book
- pens
- two-hole punch
- fasteners for file folders (or buy folders with fasteners)

- miscellaneous office equipment or services, such as speakerphone, shredder, word processor or computer, printer, writable CDs, e-mail service, copier, and fax machine.

You can, of course, use commercial copiers and fax machines. However, having your own office equipment will save you time and energy. You'll include these costs of purchase in your logs of out-of-pocket costs. Letter writing will get tedious and time-consuming to write and copy, so consider buying or borrowing a computer if you don't already own one.

Remember that anything you buy that's necessary to regain your credit is considered an out-of-pocket cost and may be reimbursable. (You may negotiate for reimbursement costs from negligent credit grantors, and if the perpetrator is caught, you should also ask the court for restitution from the defendant, and this may be tax deductible, depending on your situation.)

In any event, record all such expenditures in your expense log and keep receipts attached to your logs. (See and complete Appendix A - Document 12.)

2. Be ready at the start.

Have a legal pad, pen, and master log (see below) in hand for the very first phone call you make.

3. Log your phone calls. (See Appendix A.)

Be sure to record:

- name (get correct spelling and title) If you get no help demand to speak to a supervisor. Don't waste your time with those who cannot help you!
- direct phone number (ask for an 800 number and the specific extension)
- fax number
- e-mail address
- mailing address
- date and time of phone call.

4. Record the substance of your conversations.

Make a note of:

- Date of conversation/time/how long
- what's said by both parties
- instructions as to what they say you are to do
- pledges the other parties make to you
- information they request from you
- timeline of when they will respond to you
- what documents they promise to send to you (i.e., billing statements, affidavits, reports, original credit application, forms to complete)

Remember to repeat back to them from your notes to clarify what they said so you are clear. Also, they often tape these phone calls so make sure you verify what you thought you heard. Reflecting what they tell you will reinforce the information you received as well as get a commitment to follow-through by all parties.

5. Establish a filing system (both in hard copy and on a CD.)

Here are the essentials:

- Start by immediately setting up a file folder with an appropriate label for each company, bank, or agency you speak with.
- On the inside of each folder, write the following information about your contact there: name, title, address, phone, fax, and e-mail numbers for easy access. Each time you speak with this company or write a letter, make sure you have this file in front of you. (Enter this information in your contact file and on your computer or PDA.)
- File all notes in the appropriate folder using a two-hole punch and fasteners.
- Write a confirming letter regarding each phone conversation and send the letter U.S. Mail/Certified, *Return Receipt Requested.*

- Record the certified-mail information in your log; note date mailed and received. File the certified-mail *return receipt requested* postcard by stapling it to your copy of the letter immediately upon receipt. Then put it in the file folder.

- Make hard copies of all correspondence and file in folders. File these letters immediately so you're not overwhelmed and can find information quickly. Put the file in locked filing cabinets or banker boxes in a locked closet. Because this information will include your Social Security number and other confidential information, you must keep it under lock and key. When you get a phone call, or make one, you'll have the folder updated and be ready to discuss your situation.

- Set up your master log/file (see Appendix A) to record information as you receive it. Your log should include:

√ Date

√ Company/Agency

√ Name of person/title

√ How contact was made (phone/fax/e-mail/letter)

√ Time sent/received

√ Expenses, if any, incurred by you

√ Response date

√ Call-back date

Place this log on a clipboard and the individual file folder for the company, agency, etc., and take them with you to the phone for each conversation. Make sure you have your legal pad. After your conversation, tear the notes you took from the pad and clip them in that file so you don't misplace them.

It's important to record the following each time you speak to someone: date, time, and when you're next supposed to speak to them or when you're to receive a response. Make sure you are talking to a supervisor who can help you before you tell your story over and over to underlings. Note the person's name, direct phone line, address, etc., and be sure to get the correct spelling of his or her name and title, and the company name.

- Make a master list of telephone numbers of all important contacts at the various agencies. Keep this with your master log. If you have a database on your computer, enter the names and addresses in your contact file to save you time in calling and e-mailing.

- Set up storage boxes or a file cabinet drawer for your files, so you don't get this information mixed up with your business or other files. Safeguard these folders in locking files, since they contain sensitive information.

- If getting physically organized is too overwhelming, enlist family or friends, or hire a trusted college student to help set up these files and folders. Keep in mind that you can't just delegate; you must work in tandem with whoever is helping you, because only you know what's fraudulent and what's not. It'll also be more enjoyable to be working with someone. Be honest with yourself about your need for help — it's hard enough to keep up with your ordinary personal records. So don't be shy about asking for help or hiring an assistant. Also, you need moral support!

- Make sure you keep electronic copies as well as hard copies. You should be using the forms and letters from the CD attached to this book to save you time and money in creating your letters and completing your logs. After you complete the letters, either encrypt them completely or save them on a CD. The reason is, you have personal information and you must keep it safe from hackers, spyware, and others who may get access to the files on your computer.

6. Complete your affidavit and historical chronology.

Make sure you have completed your "Uniform Affidavit" (approved by the Federal Trade Com-

mission). Please see and complete the affidavit. (Appendix A, Document 10.) It verifies who you are and what happened to you. Also prepare and attach to your affidavit a bullet point (or numbered) chronological history of:

- What you learned.
- What you've done to deal with the situation.
- Who you spoke with.
- What the current problems are.

In the chronology, try to clarify approximate dates and what happened.

Below is a brief sample beginning of a chronology of a fraud case:

Victim's Chronology

Our understanding of the facts goes like this:

1. October 14, 2003: We pay off a line of credit with bank. We believe the account is closed. We don't learn of the following events until much later. We don't know any of the people whose names are on the checks. (See below.)

2. December 13, 2003: Fraud Check #110 for $12,980 to Michael Love drawn on our line of credit from ABC Bank. (Between Oct. 14, and Dec. 13 our bank changed the address without verification and sent checks to fraud address.)

3. December 28, 2003: Fraud Check #112 for $19,980 to Tom Jones drawn on our supposedly closed line of credit.

4. January 24, 2004: Fraud Check #113 for $898 to Capital One drawn on our line of credit. We don't have an account with that company.

5. January 28, 2004: Fraud Check #114 for $39,980 to Susan Smith drawn on our closed line of credit.

6. March 1, 2004: Fraud Check #116 for $29,980 to Doug Gordon drawn on our closed line of credit.

7. March 15, 2004, we try to refinance our home with XYZ Bank. Our credit reports show an unpaid credit line, and we find out about the fraud. We called the bank and speak to George Dogood in the fraud department at the following phone number XXX-XXXX. He tells us that someone claiming to be us called to change our address to Miami. We tell them that we have never been to Miami; we've always lived in Houston. We tell them this is fraud and demand copies of the checks.

The above sample is only the beginning of the chronology; with each new event or incident, add to your explanation. Make several copies of your affidavit and chronology and keep them in electronic form. That way you don't have to rewrite it each time you need to repeat your story. Update the events as they evolve — using the computer will save you time.

7. Keep track of all expenses.

Set up an "Expenses" log as shown in Appendix A. This is critical if you are going to ask for reimbursement from creditors, reporting agencies, or the defendant in court. It's also required for settlement negotiations or for evidence in a lawsuit or for restitution from the criminal. Keep copies of all bills and receipts in your hard copy file. You must also annotate time logs if you're going to ask for reimbursement for your billable time, loss of earnings, lost wages, and lost opportunities.

Include in your expenses file:

- Any costs incurred, including postage, copies, etc.

- Time spent on the phone (even to 800 numbers, which won't show on your phone bill) and writing letters.

- Payments to anyone you hired to help you with setting up files, filing, typing, etc.

- Costs of self-help materials/supplies — even the cost of this book and CD!

- Bills from physicians, therapists, or medication related to this effort.

- Travel and mileage expenses.

- Lost wages or time off from work.

8. Stay calm, cool, and credible.

Don't panic, and try not to let the situation overwhelm you. This challenge is an opportunity for you to learn! Instead of getting frustrated, follow the steps above and stay organized. This will save you hours of aggravation and stress. Remember to keep all your documents containing your personal information in a safe place so others can't access them.

Set up a time each day to check your log and calendar to review what you have to do next. Priorities are very important. Don't try to do everything at once. One step at a time!

9. Innovate.

If you discover new or more efficient ways to organize the credit-recovery effort, please e-mail me with your success tips at our web site (www.identitytheft.org). I'll update these suggestions in future editions or newsletters.

10. Persist.

I've said it before and I'll say it again: The process, including the filing and organizing, may seem arduous and involved, frustrating and tiring; however, once you have your system in place, the tasks will become routine and will seem much easier. You'll have more confidence and peace of mind.

It's important that you persevere in the face of fatigue and, sometimes, despair. This whole effort to restore yourself to financial and emotional health will be a test of your endurance. No pain — no gain!

Identity theft is "not going to go away without some real effort. Consumer Attorney Andrew Henderson told us, "Unfortunately, I have seen a lot of people who struggle for a while and then get exhausted and sort of ignore the problem.

Then, of course, it gets worse. Then they try and fight it again. So my personal advice is to deal with it now — don't be in denial. Confront the problem and plow through it as quickly as possible."

Please know that your efforts will be rewarded – you can do it!

Chapter 6

What to Do If They Won't Clear Up Your Name?

You've learned by now that you must be persistent, confident, and assertive (not angrily aggressive, of course, because no one will want to help a nasty person). But if you feel upset and frustrated, it's O.K to admit that. To anyone who's been through what you've been through, your feelings are very understandable!

Now the trick is to use your anger constructively to propel you to take conscientious action to protect yourself.

A lot of your effort to date has been put into writing letters and making phone calls. That's good; however, sometimes that doesn't bring the results you hoped for. You may have found, for example, that often one letter to each company or government agency is not enough. Even repeated letters may not suffice. Companies may comply with some of your requests, but they resist providing all the documentation you need.

If this happens, you may need to up the ante. This chapter describes other techniques you can use if you're still running into stone walls after having sent your letters and made your phone calls as suggested in earlier chapters.

What to do when the going gets rough:

1. Don't give up — move up the ladder.

If your letters go unanswered, or only partially answered, and the problems continue, get the name of the company president or agency head. Write to him/her, with a copy to the person you were dealing with.

If, still, no one will resolve the problems, here are several options:

- Ask in writing for formal negotiations or mediation with a neutral third party to assist in settling the issues quickly. You'll need to get negotiation coaching from an experienced attorney to do this. (See below about hiring an attorney.) You will also want to request monetary damages if the firm or agency has been negligent, so your loss in expenses and your time will help you in assessing your damages. Also consider the affect on your credit reputation if you lost the opportunity to buy a house, etc. Consider discussing how to assess damages with an attorney.

- Write to the president of the company and copy the appropriate regulatory commission that deals with complaints (e.g. Federal Trade Commission, your state Office of Consumer Affairs, your state attorney general, and your legislature). In a cover letter, directed to the Federal Trade Commission, lodge your complaint. You may also make a complaint by e-mail or phone.

2. Get help from outside sources.

You'll need support, information, and perhaps some consumer advice. Consider the following:

- Call The Federal Trade Commission Identity Theft Clearinghouse at (877) IDTHEFT, or write your complaint to www.consumer.gov/idtheft.

- Call and/or write (copy the letter that you sent above) to several organizations that may help you:

  ⇒ The Identity Theft Resource Center at www.idtheftcenter.org, (858) 693-7935 (see contact in our resources section).

  ⇒ The Privacy Rights Clearinghouse at www. privacyrights.org, (619) 298-3396.

  ⇒ The United States Public Interest Research Group at www.pirg.org.

- You can call and write to the Department of Consumer Affairs in the state where the company is located and to the attorney general in your own state.

- If you still don't get results, you should get some legal advice. You don't necessarily need to file a lawsuit; in fact, as you'll see below, that should be a last resort. Make sure you get the legal information in a timely manner. Be careful to see an attorney within a year of the date that the first fraud inquiry was made on your credit report. Under the Fair Credit Reporting Act, you have *two* years from the date of the discovery (when you learned of the fraud) with a time limit of no more than five years from the date of the violation. It may take you time to discover when a company violated the FCRA.

- Call your state and federal government representatives to find out if they can help investigate the issues.

3. Hire a reputable lawyer and get good legal advice.

Information is power! Legal information gives you leverage to obtain a favorable settlement if your issues aren't resolved. You must obtain up-to-date legal information that applies specifically to your situation.

Most reputable lawyers offer a free consultation by phone or in person. You should interview several lawyers with experience in identity theft. They must have knowledge of the Fair Credit Reporting Act and identity theft. If you suffered a criminal identity theft, you may need a criminal defense lawyer or public defender. You may need help from the prosecutor, as well, if there is a criminal record in your name. Remember to bring copies of your *organized* files, including completed logs and letters to the lawyer's office. Also, the lawyer will need copies of original correspondence you have received from companies and agencies. Don't give away your *original* records!

One option is to call your family's lawyer and ask for a referral. (*Remember*: You need someone who's familiar with identity theft and the Fair Credit Reporting Act). If you don't know an attorney, call your local bar association. Also, look at the resource list of attorneys in Appendix B for lawyers who claim to specialize in these types of cases. They belong to a listserve from the National Consumer Law Center dealing with Fair Credit Reporting Act issues, and have had experience with these cases.

Before you hire an attorney, interview several by phone or in person. Learn what their experience is in these types of cases. Also, find out what your rights are and ask about your pending timelines (called statutes of limitations). These timelines, if violated, preclude you from filing certain causes of actions. In Chapter Three, I explained that under the FCRA there are limited remedies for an individual, but your consumer law attorney may be able to creatively work around those limits.

Ask about fees and costs. These are very difficult cases to resolve. If you pay on an hourly basis it will probably be prohibitively costly. But if you have a strong case, ask for a contingency fee agreement (i.e., you only pay if you win, except for the attorney's out-of-pocket costs). Find out what those out-of-pocket costs will be. Ask if the costs will be paid as you go or taken out of the settlement or award. Also, ask if you can speak with another identity-theft victim whom the attorney has represented. (This is a privacy issue, so the victim must provide permission.)

Ask the lawyer how timely she/he is about returning phone calls. Notice how the attorney treats you. Is there positive personal chemistry between you? You must feel comfortable with the attorney you choose. You must also be *completely* honest with your lawyer.

As an alternative to full representation, it may be to your advantage to hire the attorney on a limited basis to advise you on how to negotiate a settlement. If the attorney is comfortable working with you on such a strategy (as a coach or negotiator) for a limited basis to help you in negotiations or mediation, you may consider paying on an hourly basis up to a certain dollar figure. If negotiations fail, then you could hire counsel to take over the case and file an action. Or, if you wish, you could seek other litigation counsel.

Caution: Litigation can be injurious to your health. A lawsuit is very stressful, perhaps even more stressful than what you've already gone through with your identity theft! You'll be required to re-live the ordeal, document everything in interrogatories (written questions), participate in depositions (sworn testimony under oath), and testify in court. If you claim emotional distress, your whole private life, and possibly medical records, will be debated. Remember, court filings are public records and information brokers gather this data and it make it available on the Internet. Your financial situation may also become public. You'll lose more time from work and your family. Your already stressful situation will intensify.

Under certain circumstances, though, it may be worth it to take your case through the courts. This is especially true if you've been outrageously wronged and if precedent must be set to change the law. But understand, it's rare that litigation clients have a great win, and there's so much for you to lose in the process — peace of mind, time, your privacy. Just because I recommend against litigation, unless absolutely necessary, you should not acquiesce and file bankruptcy or live with your credit unfairly tarnished. There are ways to get your life back.

Keep in mind that the companies don't want litigation, either. Although they'll play hardball, they'd prefer not to spend the time, energy, and money to fight in court. But they *will* fight to the end if the stakes are high. So, unless your case is very strong, you won't have leverage. The companies usually have lots of money to spend on litigation, and their attorneys will "paper you" beyond belief.

However, the story could be different; if you do have a strong case and the company isn't in compliance with the laws or the reasonable standards in the industry, or if it's been grossly negligent or willful, the company's risk of loss at trial is great. The company also could suffer damage to its reputation and, thus, its profits. (That's why getting the media involved adds very good leverage.)

In addition, a lawsuit will be stressful and very time consuming for the company, too, and could make its leaders look bad in the eyes of their stockholders. Further, if you win, a bad precedent may be very damaging to the firm financially in the future. So, if you have such leverage, try to use it to *negotiate* a fair and reasonable settlement.

Again, remember that these lawsuits are costly to litigate, so you may not be able to get an attorney to take your case unless you have very extensive financial losses or lost opportunities. Remember under federal law you won't be required to pay the fraud charges — so don't! There's currently no provision in federal law (or most state laws) for class-action suits in which an attorney could represent many identity-theft victims at once, making the litigation more feasible. That needs to change. Unfortunately, the lobby for the banking industry is strong and opposes class actions. So for the time being, at least, it will remain prohibitively costly for most victims to get representation by competent counsel unless they prove great loss.

4. Contact the media and expose the problem.

Another way to get leverage is by calling your local newspaper and television news stations that deal with consumer problems. Ask to speak to the consumer affairs reporter or editor. You may also want to do this in the town where the company is located. Many local papers look for human interest stories.

Tell the journalists your story and see if you can interest them in investigating and then printing or broadcasting a story about the issue. Bad press alone may get a company to clean up its act and offer you a *nice* settlement.

Also contact us, or let Linda or Jay Foley of the Identity Theft Resource Center know about your case at (858) 693-7273 or go to www.idtheftcenter. org. They get calls all the time from reporters who want to talk to victims. Tell them your story in a concise manner. Give them the names and telephone numbers of the persons and entities you are having trouble with at the various companies. Give them permission to share your story, name and phone number with the media, to see if that helps bring leverage. You may also e-mail us with concerns about a very complex case at www.identity theft.org.

5. Complain to the appropriate commissions.

Write a concise, one or two-page list of the problems you're having with a particular company(s), attach your chronological history, and send with a short cover letter to the appropriate commissions. Call your state Office of Consumer Affairs and the Federal Trade Commission in Washington, D.C., 1-877-IDTHEFT, and ask to be referred to the regulatory agencies that govern the company you're at loggerheads with. Also, see our resources in the back of this book to assist you with contact information.

You may also want to make a written complaint to the Federal Trade Commission, since it is the central clearinghouse for identity theft issues. The FTC will take complaints, gather them, and if there are enough victims with similar problems, they may file an action against a company to enforce the laws. They also make reports to Congress and work with law enforcement. If your complaint is with the CRAs, the FTC must forward that complaint to the agencies and require a response as to what actions were taken.

6. Send or fax appropriate pages of this book to difficult companies.

This book is meant to be used, not just read. I want it to assist you in any way possible. Published material gives added support to your position. You may copy appropriate pages of this book with a copy of the front and back covers to lend power to your letters demanding resolution. If you get totally stuck, e-mail us at our web site at www. identitytheft.org.

7. Focus on a fair outcome.

I hope that one or more of the above methods will allow you to clean up all the fraud and restore you to wholeness again. If the companies don't believe you — if they still suspect *you* are the imposter or that you actually are *not* a victim (they may accuse you of not wanting to pay your bills or, if a victim of criminal fraud, that you are really the criminal) — you may need to have your congressman intervene. If you have carefully documented all your letters and your costs in your expense log, you should be able to negotiate compensatory damages and compensation for emotional distress.

If you're reasonable yet confident and firm, you will be able to settle on a favorable deal without litigation. Your ability to negotiate will depend on how much information, documentation, and leverage you have. If you need advice in developing a negotiating strategy, get an attorney to coach you. (See the list of attorneys in our resources section, or call your local bar association)

Again, don't let your anger interfere with your focus. Keep your eyes on the prize — peace of mind and regaining your creditworthiness, your clean background check, your identity, and your valued name.

In short, *be hard on the issues of the problem and gentle on the people you are dealing with.*

Good luck. Use your knowledge of the facts and your rights to gain a fair outcome — you can do it!

Chapter 7

How to Protect Yourself in the Future!

Yes, you will recover from having been robbed of your identity; just know, however, that a part of you may never be the same. You may not be as trusting, and I hope you will be more privacy cautious!

If you persist, if you follow the steps outlined in this book and write the letters using the CD, you'll eventually get your credit back on track. And if you write enough letters and make enough phone calls, you *will* clear your name. If someone has worked or committed crimes while using your name, our steps and letters should help you rectify the situation, and even achieve a certain peace of mind.

Figuratively speaking though, you'll always be looking over your shoulder. You'll always be a little more suspicious, a bit more vigilant and a great deal more aware! That's a shame, in a sense, because it would be a better world if we could all let down our guard. But, we have to face reality in our society. There are malicious-minded individuals who take advantage of good innocent people like you. There are also many insensitive bureaucracies, public or private, that favor the status quo or the quick buck, so perhaps that dollop of extra precaution will act as a lifesaver for you.

"Many are the uses of adversity," Shakespeare tells us. I hope one of the positive benefits of your experience with adversity is that you do become more careful, more aware of how vulnerable you are, yet confident that you can handle whatever comes your way. We must remember that it is not what happens to us in life – it is our response that makes us calm or crazed. All challenges in life are lessons and great opportunities for growth. Look how much you have learned already!

As you know by now, identity theft is frightening and can be an overwhelming experience. It's like a cancer, in many ways; it often strikes without warning. It disrupts your whole life. Early treatment is advisable, and the scourge can, with a good attitude and the right help, be stopped. But, sad to say, it doesn't always stay in remission. You, the victim, must be proactive to prevent a recurrence, and vigilant for any signs that the "disease" is recurring.

In this chapter, I'll outline what you can do to prevent this crisis from happening again. I'm going to suggest steps to take on various fronts. Some of these may seem a little extreme, but as you know by now, the risks are high and a minor inconvenience may be a small price to pay. You decide. Go through the bulleted list of safeguards and check off what you are already doing. Then, you might want to make note of those things you wish to implement right now and what you wish to do later.

Bear in mind that nothing you do will guarantee that a criminal won't get access to your information — no matter how many letters you send, no matter how careful you are with your Social Security number, credit card numbers, and other personal information, no matter how many documents you shred or passwords you memorize. In our increasingly data-saturated society where information can be accessed, retrieved easily, and shipped anywhere by computer in a nanosecond, criminals have a leg up.

Your personal and confidential information is accessible by identity thieves off-line in the real world, (dumpster divers, and unscrupulous employees who work in banks, credit card companies, doctors offices, the IRS and other places where your information is stored on hard copies) and online — or electronically — by hackers who break into the major computer systems of government agencies, corporations, hospitals, and other institutions that maintain databases with our sensitive information. We cannot be responsible for our information that is stolen when it is out of our control. This is frustrating, since we have limited power to reduce access to our information in commerce (until we join together to demand that laws be changed). But, there are some things you can do to protect yourself, actions you *personally* can take to minimize your risk. These actions will empower you (after having been victimized), because they're proactive steps you can take to put up barriers against the identity thieves and establish your own privacy protection plan. Below *I* have provided you with a list of personal actions that you can take to protect your privacy and avoid future identity theft:

Personal Identity Theft Safety Measures

1. Review, access, and correct your credit reports.

• Order your credit report from all three major CRAs at least two times a year, or sign up for a credit-monitoring service.

You are entitled to *one free* credit report from each of the three major *CRAs* per year. You'll need to call toll-free:

877-322-8228 or visit:
www.annualcreditreport.com.

I suggest you order them twice a year, or sign up for a credit-monitoring service that accesses *all three* companies. If you've already been victimized, you know how important it is to check your reports for fraud.

Look for any debts you don't recognize and any credit inquiries that don't look familiar. As you know by now, unfamiliar inquiries might mean someone has used your name to rent property, buy a house, or get credit. It could also mean someone has applied for a job or a loan in your name.

If there are errors, make sure you immediately write to the CRA to have the items corrected or removed. You already have sample letters with this book that show you how to dispute information. You may use the forms to write correction letters, as well as to block fraud. You can even write to the companies via e-mail, but ask them to send you a confirmation of receipt, and follow-up with a copy in the mail.

To order additional credit reports, contact the following agencies:

Equifax: www.equifax.com
   or phone (800) 685-1111
Experian: www.experian.com
   or phone (888) 397-3742
TransUnion: www.transunion.com
   or phone (800) 888-4213

• Immediately correct all mistakes on your credit reports — in writing.

Send a letter, like the ones in the Appendix, to the *CRAs* by certified mail, *return receipt requested*, identifying the mistakes item by item on a copy of the credit report. You should hear from each agency within 30 days (mark you calendar). A study performed in June, 2004, by the U.S. Public Interest Research Group (USPIRG), found that 79 percent of the credit reports analyzed had errors; one in four (25%) were severe enough for consumers to be denied credit, a loan, an apartment, or a job. So even if you have cleaned up the fraud on your reports, you may still find errors with your *true* accounts. Don't ignore these!

Think of your credit report as a snapshot. By the time you request and receive it, it has probably changed, because new information is being added all the time. The fact that it's good today doesn't mean it's going to be good tomorrow or the next day. In fact, new fraud could reappear without notice! So, check it often, at least two times a year. You are entitled to get a free credit report once a year from each of the three major CRAs (Equifax, Experian, TransUnion). It should also be sent to you at no cost if you have been denied credit, are indigent, unemployed, or if you are a victim of identity theft. (If you're a victim, you may request *two* free reports in the year of the fraud.) It's best to check your profile with all three companies since, as you know by now, they don't all have the same data. Before you apply for a job or credit, make sure you check your profile for errors or fraud, and make corrections in order to raise your score. Also, it's a good idea to do a background check on yourself if you have been a victim of fraud. This is especially important to do before you apply for a job in case a company intends to do their own background check. If you were the victim of fraud, you may be able to ask the police who issued you a police report to check your criminal background to look for fraudulent criminal activity. Otherwise, you may either utilize a private investigator or use a reputable background-checking company. For a once a year free employment screening company report call 866-312-8075 or visit www.choicetrust.com.

2. Safely store, protect, and discard personal information

Contrary to popular belief, most identity thieves steal information about you the old-fashioned way …"off-line," not from your computer. But the reason we have such an epidemic of this crime is because thieves can *use* the information so easily and quickly on the Internet, where vendors have no face-to-face interaction with buyers. Your evil-twin can make purchases with *your* information and credit from the seclusion of his bedroom in another state or a far off country. To protect yourself from this:

• Don't share your personal information with people who don't need to know it.

If you've been victimized by fraud, you have had to share quite a bit of your personal information when dealing with all the agencies to prove who you are — so this suggestion may seem ridiculous! But still, you must always ask "why" before you agree to share confidential data in the future. If there is no good legal reason, politely decline.

• Keep your financial records under lock and

key, at home and while traveling.

Burglars may be more interested in your bank and credit card information than in your VCR. Furthermore, you'd be surprised at how many cases of identity theft involve a perpetrator known to the victim: a relative, client, roommate, cleaning service, tenant, or someone else who has easy access to the victim's house and to his or her account numbers, Social Security number, and driver's license number. If a friend or family member takes your identity, it's very tragic. So, you'll need to be extra cautious on this one! Don't leave *any* personal information in plain view in your home, car, or on your computer!

Invest in locking file cabinets for your confidential documents. Put padlocks on the doors of any closets that contain boxes of old tax returns and financial statements or identity theft correspondence. Secure briefcases containing private documents (with a locking device and alarm) in your locked trunk. When using a parking valet, provide a key that doesn't open the trunk. Consider a burglar alarm for your home and automobile (make sure you place a sticker on your window to warn potential thieves of the alarm — it may just frighten them away). And think about getting a dog with a loud bark to ward off unwanted visitors!

Log these costs for reimbursement or restitution since you were already victimized. For that matter, it may be deductible under 165e of the U.S. Tax Code for Fraud and Theft.

• Buy and use a shredder.

Any papers you don't need to keep that contain private information should be destroyed. Be careful with all the draft letters you write to the various agencies and creditors, since they contain your Social Security number and other sensitive data. So shred what you intend to discard. For a small investment, you can purchase a shredder to destroy those old records, and all pre-approved credit applications and convenience checks. In fact, write to your credit card companies and ask them not to send you those convenience checks, which often arrive attached to your billing statement. Fraudsters can use those "hot checks" very easily.

The Postal Inspector's office told us that *35* percent of those convenience checks are used fraudulently. So stop them from coming in your mail. For security reasons, make sure you use a *crosscut* shredder that cuts paper into small dots, virtually impossible to reconstruct.

• Be careful of "dumpster divers."

Your trash tells a lot about you — sometimes *too* much. Make sure that you don't throw away anything that someone could use to assume your identity: credit card, checking account, or investment account statements, insurance policies, credit card receipts, old tax returns, escrow documents, or brokerage statements. Utility statements provide enough information to enable a hoaxer to open utility accounts in another location. Anything that contains your financial or confidential information must be completely destroyed, or you could be re-victimized.

• Take extra precautions when you move or do spring cleaning.

When moving, take your old files of tax returns, loan applications, escrow documents, identity theft correspondence, and all other old confidential files and burn or shred them. To make it easier, call a bonded shredding service to take your boxes full of sensitive documents and pulverize them. Better yet, some services will bring a shredding truck to disintegrate your boxes of data right in your driveway, and then you can rest assured that your sensitive data has truly been destroyed.

• Tell people who fax to your home not to send confidential information in a fax to you unless they call first to confirm that you are there to receive it.

If guests, repairpersons, or babysitters are in your home when faxes arrive, they may retrieve this information without your knowledge, to your detriment.

• Quiz every firm or organization — banks, brokerages, doctors' offices, accountants, lawyers, and even your own employer —

about what they do with your private information.

Many companies you deal with still are not conscious of the risks of identity theft and fail to recognize the privacy issues. Unfortunately, identity theft is often caused by shoddy information handling practices. When dealing with merchants, vendors, and professionals, insist that they guard your personal information, secure data in locked files, and shred before putting your documents in the trash. Several states require companies to completely destroy sensitive documents before discarding. California, Wisconsin, and Georgia were the first to pass document destruction laws. The Fair Credit Reporting Act requires document destruction for personal and financial information contained in credit reports. Find out what security procedures the offices you deal with have in place to protect your files both online and off-line. If you are comfortable, tell them you have been a victim of fraud, and that you expect them to secure your information and provide a fraud flag.

• Don't co-sign for car loans, credit cards, and other credit with a friend or adult child.

You may be generous, but once you do this, your information may be used without authorization to apply for new accounts using your name. Or, the former co-signed agreement may be shown to obtain new accounts, loans etc. *I*'ve helped many individuals who were victimized by their own children in this way. Sad, but it happens.

3. Managing your credit cards after ID theft.

• Get credit cards with your picture on them.

Not all credit card issuers will do this, but some will. Shop around.

• When you order new credit cards or your current ones are expiring, keep an eye on the calendar.

Be alert when a new card ought to be arriving. If it doesn't arrive when you expect it, call the credit card issuer immediately and find out if the card was sent. If it was sent more than 10 days before your call, but you still haven't received it, cancel it at once.

- Mark your calendar for credit card bills.

If you haven't received your billing statement, you may find out that it was sent to an imposter.

- Put new passwords on all your financial accounts.

This may be bothersome and may not win you friends at the bank or with your creditors, but it's important. Make it something other than your mother's maiden name, a pet's name, or the name of someone in your family. If you think you might forget the password, ask if the bank or creditor will record a question they can ask to help you remember. Consider using at least eight letters and mix them with numbers.

- Cancel all credit cards that you haven't used in six months.

If you don't pare down your unused cards, you might as well be carrying around dynamite while waiting for a match. If you carry a little-used card, you are not likely to quickly notice if it's lost or stolen. Also, if the thief has your credit report, he or she has notice of an account that is ripe for extensive use. You have now seen your credit reports — so carefully scrutinize the real accounts listed and call to cancel old cards that you aren't using. When you cancel the cards, ask that the record say "Closed by consumer request." Then cut the canceled cards into small pieces that will render the numbers unreadable.

- Monitor all statements from every credit card company and bank.

If there's anything on the statement you don't recall buying, call the credit grantor to verify that the debt is truly yours. If it's not yours, cancel the card and get a new account number using a unique password.

- Carefully review all bank and financial statements.

Many victims learn too late that fraudsters stole money using the victim's checks or debit cards. If this has happened to you, try not to use checks or debit cards. Use a credit card instead, whenever possible — it's safer!

- Don't put your address, telephone number, or driver's license number on the credit card slip from restaurants or stores.

In fact, this practice is a violation of law in many states. It is also contrary to most credit card companies' policies. Of course, for ordering by mail you will need to provide complete address information on the order form. But you don't need to write your driver's license or Social Security number on the order form. Be stingy with your information — you are well aware of the problems!

- Don't put your credit card account numbers on the Internet (except on a secure site). In general, be careful to whom you give those numbers.

Guard those numbers zealously. Never give out a credit card number unless you have a trusted business relationship with the company, and *you* call them, not vice versa. If you shop on the Internet, use a secure browser that encrypts or scrambles account information or, better still, place your order by telephone, fax, or mail. Make sure the Internet merchant stores credit account data in encrypted form.

- Don't allow a merchant to print your credit card number on checks.

It's against the law in many states. With your credit card number and bank account number all in one place, an identity thief can do a lot of damage.

- If you think you've misplaced or lost a credit card, assume the worst.

Call the issuing bank *immediately*. Don't spend three or four days looking for it. The bad guys use it up in two days. So call immediately to cancel your account…better to be safe than sorry.

- Keep a list of all your credit cards and bank accounts.

Include the account numbers, expiration dates, and phone numbers of the issuers' customer service departments. Update the list as needed and keep it in a secure place so you can quickly contact your creditors if your cards are lost or stolen. Don't keep this information on your computer or PDA; keep it on a CD and hard copy. Then lock it in a secure filing cabinet. Make Xerox copies of each card and store these in a locked file, too.

Jeff Levy, computer expert and host of a syndicated computer talk-radio show tells us, "Avoid storing your personal information on your computer. Things that require your name and your Social Security information should never be kept on your hard drive." Quicken, Microsoft Money, and other programs that track our financial information all allow us to store data on CDs, not on the hard drive.

For Internet users who travel extensively: create a list of all your credit card companies (*don't* list the account numbers) with the toll-free numbers. Save it in a file folder with a Web-based e-mail account like Yahoo. This will provide you instant access to your credit card companies to cancel your accounts in the event of loss or theft of your wallet, even when you are away from home. As an alternative, sign up for a service (with your credit card company) that lets you cancel all your cards with one call.

4. Protecting your financial transactions.

- Use checks only when necessary.

You are safer using a credit card to buy groceries, gas, products, and services than you are using a check. Your account number and routing numbers are printed on your checks, so fraudsters can easily use commercial software to create new checks and drain your account.

- Don't print your Social Security number on your checks.

Don't allow merchants to write it on checks, either. Retailers don't need it — thieves *do*. Also, don't print your Social Security number on your business cards, address labels, invoices, or other identifying information. Try to convince your employer to follow the same precautions.

- Don't print your telephone number or full name on your checks.

Put your initials and last name on your checks. If a merchant asks you for your phone number, you can decide to add it at that time.

- When you order new checks, have them delivered to your local bank branch, not to your home.

Boxes of blank checks are readily recognizable and an easy target for mail thieves. Since you've already been victimized — you need to be extra careful with your mail.

- Don't give your checking account number to people you don't know.

Be equally suspicious if they claim they're from the bank. Don't allow automatic deductions from your bank account; if you want the convenience of automatic payments, authorize them on your credit card. If there's a problem, you are protected from fraud.

- Take precautions against illegitimate access to your accounts.

Write to your bank and ask them to notify you in writing before they provide any information or make changes for someone who requests them (i.e. address change).

- Store cancelled checks in a locked file.

When you discard them, shred or burn them. Your checking account numbers can be used to impersonate you. Fraudsters use the account numbers to create new checks and drain your account.

- Consider replacing your ATM debit card that has the Visa/MasterCard logo. Use a regular ATM card instead.

It's safer to use a credit card than an ATM debit with a Visa/MasterCard logo. If your debit card is used without your authorization, the money is directly withdrawn from your bank account. If someone uses your credit card, you have the opportunity to dispute the charges before you pay the bill. All you need is a regular ATM card to get cash or make deposits anywhere in the world. For purchases use a normal credit card — it protects you from future fraud.

5. Protect information by phone.

- Establish an unpublished phone number so that your name and home address won't be in the phone book and so you'll be removed from reverse directories.

Make sure you also opt-out of having your cell phone listed in a 411 directory.

- Sign up for the Federal Trade Commission National Do Not Call List.

Call (888) 382-1222 or visit www.donotcall.gov. Stop unsolicited calls from unknown people.

- Stop unwanted or unsolicited faxes.

Call the Federal Communications Commission to complain at (888) callFCC (888-225-5322) or visit www.fcc.gov.

- Block your phone number from showing up on Caller ID. (Order this option from your telephone provider.)

Your number will not show on Caller ID if you have indicated this option with your local phone carrier. You'll need to input *82 to unblock your number to place calls to numbers that do not accept blocked calls. Be aware this will then disclose your phone number so you can make the call.

- Never give out any personal information over the phone to someone you don't know.

If someone tells you he or she represents a credit grantor of yours, or a government agency, call the person at a telephone number that you know is the *true* number and ask for that person. Even then, provide only information that you believe is absolutely necessary. Only give your credit card on the phone when you initiate the call to a trusted number.

- Tell your children not to give out information to anyone on the phone, at the door, or on the Internet.

Children are very trusting and inexperienced; they need your guidance to protect simple personal information.

- Check to see who is listening when sharing confidential information on a speakerphone.

Persons who could use the information to commit fraud may overhear you. If someone calls you and he is on a speakerphone, ask him to pick up the receiver.

6. Defend yourself against new identity theft when using a cell phone.

- If your wireless phone is lost or stolen, immediately de-activate it.

If you find it within a few days, it can be re-activated.

- To be safe, don't give out personal, financial, or confidential data while on your wireless phone.

Current cellular phones are much more secure than the old-style analog phones. However, our cell phone communications can be unscrambled by law enforcement and techies, as there is extensive cell phone fraud. Check your credit reports for cellular service inquiries — if you see the name of a company that doesn't provide you service, you may have been re-victimized.

Cell phone fraud has become epidemic. A fraudster will open an account in your name with your Social Security number, and the bills will be sent to the impostor's address. When no bills are paid, the victim learns of this account from collection companies demanding payment. Here are some things you can do to minimize your risk:

⇒ Carefully monitor your cell phone bills each month: Look for phone calls you did not make and report them immediately to the phone carrier.

⇒ Unless you are traveling overseas, contact your cell phone carrier and ask that the phone be limited to calls within the United States.

⇒ When you aren't using your phone, use the phone's locking feature: Don't let others borrow your phone, and keep it in your possession at all times when you are away from home. If you are on vacation, lock your cell phone in the hotel safe. When you're at home, and not using the phone, secure it in a locked drawer.

⇒ Never give out confidential or financial information over a wireless or cordless phone: Persons with scanners may be able to listen in on your conversations when you least expect it. Your wireless transmissions are not secure. It is best to use a "landline" for confidential communications.

⇒ When using a wireless phone in a public place, be careful to speak quietly, and move to a secluded area when speaking about your sensitive information: Many people speak louder than normal when using a wireless phone. It's easy to eavesdrop on cell phone users' calls at a restaurant or standing in line for a theatre.

7. Guard your identity when using other wireless devices.

In this age of high tech gadgets, we find many wireless devices make our lives easier and more enjoyable, but we tend to be oblivious to their dangers and don't know how to protect ourselves. The following devices operate on radio frequencies that can be picked up by radio scanners, cordless phones, and other monitors; be aware when using these devices:

Walkie-Talkies: Families use these to communicate all the time on vacation, at festivals, and anyplace where it's easy to lose each other. But if you aren't careful, you may lose your identity.

Home intercom systems: Make sure the intercom is off when sharing confidential information.

Baby monitors: Consider using the wired version to be more secure. Neighbors can pick up conversations on baby monitors.

Wireless video cameras: Many security-minded people have installed these devices to provide security at home. The camera sends the images to be viewed on a computer or TV, but these devices are easy for criminals to monitor, so they may view the images as well. Consider using wired cameras and tapes for safety.

Airplane wireless phones: These are vulnerable to radio scanners. When using airplane phones, others around you can also hear your conversations. Wait to use a landline to have confidential conversations.

8. Secure your Personal Data Assistant (PDA).

People use these devices to check e-mail, surf the Web, maintain calendar and contact files, and some people use them to store their credit card numbers and other sensitive information. Those of us concerned with identity theft consider the following to be the biggest threats:

♦ Theft of the PDA itself (especially if it contains sensitive data)

♦ Password Theft

♦ Viruses and data corruption, and

♦ Wireless vulnerabilities.

As *I* suggest for wireless connection to the Internet, don't keep sensitive information on the PDA. If you choose to keep private information on your PDA, there are encryption solutions.

• To protect data if the PDA is lost or stolen, utilize user ID and password level security.

To find out more on how to protect your information on your wireless devices, and to access reviews of Internet security products, including wireless computer networks and PDAs, visit the Web at www.firewallguide.com/index.htm.

9. Protect your mail and mailbox.

• Don't mail checks from your home mailbox.

When you pay your bills, make the effort to drop them off at the post office. If you leave them as outgoing mail for the letter carrier, you create an easy target for a thief who can learn a great deal about you from that handful of envelopes. Also, it's not hard for a crook to steal a check, acid wash the name of the recipient, and make himself or herself the payee.

Consider using an alternate means of paying bills. Pay-by-Phone, initiated from your own bank, is a secure transaction. The bank sends the payment electronically or by draft to the payee. You won't have to use your checks and you'll save money on postage!

• Get a post office box or a locked residential mailbox.

Stealing mail is so easy — and the aftermath is so potentially ruinous to your identity. This is a simple precaution that pays big dividends in peace of mind.

• Don't throw away pre-approved offers that you receive in the mail.

Some privacy advocates suggest marking the mail "refused, return to sender." *I* suggest shredding and opting out instead. (Call 1-888-5-OPT-OUT to stop receiving pre-approved offers from the CRAs)

10. Block your name from marketing lists.

• Protect your financial privacy

Financial companies are required by law to mail a privacy notice to you once a year under the Federal Financial Modernization Act. Don't throw out those privacy brochures or letters, write or call the number provided in the notices and stop your financial institutions from selling your personal information or sharing it with third parties. Some companies will also allow you to opt out of sharing information with affiliates. California and North Dakota have passed more stringent privacy laws, which require financial institutions to get prior permission before selling/sharing your information to/with third parties (called opt-in). Those states also permit you to opt out of sharing your information with company affiliates.

• Opt out of unsolicited credit offers.

Choose to exclude your name from credit bureau lists for unsolicited credit offers. (*"You've been pre-approved!"*) This will limit the number of pre-approved offers of credit that you receive. These, when tossed into the garbage, are potential targets of identity thieves, who use them to order credit cards in your name.

The CRAs are required by law to provide a toll-free number that you can call to request that your name not be sold for credit solicitations. Call (888) 5OPTOUT, or (888) 567-8688. Your request is shared with all three credit bureaus. You will have to give your Social Security number in response to a voice prompt. You may opt out for five years.

• Don't forget to ask companies not to share your information with their affiliates.

Unfortunately, the federal law is weak regarding sharing with affiliate companies. Federal law allows companies to share your information with affiliates without the right to opt out. Write to your banks and credit card companies (*return receipt requested*) and ask them to remove you from their promotional lists. Ask them not to sell your name or information on your creditworthiness or spending habits to any third party (or affiliate), or to other companies without your permission. Demand that they protect your privacy. They may not comply. If that's the case, write to your congressperson and tell your story and concerns.

- Alert your professional or trade associations not to sell your data.

Many professional organizations sell their member lists for marketing purposes. Write your professional associations and ask them to stop selling your name and other information to other entities. Alert them to your fraud.

- Don't participate in phone surveys, marketing surveys, or contests.

Phone surveys and contests hook you in to gather your information to sell. Also, don't fill-in personal information on product warranty or registration cards. Information about your income is not needed to warranty your new TV. Remember, information you provide could be used to steal your good name again.

- Notify your state's Department of Motor Vehicles that you don't want your personal data sold.

To save money for the state, Illinois prisoners were data processing the personal information provided for vehicle licenses. These criminals, armed with private information, had many opportunities to commit identity theft.

Find out how your personal information is entered into your state's databases and complain where appropriate. Ask to have your name removed from lists that are sold to marketers.

Some states still use the Social Security number for the driver's license number. If this is the case in your state, ask for an alternative number.

- Take your phone numbers off of marketing lists: (888) 382-1222 or www.donotcall.gov.

Stop unwanted telemarketing calls. This will also reduce pretext calling … where someone pretends to be an agency or company asking for your confidential information. Never give out sensitive information unless you call the number you *know* to be true.

- If a company you already do business with calls you, and you don't want to be called, ask them to add you to their *internal* database as a Do Not Call.

Most companies will honor that request.

- Stop the selling of your information, which produces junk mail.

Contact Mail Preference Service, and sign up for the opt-out list.

Direct Marketing Association
Mail Preference Service
P.O. Box 643
Carmel, NY 10512

It costs nothing to opt out by mail, but you are charged $5 to sign up at their web site. Visit: www/ dmaconsumers.org/consumerassistance.html

- Find out what the Insurance Industry Database of Property Loss Claims is selling and sharing about you.

You can obtain your homeowner's or automobile insurance claims history, by contacting an information broker: Choicepoint, P.O. Box 105108, Atlanta, GA 30348. Phone: (888) 497-0011. Web: www.choicetrust.com.

- Don't let tax assessor records be sold with your property information.

Contact these companies and opt out of having your information made available online for fraudsters to use.

⇒ Axiom: Opt-Out Hotline (877) 774-2094, or e-mail optout@acxiom.com.

⇒ DataQuick: Opt-Out Hotline (877) 970-9171.

• Learn what the public records show potential scammers about you.

Public records are documents that are open to inspection by any person. In fact, now they are easily downloadable on the Internet from myriad information brokers; many are available at no cost. Depending on your resident state, certain records may or may not be public. Normally, birth records (has your mother's maiden name), marriage certificates (your Social Security number and other personal information), death records (the decedent's Social Security number is included in the death index), court files, divorce files (court records often have sensitive financial information and personal identifiers), arrest records (Social Security number), property ownership, tax information, minutes of meetings of government entities, driver's license information, occupational and professional licenses, Securities and Exchange Commission filings, and government contracts are considered public records. Once a record becomes public, there is usually no restriction on use in the public domain. This information, available to criminally minded persons, exposes you to the risk of identity theft.

When commercial profilers buy and sell your public information for marketing and targeted advertising, they also make your data accessible to those who would use this information to commit fraud. Information brokers such as ChoicePoint and many others collect and assemble your data and then sell detailed dossiers to law enforcement, attorneys, government agencies, and others. It's impossible for you to know how many persons have had access to your personal information thanks to the re-selling of that information. Additionally, these databases often contain errors, and such errors could be severe enough to falsely identify you as a criminal. Also, since you are already a victim, you need to know what these public records say about you. Faulty records may result in a case of *unintentional* identity theft. Additionally, public records provide all the information necessary for an impersonator to pose as you and obtain financial records from your bank (or other private information from companies with which you do business) by practicing what is called "pretext" calling. The fraudster can then steal money from your bank.

Two Brooklyn men allegedly usurped the identities of such luminaries as Oprah Winfrey, George Soros, and Ted Turner to steal millions of dollars. Clearly, no one is immune to identity theft, a range of crimes that runs from stealing credit card numbers to concocting phony personas, complete with credit reports and college degrees.

Under present federal law, you have no right to opt out of having your public record information sold, shared, or transferred; nor are you notified when vast profiles are being amassed about you. You have no privacy (control over the sharing of this information) when it comes to public records. This is one of the many reasons that, even if you are able to execute all of the actions in this book, there is some information dissemination that is beyond your control. It's critical to minimize your risk where you can, but also be aware of the dangers lurking in these public records. Some states are beginning to see the vulnerability of these records and have passed laws requiring that sensitive information be redacted for the general public like the Social Security numbers of parents on birth certificates. This is a healthy approach to allowing public access without divulging riskier data. Urge your legislators to consider more protections for sensitive information in public records. If you find errors in the public records, you will need to go to the original agency that reported the error and make corrections. You will need to use the letters on the enclosed CD to document all issues in writing.

• Order your free specialty consumer report.

Under recent changes to the Fair Credit Reporting Act, you are entitled to a free annual disclosure of your consumer report that is compiled by a nationwide specialty consumer reporting agency.

Potential employers often order these reports as background checks. Per federal law, the big companies must set up a toll-free number to give you instructions on how to order these. At the time of this printing, the companies had not yet done so. You will be able to find which companies will do this and other information including the toll-free number by going to www.ftc.gov. As a former victim of identity theft, you may also call 1-877 IDTHEFT to find out more about the companies who prepare these reports.

11. Protect yourself while using your computer.

- Set up a system password to get into your computer

Set up a system password (for your computer and laptop) that must be entered before Windows even begins to load. It will prohibit any access to the computer except by the person who enters your password, which should only be you! Check your computer manual to set up the password.

- Install Firewalls

Hardware firewalls block all traffic between the Internet and your network that isn't explicitly allowed. A hardware firewall keeps unauthorized programs and people from remotely accessing your computer. These firewalls can also hide the addresses of the computers behind your firewall, making individual computers on your network invisible to the outside. You can purchase an inexpensive hardware router/firewall from such companies as LinkSys, Microsoft, and D-Link.

Software firewalls, such as the Microsoft Internet Connection Firewall, ZoneAlarm, and Norton Personal Firewall protect only the computer they're running on. It's a good backup defense to hardware firewalls, but software firewalls on their own cannot protect your entire network if you have several computers linked in your home.

- Install, use, and continually update antivirus software

Antivirus software screens all incoming data and files to determine whether a known virus is trying to infect your computer, then gives you a choice to delete, repair or quarantine the file. Every time you download files, receive e-mails, or even put a CD or floppy on your computer, you need to scan for virus infections. Viruses can be coded to scan your computer for financial information like your tax return, which could subject you to identity theft.

- Don't just give your computer away when you purchase a new one.

Some people think deleting the files will clean them from the computer; but computer-savvy crooks can easily retrieve this information. So instead, use an overwrite or erasing program to override the entire hard drive. Go to www.hq.nasa.gov/office/oig/hq/harddrive.pdf on the National Aeronautics and Space Administration web site for more information.

- Use hard drive eraser software.

If you have sensitive files with your personal information on your computer or laptop, you can use a program called Erasure to erase just those files. You can use the security level you wish, and you can also remove sensitive information stored without your knowledge. Go to www.east-tec.com and you can find erasure software for your computer as well as for your CD's or other removable media. You can also find an East-Tec disk sanitizer, which can securely destroy all data on any hard drive or floppy disc.

- Don't store financial or sensitive information on your laptop.

In fact, if you have any personal identifying information or any financial files or confidential files that you must keep on your laptop, encrypt them. Remember that your fraud resolution letters and sensitive documents have all the data that an imposter needs to do this to you again! Store your unencrypted, confidential files on a CD.

- Secure your laptop while traveling on airplanes.

Use caution when putting your laptop through the security screener in the airport. Make sure that you place your other bags first, so that you'll have time to get through the screening before someone steals your laptop.

Once onboard your flight, stow your computer in your bag under the seat in front of you. Avoid putting it in the overhead bin where others will have easier access to it.

- Encrypt your confidential data.

If you have sensitive information on your computer, encrypt it. Programs such as Pretty Good Privacy (www.pgp.com) make the job easy, and if you have Windows XP, you already have the tools needed. If a thief gets your machine, these extra steps will make it much more difficult to access the laptop's data.

- Back up your data before you leave for your trip.

If your laptop should be stolen on your trip, you may be able to get another computer at your destination and download your important files — at least you'll have your data on CD. Don't keep the backup file in the same computer case as your laptop.

- Trace a stolen laptop's location.

There are now programs available that can locate stolen laptops. They are activated when the laptop connects to the Internet. Tracing programs include zTrace (www.ztrace.com), CyberAngel (www.sentryinc.com), and ComputracePlus (www.computrace.com).

Also, engraving your name on your computer will make it more difficult for the thief to sell.

- Be on the lookout for charlatans who can access your home computer even if you are *not* connected to the Internet.

Your home is your refuge — so it's easy to forget that a crime could be committed there without a physical burglary. If you keep identifying information and confidential data on a computer without protecting it from the view of others, you are at risk of identity fraud once again. Ask yourself the following questions: Who has access to my home computer? Do my children bring friends to our home to use our PC? Do I use a cleaning service? Are repairpersons or household workers entering our home? Do guests and roommates have access to our processor? Are we using a wireless connection so that several computers in our home can network?

12. Protect yourself on the Internet.

There's a lot of things you can do with the Internet to destroy someone from the comfort of your own home.
— Dave Gordon, Maine police officer

- Strengthen your computer's login security.

Your passwords are the keys to unlock the door to your identity — guard them well. Don't forget and store them on your computer or on the web site itself. Type them in each time you access a particular site.

Learn how to browse the Internet and send e-mail messages without leaving a trail. (See PC World at www.pcworld.com and other computer magazines for ideas on how to protect your privacy when using the Internet. Also visit www.anonymizer.com.)

In addition, don't give out your Internet account password to anyone. If you do, you may find unexpected charges on your bills and lots of other problems.

Here's a suggestion for effective password creation: Use the first or last letters of each word in a favorite line of poetry that you'll easily remember. Intersperse these letters with numbers and punctuation marks. Example: "Mary had a little lamb." M*HA2LL or Y!DAE9B. Upper and lower case can also be varied. M*ha2LL.

- Create two passwords.

I suggest that you have at least two passwords: One password (using letters and numbers, at least eight characters long, as above) for your very sensitive and private information, and another one for your less sensitive web site entries. Make sure that you lock up your passwords in a locked drawer, cabinet, or safe. Change your passwords every six months

- Tell your Internet service provider that your personal data is not for sale.

Find out the company's privacy policy. Inform the service that any information you provide is not for sale and that you will hold the service accountable if it fails to maintain your privacy.

- Look for and read privacy policies.

For every web site that asks you to register or provide information, take a minute and read their policy carefully. It should be easy for you to find and if it is not, then *I* advise you *not* to fill in any information. The privacy policy should tell you what information they're collecting, what they're using, and how they're sharing it. You can also find out what kind of security they're using to protect your information. If you still want to do business with a company that doesn't have a privacy policy, then e-mail their web site and ask them to specifically answer you in writing what the policy is, and ask them to post one. Some states, like California, require companies to post a privacy policy.

- Look for a privacy seal.

TrustE (www.truste.org) and the Better Business Bureau (www.bbb.com) provide seal programs that are backed up by that company's willingness to handle complaints by consumers who feel that their privacy has been violated. This helps companies institute a system for "walking their talk" in protecting privacy. Unfortunately, a privacy seal doesn't necessarily mean that the company is not a fraud, because sometimes the bad guys can steal a privacy seal and place it on their web site, as well.

- Don't register when visiting web sites on the Internet, unless you are certain it's not a hoax site.

Web page owners have the ability to collect data about you when you visit their site and store that information in "cookie" files on your computer, which they can also share with other web sites. Ask web site operators what they do with your personal data before you give them too much information. The more information someone can access about you, the easier it is to assume your identity.

Watch out for fake sites that purport to offer services or sell goods, but which are nothing more than vehicles for collecting Social Security and credit card account numbers for identity theft purposes. Always heed the old adage: only do business with known, reputable companies. Check out the company and make sure it has a real address and phone number. If it is a well-known company, double check the web site address by doing a business search on the web. Some fraudsters will copy reputable web sites to fool you

- Don't display your personal or family information on the Internet.

Think twice before creating your own homepage, family tree, or photo web site with identifying information about your family. These web sites give the imposter lots of data with which to create his or her new identity, including mothers' maiden names and dates of birth.

- Shield your children online.

⇒ Place the computer that your children will use for school in a family-oriented space in your house, such as the kitchen, family room, or recreation room. That way you don't have to worry about your children in their bedroom and who they're "chatting" with.

⇒ Explain to your children about identity theft and the dangers of giving out personal information online. Remind them that when they register for a newsletter or products, they should use a temporary e-mail address from Hotmail or Yahoo.

⇒ After your child has used the computer, check it for downloads from e-mail or on-line sources.

⇒ Remind your children never to put personal information about themselves or any information or photos of their family on the Internet.

• Set limits for your children.

Warn your children about peer-to-peer file sharing. Not only is there a problem with sharing music (parents may be sued for copyright infringement) but also make your kids aware that viruses and hackers use the peer-to-peer file sharing to access sensitive files on your computer.

Also, warn your children to be careful when letting their friends use your PC. Unfortunately, computer privacy intrusions and fraud are often committed by people who have the opportunity to do it, such as friends and family members. So warn your children never to let someone else use your computer, unless they're sitting right there with them. For more information go to www.safekids.com.

• Don't trust charming people you meet online.

Use extreme caution when participating in chat rooms. True, you may find the love of your life, but you might also run into an evil-minded criminal. So don't give out personal information to people you do not know. Remain anonymous and use a nickname for your screen name.

• Remove your name from Internet online directories.

If you're in the white pages of the phone book, you're likely to be on any number of Internet directories. Most online directories provide opt-out opportunities. Take advantage of them. Below I've listed several such directories, but there are many more.

www.bigfoot.com
www.Four11.com
www.InfoSpace.com
www.Switchboard.com
www.whowhere.com

• Opt out of "look-up" companies' databases.

Take advantage of any of the opt-out opportunities of the major information vendors such as Lexis-Nexis (www.lexis-nexis.com).

• Opt out of the sharing of online cookie data with advertisers

Network Advertising Initiative: www.networkadvertising.org.

• Use a secure browser that complies with the industry security standard, such as Secure Sockets Layer (SSL)

The little lock that will appear at the bottom right-hand side of your screen will show you that the file will be encrypted or scrambled as it goes through cyberspace. Please remember that some fraudster sites also can use SSL, so you need to verify whom you are really dealing with.

• Make purchases on the Internet only from reputable companies.

At a minimum, be sure that the company has a physical address, not just a post office box, and a telephone number where you can call and talk to them directly off-line. Check with your state's attorney general for any adverse reports regarding the company you are dealing with. (This is not always an absolute guarantee, though, since your attorney general. or the FBI, is not always familiar with the new fraudulent companies that arise.) If possible, find the item you wish to purchase, then order by calling the 800 number to give your credit card number by phone.

• Make sure you are on the web site of the company that you really think you're doing business with.

Online fraudsters create web site names (URLs)

very similar to those of legitimate companies. To check whether the site that you're on is really the legitimate company, go to www.whois.net, which tells you who has registered the URL and the physical address of that company.

If the URL in the address section of that Web page doesn't exactly match the site you think it is, go to the front page of the actual site (i.e., eBay.com, PayPal.com, Best Buy.com, AOL.com) and scroll down to the billing section. Whenever you are questioning the URL, it's best to call the customer service number on your bill or on the real web site that you have found to ask them if, indeed, the URL you are dealing with is correct.

• Only divulge information that's necessary for the transaction.

Don't give out more information than is necessary for your purchase. For example, if you buy something with a credit card, you'll most likely be required to give your name, address, credit card number, expiration date, and perhaps the security number on the back or front of your credit card; but you should never be required to give your Social Security number, birth date, or mother's maiden name.

• Use your credit card to order, it's safer than sending a check or cash.

Never send cash, because it doesn't create a record of your payment. Also, don't send a check because if the company is fraudulent, your money is gone. When you use a credit card, if you haven't received the product by the time your credit card statement arrives, you can let the credit card company know that you have not received the product, and you can dispute the charge until the merchandise arrives.

• Consider a one-time-only credit card for shopping online.

Consider using one-time-use credit cards. Many credit card companies now offer a single-use credit card, which gives you a unique number that links to your regular credit card number, but is only good for a few transactions. Your true credit card number is never placed online. Therefore, you can use the credit cards for a limited amount of purchases. The charges will show up on your monthly statement, but the vendor will never see your true credit card number. Go to your credit card company's web site and see if they offer this service. This will protect your real card from fraud.

• Manage junk e-mail.

You can use your delete key to manage incoming junk mail, but it takes forever, especially if you get a hundred junk mails per day. Consider using a junk mail filter. Microsoft Outlook, Eudora for the PC, Entourage for Macintosh, AOL, and Hotmail all have junk mail filters. Get information on this and save yourself a great deal of time and also protect your identity. A great deal of junk mail is a "come-on" by fraudsters. Don't be fooled. For junk mail and spam, forward e-mails to spam @uce.gov.

• Use disposable forwarding e-mail addresses.

It is a good idea to create separate addresses or accounts that can be used for online purchases, chat rooms, and other public postings. You can create such e-mail addresses with Hotmail or with Yahoo that will protect your identity.

• Protect yourself when you are "always on" the Internet, with connections like DSL and cable networks.

"Always on" users have permanent addresses that are easy for hackers and fraudsters to find and exploit. Make sure you use a router and other firewall protection.

• Applying for a job online.

If you post your résumé online, include only the most relevant personal information and keep details of your work history to a minimum, since someone else can steal your identity again and apply for the same job.

Don't give your Social Security number until you

are ready to be hired and only after you have checked out the company.

Approach every data request with a great deal of skepticism and with these questions: "Why do you need that information?" "How will you use that information?" "What happens if I don't give you that information?"

• Look over your shoulder when online.

Look around to see who's watching you when you go online at work, at a friend's house, or at Starbuck's. People around you can see what you're doing. Never let anyone see you input a password on your computer. Use your hand to shield the keyboard so no one can see the letters that you're inputting.

• Never use a public computer, such as an Internet café, a library, or airport computer to access your sensitive financial information.

Fraudsters love to access these public computers. They visit a public computer, download key logging software, or attach key logging hardware that records every key typed in and every web site accessed, then they leave. You have no idea that your keystrokes are captured. When the fraudster returns (after you're gone), he accesses the hidden key log and has all the information you input. If you typed in passwords and confidential information, he can steal your identity and transfer money out of your accounts.

• Never buy anything from spammers.

People who send out these unsolicited e-mails are not to be trusted.

• Be careful when buying from Internet auctions.

Make sure that the seller has a telephone number that you can call, because you should be able to talk with the seller if you win the auction. Before you send any funds, talk with the seller. Beware that they may have only a temporary cell phone number, which they can cancel quickly. Ask questions that help you find out more about their authenticity.

• Use a reliable pay service such as PayPal.com or escrow.com.

If you're shopping on eBay and other auction sites, carefully read the section of their web site that gives tips for safe purchasing. Get consumer advice when shopping online and call (877) FTC-HELP or visit The Federal Trade Commission at www.FTC.gov.

• Complain at the FBI's web site for fraud.

Internet shopping is a blessing and a burden. You can get a wide variety of goods and services that you can't find locally, but at the same time, you don't really know whom to trust. It's easy to be defrauded, so if you become a victim again, make a complaint at the FBI web site at www.IFCCFBI.gov. Unfortunately, so many people are ripped off on the Internet that you probably won't get an investigation and, most certainly, you won't get your money back. However, if these fraudsters create a pattern of crimes, the FBI just might hear from enough victims so that they will investigate and find these criminals.

• Never download any file that you don't recognize.

It's best to run your virus scanner over all attachments before you open them. Even with this precaution, you could become infected with a virus that literally steals information out of your files. If you receive a file that is not described in the subject of the e-mail, even if it's from a good friend or trusted person, delete it. It's best to e-mail back to the person who sent you the file and find out before you download it if indeed they sent you an attachment, including what was in it. Beware that even the virus scanners and antivirus software can hardly keep up with new, malicious technology. There may be times when the software misses a virus and your computer could become infected.

- Download all patches for your programs.

Get on an e-mail notification service (like Microsoft or Intuit) so that you know to download all new patches in Windows and other programs you use. These patches will provide a defense for the vulnerabilities or holes that are in the software that the bad techies find out about.

- Delete cookies or use anti-cookie software.

Web sites use cookies, or little pieces of data, that they place on your hard drive to keep track of your visits. These cookies tell the company you are visiting what pages you visited, and also can keep track of what you purchase online. With companies you trust, a cookie is helpful because it saves you from having to identify yourself with the web site and the company each visit. It may often capture your user ID and password. It also can collect personal information to do market research. Even though a cookie doesn't have very much text, it provides your user ID when you visit a web site. The little data files reveal all the things that you've done on that company's web site. So, if companies surreptitiously put these cookies on your hard drive, and you're not comfortable with that, you can delete them. You can click on the cookies that you wish to delete, and keep those from companies that you regularly do business with. For example, if there's a cookie from American Express or your bank or another trusted company that you deal with, you may not want to delete it, instead just remove those cookies from companies that you don't wish to continue to do business with. You can also set your cookie warning level so that you are notified on screen before you accept or reject cookies.

- Protect yourself from spyware.

Spyware programs capture information about you from your computer. These insidious programs are usually embedded into other programs that you download. Good and bad guys collect data about us when we're online. We don't even know or give our consent, so that's why this is called spyware. Deleting spyware can be very challeng-ing. To rid your PC of spyware and pop-up adware, download free software called Spybot. You can get this at www.download.com at no cost. There is also Spy Cop (www.spycop.com), which will alert you if you're being watched or if key-logging programs are on your computer. Spyware and key-logging programs can watch you as you use online bill paying services, make deposits, or review your financial statements online, and can steal your secret data.

- Rid yourself of pop-ups, or adware.

These pop-ups are irritating and also may carry viruses. Go to www.ada-ware.com to download the software to eliminate them.

- Other tips for keeping your e-mail safe and personal information out of the hands of identity thieves.

Minimize the information that you put in your e-mail signature file. If your e-mail is used for your business, of course you're going to want to put your contact information so people can do business with you. But you should not be putting your home address, and home phone number and other personal data in your signature file.

- Don't put your e-mail address on your web site.

If you put your e-mail address on your personal web site or your business web site, you will get thousands of spam e-mails. Instead, create a contact box where visitors can fill in information and send e-mails without seeing your e-mail address. Once you have a relationship with them, then of course, they'll see the e-mail address you are using when you write back to them. Then it is your choice to provide it to them.

- Search out your name on the Internet to find what information is circulating about you.

Misinformation might be reported about you that could be a result of someone else using your name.

- Don't get hooked by a "phishing" expedition.

"Phishing" is an e-mail scam that involves deception and identity theft. The imposters create bogus e-mails, pretending to be from reputable companies or government agencies to trick victims into revealing personal information including Social Security, credit card, and personal identifying numbers, and online banking passwords. The con gains the confidence of the victim and appears real, using authentic-looking logos and Web addresses (URLs) that look impressively similar to the real Web address for the company they are impersonating. In April 2004, a survey conducted by the Gartner technology research firm estimated that 52 million American adults had received phishing e-mails within the past year. Of those surveyed who received such e-mails, three percent, (representing about 1.8 million individuals), said they disclosed personal or financial information. Gartner concluded that at least another million have unwittingly fallen for phishing lures — don't be one of those who gets hooked.

Here's an example of an alarming, authentic-looking "phishing" expedition that pretends to be from Wells Fargo Bank:

Dear Wells Fargo Account Holder,

We regret to inform you, that we had to block your Wells Fargo account because we have been notified that your account may have been compromised by outside parties. Our terms and conditions you agreed to state that your account must always be under your control or those you designate at all times. We have noticed some activity related to your account that indicates that other parties may have access and or control of your information in your account. These parties have in the past been involved with money laundering, illegal drugs, terrorism and various Federal Title 18 violations. In order that you may access your account we must verify your identity by clicking on the link below. Please be aware that until we can verify your identity no further access to your account will be allowed and we will have no other liability for your account or any transactions that may have occurred as a result of

your failure to reactivate your account as instructed below. Thank you for your time and consideration in this matter. Please follow the link below and renew your account information.

   https://online.wellsfargo.com/cgi-bin/signon.cgi

Before you reactivate your account, all payments have been frozen, and you will not be able to use your account in any way until we have verified your identity.

This authentic looking scam caught many people. Are you protecting yourself from getting scammed by a hoax like the sample above? Here are some safeguards:

- Never answer any e-mail that asks either directly, indirectly, or through a web site for your personal or financial identifying information.

If you are told that you need to update your information online, don't update it. Don't click on the web site in the e-mail. Instead, go to the Web address that you know and write an e-mail asking if there is any account maintenance needed on your account. Or call the 800 number that's listed on the true Web page. Make a copy of the questionable web site's URL and forward it to the legitimate business and ask if the request is legitimate. You may also forward it to spam @uce.gov.

- Don't ever respond or reply to the "phishing" e-mail or the fraudster will have your real e-mail address, and perhaps your contact information that you include with your signature.

- Don't be gullible.

There are many hoaxes, scams and outright lies on the Internet. You don't know who you're dealing with or where they are located. If you are like most honest people, you are eager to help someone in need. Unfortunately, the Internet is filled with requests for help and sympathy letters asking for donations for Make-A-Wish, The Diabetes Foundation, American Cancer Society, etc. If you want to make a donation to one of the legitimate charities, call the nonprofit organization that you'll find listed in your yellow pages and make a donation to a legitimate company with a verifiable address.

- Be cautious of scam letters.

One hoax is the Nigerian scam letter. The FBI reports there have been millions of scammed investors who have responded to various Nigerian scam letters. You may have received an e-mail asking for your help, explaining that hundreds of thousands of dollars are currently stashed in a foreign country. The scammer contacts you and asks that you allow the money to be transferred to a bank account in your name and then you get a portion of the funds. If you lose money to a scam, you will never retrieve it, and you may lose more than your identity; you may lose your life.

To find out about more of these financial scams, go to the United States Secret Service web site at www.secretservice.gov. If you receive any of these letters, forward them on to the Secret Service, the FBI, or the Federal Trade Commission, but *never* reply to sender. Forward this and other types of spam to Spam@uce.gov.

- Don't put confidential or controversial information in your e-mail.

Your e-mail is like a postcard; so before you write any information in e-mails to a friend, colleague, or family member, ask yourself if you would display this information for anyone else to see. If you wouldn't want other people to see this e-mail, don't send it. If you want to send confidential information in an e-mail message, then your best bet is to use encryption software to protect it (*e.g.*, www.pgp.com).

- Be cautious when participating in instant messaging.

Often people think because they're sitting in the privacy of their own kitchen, bedroom, or office that their IM conversations with a friend are confidential. First, ask yourself is this person really a friend? Have you ever met this person? Is the person that you think you're talking to really who he says he is? Don't trust any stranger online, and if you are corresponding with a good friend, don't share secrets online. Be cautious — you've already been through identity theft hell!

- Take extra precautions to hide on the Internet.

Remember not to reveal your gender, age, where you live, or anything personal about yourself when posting messages online.

- Sign up for e-mails that are disposable.

If you get a temporary e-mail address at Hotmail, Yahoo, or Google, then after awhile if you're not comfortable or you feel that you're being harassed, or your identity is in danger, you can close that account. Also, this will help you to reduce the spam that you receive from giving that e-mail out on list servers, posting boards, etc.

- Re-read your e-mail several times before sending.

In our haste to write e-mail (because it is such a simple means of communication), we may often send out more information than we need to or make silly errors. So take your time and re-read your e-mail before you push the *Send* button. Once it's in cyberspace, you can't retrieve it.

- Visit an Internet safety organization such as Cyber Angels (www.cyberangels.org) or the Federal Trade Commission (www.FTC.gov), for additional precautions.

New scams are created each day, and *I* can't list them all. The bottom line is, just be skeptical of everything online — and off-line, too, for that matter.

- Don't fall in love too quickly with online matchmaking.

Cyber dating and matchmaking services are very

popular these days. But your cyber date may be impersonating another person or even lying about everything from age to gender to career, etc. So ask yourself these questions when communicating with a potential love relationship online: How much information do I really want to give out? Is this person in too much of a hurry to meet me? Is he or she wanting to become intimate too fast or asking too many personal questions before we get to know each other? Have I done a Web search with this person's name on the Internet to find out who he or she really is? Have we considered running background checks of each other? If I set up a time to meet this person, will it be for lunch or coffee in a public place? Use your own transportation so that you can leave immediately if you are uncomfortable. Let friends and family know that you are going to meet someone (bring your cell phone) so if there is a problem, they can reach you or you can reach them, or the police.

• Anonymous Internet connection.

Normally, when you're connected to the Internet, you're transactions are visible to various ISP servers. If you wish to surf the net anonymously, then shield yourself from Web bugs, viruses, cookies, and others. You may wish to use Anonymizer software. Go to www.anonymizer.com.

* * * * *

You've now taken an inventory of what tasks you need to perform to protect your personal information, and limit your susceptibility to becoming victimized by identity thieves again. You've already experienced the challenges of dealing with fraud, so you're probably feeling that it's an intimidating mission to take all these actions. But I'm sure you are also eager to protect yourself from further fraud. You now have the knowledge, the insight, and ability to implement these tools to protect yourself and your family now and in the future.

Since you have purchased this book and CD, you are either very concerned about identity theft or you have lived the nightmare of identity fraud yourself. Either way, you have a heightened sensitivity to guarding your confidential information … and rightly so. You're more informed than most people as to how to be proactive and take precautions when necessary. Review a few pages at a time of these safeguards to begin to implement these measures. If you wish to learn more ways to protect yourself in commerce, in the workplace, and in dealing with government agencies, you may wish to read my book *Safeguard Your Identity: Protect Yourself With A Personal Privacy Audit*. (Porpoise Press, 2005). You will find it at www.identity theft.org, or you may call Porpoise Press at (800) 725-0807 (for fast service by mail), or you may visit your favorite bookstore.

This chapter gave you many suggestions to guard your identity from future theft — but the bottom line to remember: no matter where you are — at home, at work, on vacation, surfing at the beach, or surfing on the internet — don't trust people you don't know and don't believe information you receive without checking it out for yourself! Don't share your confidential data unless you absolutely must, and you are comfortable that you know how it will be used, who will have access to it, and how it will be secured. You already know the dangers of abuse of your confidential information, so stay conscious of what you are doing whenever your identifying information is involved.

Implement your own privacy-protection plan to be victorious!

Chapter Eight

What Needs to Change

The information age has brought us wonderful opportunities to increase our knowledge and share information. Over the Internet, we can instantaneously purchase goods and services and meet new friends all over the world. But the evolving technology has not only created global communication innovations and brought with it tremendous economic benefits, it has also introduced worrisome vulnerabilities. In a nanosecond vast databases, containing gigabytes of information about us, are bought, sold, shared, transferred, and profiled without our knowledge or consent. We have little control over who has access to our very sensitive data — we have lost our privacy.

In the late 1800's, Louis Brandeis (who later became Chief Justice of the U.S. Supreme Court) described the right to privacy as "the right to be let alone — the most comprehensive of rights most valued by civilized men." The privacy definition must be expanded and redefined in the technological era. as the ability to control the collection, distribution, and use of our personal information.

If you've been victimized by identity theft, you're well aware of how it felt to be powerless to control how your information was accessed, transferred, or utilized for fraud purposes.

Our nation needs a comprehensive federal policy and legislation that covers all aspects of privacy, both online and off-line — one that protects personal, financial, health, and other sensitive information about us. Presently we have hundreds of state and federal privacy laws pending that address the issue of the use of our private information, but there is no overall, comprehensive federal privacy statute. Most economically advanced nations (including the nations of the European Union) have very stringent privacy laws, and have established centralized governmental privacy commissions to review the concerns regarding their citizens' personal information. If we are going to address the seriousness of this issue, we must place a higher priority on our nation's privacy approaches. Until our legislators pass legislation that will protect our personal information, we will continue to take a piecemeal approach to safeguarding our private data.

Below are some suggestions for companies and governmental agencies that collect and use your personal information to help them thwart the easy crime of identity theft. These will also protect you from fraud, assist you in your recovery if you are victimized, and better respect your privacy.

Suggested Procedures for Businesses and Agencies

1. All companies should institute an opt-in standard for any sale or transfer of your personal information. For example, before any potential creditor sends you a pre-approved offer in the mail, you should be asked for your prior consent. Any company that has your data should be required to obtain your permission before that information is shared in any way.

2. It should be illegal for credit card companies to send convenience checks in the mail prior to receiving a request from the customer. Often, consumers receive these "hot checks" along with their credit card statement. Imposters frequently steal these checks and use them — simply signing your name and making the checks out for any amount. Then after an impersonator steals

the funds, the creditor looks to the victim for payment.

3. Companies and agencies should refrain from using your mother's maiden name or Social Security number as your password. Your mother's maiden name is written on your birth certificate, in most states a public record, and is available by Internet. Instead a unique password is needed for the consumer to input to change any aspect of a profile or address.

4. Credit grantors should be required to authenticate who they are issuing credit to, and should match identifying information on the credit application to the credit report so that if there are inconsistencies, the credit grantor should call the consumer to verify the application or change. Under the new provisions of the Fair Credit Reporting Act, the *CRAs* are required to notify a creditor with an alert that the address on the application is substantially different from the address on the credit report. At that point, the credit grantor should be required to call or write the consumer before processing the credit application to make sure that an impostor didn't initiate it.

5. No agency or company should be allowed to maintain credit card numbers and other personal information on its computers without guarding that information in encrypted files. Additionally, retailers should not be allowed to store credit numbers without the customers' consent. Unscrupulous employees and others who have access to these databases can easily retrieve these credit card numbers, and other personal identifying information.

6. The use of a Social Security number should be eliminated as the record locater. That number is the key to assume your identity and all agencies and businesses must stop using this number for verification, since it is readily accessible to criminals. A password should be used instead and alternate identifying numbers. Even if biometrics are used, there should be password protection as well.

7. Creditors should be held liable to victims for extending credit to imposters. The recent provisions of the FCRA do not allow victims of identity theft to sue a creditor if they negligently issue a new account to a fraudster. Congress should create an enforceable duty upon creditors, so that they'll be more responsible before issuing credit. Although there's a duty under FCRA to take reasonable procedures to verify the identity of an applicant, there's no enforcement by the victim who is wronged.

8. A nationwide security breach law should be passed. In California, if a financial institution learns that their unencrypted electronic files (even if printed out) have been acquired by someone who's unauthorized to use them, the company has a duty to notify all potential victims. To protect our personal information, federal law should be enacted that would require all entities, (not just financial companies) commercial or governmental, who have documents (whether online or off-line) containing sensitive information to protect that information. If an unauthorized person acquires such confidential information, the entity should be required to notify all potential victims so that they can protect themselves. The entity also should be required to notify law enforcement, and provide victims assistance in securing their information.

9. If a victim learns that his information has been compromised due to negligent information handling practices by a business or agency, the victim should have a right of redress. If it happened with a government agency, there should be an ombudsman program to rectify the situation. If it is a commercial company, there should be a mediation system and a private right of action if alternate dispute resolution fails.

10. All entities collecting sensitive personal information need to adopt a comprehensive privacy and fraud deterrent policy that incorporates best practices for effective information handling practices. A task force of privacy, security, and industry specialists should develop these practices through the Federal Trade Commission.

11. Congress should pass a document disposal law that requires complete destruction by all businesses and government agencies. Whenever a company or entity discards personal or financial information about consumers, they should be

required to properly destroy those documents. This may include crosscut shredding, burning, or other means. For electronic files, destruction may include wiping or erasing files, completely destroying computer diskettes, CD roms, DVDs, hardrives, PDAs etc.

12. Businesses and agencies that collect personal information should require that job applicants who will have access to sensitive information undergo a background check. and be restricted only to the information that they need to know.

13. All companies collecting and maintaining sensitive files should restrict processing any sensitive information by outsourcing in foreign countries unless the consumer provides prior consent. If a company wishes, for example, to perhaps give a lower interest rate for a loan in exchange for allowing that information to be processed abroad, if that information is compromised, the harmed consumer should have a right to redress against the company in the United States for any failure to protect that information.

Suggested Guidelines for Protecting Credit Reports

1. Information in your credit profile should not be shared or sold without your prior consent. Presently, the *CRAs* can sell your financial profile for purposes of prescreening offers unless you "opt out." The standard should be "opt in," meaning your information can't be sold unless you give prior permission.

2. If a *CRA* violates any of the provisions of the FCRA and the victim is damaged as a result, that victim should have redress, meaning that they should be allowed to seek compensation via a private lawsuit.

As it stands now, there are many aspects of the FCRA in which an individual has no private right of action. The Attorney General of your individual state may not file an action, and only a designated federal agency can take any action. Consumer advocates believe it's necessary to implement stronger enforcement, including allowing a class action lawsuit when many victims are similarly injured by negligent practices.

3. *CRAs* should allow any consumer in this nation to "freeze" his or her credit report if he is victimized by identity theft. Presently, there are a few states, such as California, Texas, and Louisiana that allow consumers who are victimized (and other consumers) to take their profile off-line, meaning that no one can get their credit report without the victim providing a pass code to unfreeze the report. Presently, a consumer can institute a fraud alert if he's been victimized by fraud. But since there's no private right of action against a creditor who issues credit to a fraudster, in spite of the fact that there's a fraud alert on the credit report, some victims find it's necessary to stop careless creditors (who ignore the fraud alert) from issuing new credit to an impostor. Credit grantors who do issue credit to an impersonator after a fraud alert is on file, should be heavily sanctioned.

4. *CRAs* should provide victims of identity theft exact copies of the commercial consumer report that were provided to the creditors who accessed the files in order to issue the fraudulent accounts. Presently, when a victim asks for a credit report, he or she receives a different report than the creditor received. Special alerts and other data that are provided to the commercial credit grantor don't appear on the consumer's report. This evidence is necessary for the victim to understand the case and clear his credit.

5. When a creditor or an employer denies a consumer credit, instead of telling the consumer to order a free credit report from the *CRAs*, the creditor should be required to provide a free copy of the report it received to the victim or consumer who has been denied that credit. Victims shouldn't have to wait to get a copy from the agencies.

6. The Federal Trade Commission should stringently regulate the specialty consumer reporting agencies that provide background checks. Under the newer provisions of the FCRA, a consumer may obtain a free annual consumer report from the Specialty Consumer Reporting Agencies; however there are thousands of information brokers who compile background checks both off-line and online, and they are not regulated. The same duties that the *CRAs* have to consumers should be required of all information

brokers who sell personal information profiles about consumers. There should be a private right of action by consumers. Additionally, victims of identity theft should be allowed to place fraud alerts on their background check profile. It's very difficult for a victim of criminal identity theft to clear all of his/her records in these profiles. The Federal Trade Commission, upon taking complaints from victims, should be required to make public disclosures of the companies with the worst and best records for identity theft.

7. The credit header information on credit reports, which includes all of your personal information, should only be accessed for permissible purposes, but presently it is shared and not subject to the permissible purpose restriction.

8. Individual states should have a right to enact more stringent privacy protections than federal law in order to protect their own citizens. Presently, most of the provisions that protect victims of identity theft are pre-empted by federal law, meaning that the states cannot enact more protective statutes.

9. More protection is needed from the unauthorized release of credit reports. Presently, *CRAs* are only required to maintain reasonable procedures designed to prevent unauthorized release of the consumer information. This standard is quite weak, since there is a vast network of companies that easily access your most personal information on your consumer report. Unscrupulous employees obtain credit reports for fraudulent credit acquisition … even in the credit bureaus themselves. Many companies have subscription services with the *CRAs* (like real estate companies, mortgage brokers, car dealerships, attorney offices, etc.) For a *CRA* and a user of credit reports to create a relationship, the user merely completes a form stating that they will use the reports for permissible purposes. Criminals who worked for Ford Motor Credit Company stole 30,000 credit reports through Experian for identity theft purposes. There have been many cases in real estate agencies and car dealerships in which credit reports were used by fraudsters who had inside conspirators. The author of this book became a victim of identity theft when her imposter was able to obtain her credit report

through a subscription service in a law office where the imposter worked as a temporary employee.

10. Additionally, the *CRAs* should verify an address when a victim calls in a fraud alert. I am aware of many cases in which a *CRA* sends the free credit report to the fraudster's address.

11. Consumers should be notified by the *CRAs* whenever there is an inquiry made by a creditor. Presently, in order to be notified, a consumer must pay to sign up for a credit monitoring service or order his credit report. If a victim of identity theft knew whenever a creditor accessed his file, he could immediately contact that credit grantor and stop the identity thief before credit is extended.

12. Whenever an employee gives permission for any consumer report to be provided to a potential employer (for credit or background check) that employer should have a duty to provide a copy of the credit report as well as the background check to the potential employee. This should be required whether or not the employee is denied the position. Normally, a company is required to provide "results" of a background check only if there's an adverse decision made as a result of the report. Federal law should state that whenever an employee or potential employee authorizes a consumer report or consumer credit report, that person should be provided an exact copy of any and all reports, so that he may have an opportunity to correct any errors or fraud.

13. *CRAs* should be required to set up hotlines with live persons to talk to identity theft victims. A victim should be assigned to a particular employee in the fraud department of the CRA so that the victim has consistency in dealing with the issues.

14. Credit Reporting Agencies should be required to track all cases of identity theft and report all data to the Federal Trade Commission who should make that information public.

Suggested Changes with Regard to Law Enforcement's Role.

1. Federal law should require that an identity theft

victim be allowed to file a police report in the jurisdiction where he lives or where the fraud occurs, and law enforcement agencies should be required to share data to resolve the case.

2. An identity fraud case should be legally allowed to be prosecuted where the victim lives or where the fraud occurred.

3. There should be a nationwide consistant format for the Identity Theft Report. Presently, various law enforcement agencies use very different formats and under the new provisions of the FCRA, an Identity Theft Report is required and it must provide documentation of the fraudulent accounts. Some police reports just state "Victim says he's been victimized by an identity thief" and nothing else will be listed. Without information, a victim cannot clean up the mess with the financial industry. A nationwide Identity Theft Report with specific guidelines that are congruent with the FCRA's requirements would help law enforcement to work together and help a victim to get his life back.

4. Police departments should be required to track all of their identity theft cases so statistics can be gathered. These should be made public.

5. Every major city should have an Identity Theft Task Force to include local law enforcement, Secret Service, the postal inspector, the Social Security Administration inspector, and other government agencies that may be involved. Since terrorists are known to use false identities, this would be an important component of Homeland Security. To do this, more funding for training and personnel is needed.

6. The Department of Justice should be in charge of coordinating nationwide training for all levels of officer, from patrol through division head on what ID theft is, how to write a report, how to document it, how to investigate it, and more importantly, how to provide the resources necessary to investigate it. Since terrorists use false identification, the resources allocated for Homeland Security should include identity theft cases.

7. Departments of Motor Vehicle Licensing Bureaus should establish more stringent monitoring and matching of duplicate licensing and new licenses. A photo ID and a fingerprint could be matched. Rather than developing a "national ID" with various forms of biometric information, credit cards and other unnecessary information which would complicate the process and decrease privacy, this national driver's license would have a national database to help deter interstate identity theft.

8. Each state and the federal government should institute an Office for Privacy Protection; there should be a federal office of privacy protection which acts as a privacy commission. The state offices of privacy protection should institute ombudsmen programs to assist victims of identity theft experiencing challenges with companies, government agencies, and law enforcement.

9. Institute overall policies and procedures for biometric accuracy. Federal law must address the issues of accuracy of biometric systems, due to the high incidence of false acceptance and false rejection rates. If a business or agency accepts a false acceptance rate low enough to prevent impersonators, then consumers who rightfully should be accepted will be refused. This is a concern for credit granting, as well as for the airline industry screenings at airports. The intent to use biometrics for all credit applications and authentication will be costly because if the entity is cautious many innocent customers will be rejected and if not, the purpose is defeated. If companies have a low rejection rate, then they'll have more fraudsters and identity theft will increase.

10. Institute policy and laws to safeguard the collection, use, and security of biometric information. If biometric identifiers are compromised, the consequences for victims will be overwhelming. Biometric standards must be established, and safeguards must be implemented. Questions like the following must be answered: Who can gain access to the databases? Will they be altered? Who will be establishing the original biometric authentication? How will the data be stored? How will it be affected by environmental influences? How accurate will it be with body changes over time? How can safeguards are circumvented? Biometrics is gaining widespread use to replace the use of the Social Security

number as identification, but the concern for accuracy and for how that information might be corrupted, transferred, or used by a fraudster must be addressed immediately.

11. Federal law and policy should establish uniform procedures so that if a person is victimized by a criminal identity theft, they may follow the uniform steps that the Department of Justice establishes on how to correct all criminal records, clear data bases, expunge court judgments, and cleanse the data. Since the information brokers sell this data through access to public records, the court documents must be more easily corrected.

Conscious collaboration, moving forward

Our personal information, worth more than currency, can be used fraudulently to apply for credit, loans, mortgages, employment, legal citizenship, or to commit other crimes and avoid prosecution — all without our knowledge. The fraudster can do anything we can do and even things we wouldn't do, like commit crimes or terrorist activities.

We must address this problem on a national level and work collaboratively among all stakeholders to protect our vulnerable citizens. With the ease of movement and communication, a veteran in Chicago may have an impostor in New York City who then sells the data to another criminal in Miami who in turn sells the information to a fraud ring who intends to sells credit cards to terrorists. These problems are complex, perplexing, and overwhelming for the victims and our country. Government agencies and all businesses must be more conscientious. They must cautiously verify identity, confirm address changes, respect personal confidentiality, and enforce proper safeguards against unauthorized access. When we all work together to enhance privacy protection, we'll all be less susceptible to identity theft. Then law enforcement can focus on reducing violent crime and terrorism, and the financial industry will save billions of dollars.

As more personal information about us is generated, compiled, profiled, and shared, the risk of harm increases. We need to balance the benefit to society of our privacy interests, with commercial and law enforcement needs — especially in view of the fact that we're dealing with a war on terrorism. We'll see more tradeoffs between privacy and security. With these conflicting interests, and public fear for safety, we have a challenging road ahead. The overriding issue, at least from your perspective as a victim or a potential victim, is to empower yourself by exerting your privacy rights to safeguard your identity. These rights are:

1. You should have the right to obtain your personal information. As you probably know, it's a huge hurdle just to get the information regarding what happened to you as the victim of identity theft. Many times victims are denied credit or a job, and don't understand why or what has happened to them. Unless you get the fraud information, you're without recourse to address the situation or clear your good name. If you're innocent, you must have evidence to prove it.

2. You should have the right to correct any erroneous information. If data is incorrect or fraudulent, you must have a means to correct that information. Under the Fair Credit Reporting Act you can access your information in order to fix the profile. If you cannot enforce the provisions to correct your profile, you're going to be blocked from clearing your name.

3. You should have the right to become knowledgeable about and use the available technology to protect your confidentiality and the integrity of your communications and transactions. In Chapter Seven, *I* gave you many ways that you can take responsibility to minimize your risk of identity theft in both the real world and the virtual world.

4. You should have a right if you're harmed by any improper disclosure of your information, to have a means of redress. This may mean resolution through an Ombudsman Office, mediation, and regulatory enforcement by a federal agency, or a civil lawsuit. Additionally, help could come by contacting your local newspaper, the media, and

your legislators. We must enact laws that will impose severe sanctions against companies who blatantly violate your privacy.

Many of us who have experienced the nightmare of identity theft and the violations of our privacy realize we must institute stronger measures to control our private data before it's too late. In order to guarantee every American citizen's right to control the use of his personal information, we must institute a comprehensive Federal Privacy Law. We will still need to take personal responsibility for protecting our communications, using appropriate security measures, and limiting what we reveal when we're on the Internet. But government agencies and private companies in our nation must institute secure, trustworthy procedures to better insure the safekeeping of our sensitive data.

The following list of Fair Information Principles is adapted from policies that were developed by the Organization for Economic Cooperation and Development. Although technology is rapidly changing, the basic principles should still guide us for privacy laws and business practices.

All businesses and agencies should implement these steps:

1. Provide open policies.

There should be an open, written clarification about exactly what personal information is to be collected. The existence and nature of personal data held by the organization should be readily available for inspection by individuals.

2. Designate specific purpose or use.

The customer or citizen (if governmental) should be told why the information is being collected at the time it is gathered. There should be no other use of that data without your consent.

3. Describe data collection limitations.

The information collected should be limited to the information necessary for the stated purpose and nothing more. Information shouldn't be collected simply because it may be useful in the future.

4. Limit use and transfer of data.

The information collected should be limited to the use of the business or organization that collected it. The information shouldn't be revealed or sold to others without *prior* consent from the individual or legal authority.

5. Provide consumer inspection.

The individual should have a right to consent, inspect, and correct (and delete if appropriate) his or her personal information.

6. Institute quality controls.

The information should be accurate, complete, timely, and relevant to the purpose for which it is to be used. Whenever possible, the information should be collected directly from the individual, not from third party information brokers.

7. Develop strict security measures.

There should be reasonable security safeguards against risks such as loss, unauthorized access, destruction, or alteration. Only those with a need to know should have access. Audit trails must be instituted.

8. Implement standards of accountability, enforcement, and redress.

The business or government agency must be held accountable to the individuals. There should be enforcement mechanisms that provide remedies to those harmed by the lack of accountability. Privacy audits should be conducted regularly, as should employee-training programs. Sanctions should be applied for employees, companies, or agencies that violate these policies or standards.

* * *

If you've reached this point in this book, you've immersed yourself in the identity theft experience.

I hope by now if you've been victimised, you're turning your crisis around and you're getting your life back. Although the details of your individual case may be very different from what I experienced, you've probably learned, as I did, that you had to investigate the case yourself, and speak up on your own behalf. With the knowledge that you've gained, and your triumph over this crime, I encourage you to put that same energy into changing the systems that allowed identity theft to be perpetrated against you. Join with me in asking our legislators and government officials to make changes in laws and policies that will protect security and privacy for us and for future generations.

I hope this book and CD were a comforting support to you in regaining your financial reputation, emotional health, and your good name. May you be inspired by your identity crisis and use the experience as a springboard for great growth, new opportunities, and increased optimism knowing that you were transformed

From Victim to Victor.

Appendixes

Appendix A

Letters, Affidavits, and Logs

Now you are ready to begin your crucial task of letter-writing. This will empower you to:

- Document the fraud.

- Clarify your situation.

- Exert your legal rights.

- Prepare yourself for legal remedies with law enforcement (restitution) and criminal courts, possible civil legal action (if the companies don't comply with timelines and legal requirements.)

- Regain your good name, reputation, financial health, and peace of mind!

LETTER 1 - A: Dealing With Credit Reporting Agencies (Initial Letter)

Your Name
Address
Home Phone
Cell Phone
Fax (your own or local office store)
E-mail (if you have it)

Date:

CERTIFIED MAIL
RETURN RECEIPT REQUESTED

Experian
Consumer Fraud Assistance
P. O. Box 9532
Allen, TX 75013

TransUnion
Fraud Victim Assistance Department
P.O. Box 6790
Fullerton, CA 92634

Equifax Information Service Center
Customer Service/Fraud Assistance
P. O. Box 740241
Atlanta, Georgia 30374-0241

    Re: Name:
           Social Security No.:
           Date of Birth:
           Subject: Identity Fraud

Dear Gentleperson:

I called the fraud number of your office on **[date]** to inform you of the identity fraud committed against me, and requested my free credit report, a fraud alert to be placed on my file, and assistance in clearing my credit. This letter will serve as a formal summary and follow up of information I know at this time. On **[date],** I became aware that I am the victim of theft of identity. I learned about the theft of identity in the following manner:

_____

I have completed the Federal Trade Commission's Fraud Affidavit with the present information I have, and attached it to this letter. I will update it when I learn more information from my credit reports.

1. Please give me the name of the specific Fraud Resolution Investigator with whom I will be working with at your office so I can direct all my future correspondence to that same person. Please provide me a direct telephone number to call with my case number as well.

2. Please place a Fraud Alert on my credit file in a conspicuous location (in at least 14 point type) and state that no credit is to be issued in my name without the credit grantor first calling me at the following telephone numbers: [home and cell phone numbers]. Please place this alert on my report immediately. Also, please keep this for at least seven (7) years. I have provided you with the necessary identification.

3. I ascertained from a credit grantor that the credit card and/or credit line billing statements were sent to the following fraudulent address: _____. Please note that this is **not** my address. My address for the past _____ years (months) is: _____. Do **not** change my correct address (as above) on my credit report without verification in writing from me.

4. Please **immediately** send me a complete **unedited** copy of my credit report at your earliest convenience to my home address above, or by fax [*fax telephone number*], so that I may ascertain what fraudulent accounts have been opened in my name. I need to see my credit report exactly how it looked **prior** to my learning of the fraud. I understand that as a fraud victim, there is no charge to receive this report. Once you provide this current report to me, please remove any fraudulent addresses from my subsequent credit reports and maintain my current mailing address as provided above. Also, please immediately block the following accounts:

    Bank Account #_____

5. For **verification of my identity,** enclosed you will find a copy of a current utility statement showing my residence as well as a copy of my driver's license [or state issued identification].

6. Please also **immediately** cease from selling my name on promotion to any credit grantor or other agency. Take my name off all promotional lists for at least five years as per federal law.

7. Please also notify all credit grantors and/or other agencies who have received my credit report **within the last year** that there has been fraud committed against me. I understand creditors have one year to offer credit once they have received my profile. Please also send notice of the fraud to all employers who received my credit report in the last two years. Please send me a copy of the correspondence that you are sending to the credit grantors and employers for my records.

8. Please send me a list of names, phone numbers and addresses of all of the credit grantors on my credit report, including the inquiries, so I may contact them to alert them of the fraud.

9. Please notify all companies that have inquires in the last 12 months about my credit that fraud has occurred. Please confirm this was done. This is necessary so no new accounts are opened in my name.

10. I have contacted the following Law Enforcement Agency(ies): [*Name of Police Department or Postal Inspector, etc, address and phone number*]. The Police Report No. is [*police report number*]. You may contact _____ (*Investigator*) with whom I made the report at [telephone number]. Once I have a copy of the police report and a list of all fraud accounts, I will send them **to** you so you may immediately remove all fraudulent items.

11. Additionally, please immediately send me any booklets or documents as to my legal rights and additional information to help me deal with this fraud situation.

12. Please do not release my credit report *without my permission.*

13. Once I have more information, I intend to send you a *100-word* victim statement to be added to my credit report. Please send me the appropriate form and/or requirements if any.

Please do not respond to this letter with a form letter. I wish to have a response to all of my enumerated concerns.

Thank you very much for your **immediate** attention to the above. I look forward to receiving my credit report, the above items listed, and any other pertinent information from you as to how you wish me to address the fraudulent and incorrect items on my credit report.

You may reach me during the day at [*telephone number*] and during the evening at: [*telephone number*]. My cell phone number is [*cell phone number*].

Please write to me at the address on the first page of this letter.

Thank you for your prompt response. I look forward to hearing from you by no later than [*two weeks*].

Yours truly,

Enclosed:

1. State identification (i.e. driver's license)

2. Utility bill (to verify address)

3. Completed formal affidavit from the Federal Trade Commission

4. Police Report [*if available*]

LETTER 1- B: Dealing With Credit Reporting Agencies (Follow-Up Letter)

Your Name
Address
Phone
Cell Phone
Fax (your own or local office store)
E-mail (if you have it)
Case # _____

Date:

CERTIFIED MAIL
RETURN RECEIPT REQUESTED

Experian
Consumer Fraud Assistance
P. O. Box 9532
Allen, TX 75013

TransUnion
Fraud Victim Assistance Department
P.O. Box 6790
Fullerton, CA 92634

Equifax Information Service Center
Customer Service/Fraud Assistance
P. O. Box 740241
Atlanta, Georgia 30374-0241

> Re: Name:
>   Social Security No.:
>   Date of Birth:
>   Subject: Identity Fraud
>
> **Case # _____ (*Different for each Credit Reporting Agency*)**

Dear _____ (Supervisor's Name or specific Fraud Resolution Employee):

This is a follow-up to my previous letter dated _____ informing you of the fraud committed using my name. I have now received my credit report from your company.

I have not yet received the following information requested in my first letter referred to above:

1._____

2._____

Please provide this immediately.

I have enclosed a copy of my police report, which includes a *list* of the reporting of **each** of the *fraudulent accounts that I am currently aware of as listed on my current credit report, dated*_____. It is my understanding that all of these fraud accounts will be *immediately* blocked (removed) (within **4** days of your receipt of this letter) from my credit report since you now have a police report listing these accounts as fraud.

I understand you will inform the credit grantors of the fact that you received the police report and have blocked (deleted) the fraud information so that they should **not** re-report this to you. The burden should now be on the credit grantor to disprove any fraud. Therefore, it is also my understanding that you will **not** place these fraud accounts back on my file (it would be necessary on the part of the credit grantors to prove that these accounts are not fraudulent). Please inform me immediately if you intend to reinsert any of these fraud accounts into my credit profile. If so, let me know the reason you intend to reinsert.

Please immediately remove and delete permanently the following fraud information:

1. *Fraud address* _____
2. *(e.g.)* Provider Visa account #0000000000
3. *(e.g.)* Capital One Visa account#000000000
4. *(e.g.)* Providian   (1/2004)
5. Fraudulently Reported Bankruptcy (information reported on file)

Remove and delete permanently the following fraud *inquiries*, which were the result of fraudulent requests for credit. I understand that excessive inquiries negatively affect my credit rating and score as well.

1. _____ (Date)

2. _____ (Date)

3. _____ (Date)

Fraudulent Identification Information:

Please delete the following incorrect and fraudulent information from my credit profile:

1. Incorrect (fraudulent) Social Security No. _____
   Should be _____
2. Incorrect Spelling of Name _____
   Should be _____
3. Incorrect and Fraud Address _____
   Should be _____
4. Incorrect and Fraudulent Business Phone _____
   Should be _____
5. Incorrect Date of Birth _____
   Should be _____
6. Etc.

[*Optional*]

In reviewing my file, I also noted the following other errors on my report with regard to my true accounts. Please correct as follows:

(*e.g.*) My Discover card account # _____ was closed. It is not an open account. Please label "closed by consumer request."

Please immediately send me a list of the names, addresses and telephone numbers of all of the above fraudulent creditors listed on my file (if this was not done by my request). This includes all the information for the fraudulent inquiries as well. I need this information to notify them of the problems and stop the fraudulent activity. I need to cancel all fraud accounts opened and I must contact fraudulent inquiries to tell them **not** to issue new credit to the impostor.

Please continue to maintain a fraud alert on my file for at least seven (7) years, pursuant to Federal law. I understand that impersonators can reuse my confidential information at a later date or may sell that information to another criminal who may start the fraud again.

Please add the following 100-word statement as to the fraud:

100 WORD STATEMENT

I am a victim of Identify fraud. A person assumed my identity and received credit in my name at the following address: _____. See Police Report #0000, Fraud Investigator_____, phone number _____. My address at [*present address*] is **not** to be changed for any credit purposes or on this report without verification from me. Credit is not to be granted without my permission. I have learned the following: _____. Call me at _____ (office), _____ (home) or _____ (cell).

This statement should remain on my credit report until I amend it.

Please immediately send me a corrected copy of my credit report with all the deletions and amendments listed above. I understand there is no charge for corrected reports. I also understand that I am entitled to at least two additional free credit reports (in a 12-month period) to review my file (by federal law) as a victim of fraud.

Thank you for your prompt attention to these corrections. I look forward to receiving the corrected report with the fraud deleted (blocked), the names and addresses of all the fraud account creditors and inquiries and the other information requested herein by _____ (*date two weeks from postmark*).

Yours truly,

Enclosed:

1. Police Report or Identity Theft Report from another governmental agency with specific fraud accounts listed (this may be an addendum to the original police report).

2. Completed FTC Affidavit with updates

LETTER 2 - A: Dealing With Credit Grantors-With Fraud Accounts (For Creditors, Banks, Department Stores, Phone Card, Etc.)

Your Name
Address
Phone
Cell Phone
Fax (your own or local office store)
E-mail (if you have it)

Date:

CERTIFIED MAIL
RETURN RECEIPT REQUESTED
Supervisor/Fraud Department:
    Re: Name on Fraud Account
                 Identity Fraud Account No.

Dear _____:

Pursuant to my conversation with (**you** or _____ **of your office,**) I have informed you that the above account number was opened fraudulently. I am the victim of Identity Theft. Your office informed me by phone that you sent the credit cards, credit lines, etc., to the following address: _____ which is **not** my address. My address is _____ and has been for the past ___ (years / months). Please note that I notified you as soon as I learned of the fraud. I shall not be responsible for any charges to this account. As per my discussion with you, please immediately close the account and report it to the Credit Reporting Agencies as **fraud** (**not** lost or stolen). It should be **removed** from my credit profile.

I have enclosed a copy of my currant utility statement and my current driver's license (state ID) to verify that this is my correct address.

[Note: If sent to correct address, state: "You issued (instant) credit to an imposter and I received bills, which do not belong to me."]

I have enclosed a copy of my completed Universal Affidavit (Prepared by the Federal Trade Commission). I will also be happy to sign any of your affidavits under penalty of perjury. The Privacy Rights Clearinghouse and the Federal Trade Commission inform me, that I should **not** be burdened with the costs of a notary for these documents. Please do not ask me to pay any additional fees.

As per Federal Law, please **immediately** send me copies of the following:

    1. The address, phone number, and password for the fraud card opened.

    2. The original application and/or forged signature or electronic information.

    3. All copies of billing statements and any other correspondence related to this account.

    4. Any other information with regard to this account

    5. Any fingerprints, photos, or video of the impersonator.

    6. Application records or screen prints of Internet/phone applications

7. Statements

8. Payments/Charge Slips

9. Investigator's Summary — electronic or otherwise

10. Delivery addresses

11. All records of phone number used to activate the accounts or used to access the account

12. Any other documents associated with the account

As per Federal Law, I am enclosing:

1. A copy of the police report

2. The Federal Trade Commission Affidavit

3. My Government issued identification.

You are required to send all documents to me at **no cost**, by no later than 30 days from the receipt of this letter. I also request that you send a duplicate copy of the information to my fraud investigator at _____ Police Department, address _____ within this 30-day period.

I have reported this crime to the _____ Police Department/Postal Inspector at (address _____). You may contact Fraud Investigator _____ at **[phone]**_____ regarding Police Report No. _____. [Enclosed] I hereby request that you assist the police and actively prosecute the crime to recoup your losses.

Please cancel the fraud account pursuant to **my request** as discussed on the phone. Also, please notify the Credit Reporting Agencies that this is a fraud account, and that should be removed from my credit report. As per Federal Law, **do not** report this account again to the Credit Reporting Agencies. Also, in accordance with Federal Law, you may **not** sell or transfer this debt or place it for collection now that you have received notice of this fraud.

Please provide me copies of the notice(s) you have sent to the three credit reporting agencies to have them remove these from my credit file. I would be grateful for your prompt attention to this matter.

Please do **not sell** my name, address (or fraud address), or other information to anyone at any time for promotional purposes.

I look forward to receiving the above requested information at your earliest convenience. I have attached the completed affidavit from the Federal Trade Commission.

If you have any questions, please call me at   **[home phone]**   **[business phone].**

Yours truly,

Enclosed:
1. Driver's license (or other state ID)

2. Utility bill

3. Completed Uniform Affidavit

4. Police Report

LETTER 2 - B: Dealing With Credit Grantors (Collection Agencies)

Your Name
Address
Phone
Cell Phone
Fax (your own or local office store)
E-mail (if you have it)

Date

CERTIFIED MAIL
RETURN RECEIPT REQUESTED

Supervisor/Fraud Investigations
Collection Companies
   Re: Name:
           Account No.

Dear Gentleperson:

Per our phone call and/or a written notice on my credit report, I have received notice of your collection account on my credit report. This above account is **not** mine — it was opened fraudulently.

Please note that I am the victim of identity fraud. I have reported this to the _____ Police Department. Their address and phone number is _____. The Police Report No. is: _____. You may contact the Fraud Investigator **[name, address and phone number]**. (Enclosed is a copy of the Police Report). I have placed a fraud alert on my credit profile. Please report this account as fraud to the original credit grantor and the Credit Reporting Agencies, and do not share, sell, or re-report this account as my account to any credit reporting agency now that you have this information.

Please inform me of the name of the company who sold you this fraud account and inform them that they must **not** re-report this account to the credit reporting agencies.

Please provide me all documentation of the **original** fraudulent delinquent account and information in your file as to this account. This includes all evidence as to applications, billing statements, verification of identity or transactions.

Pursuant to law, I have enclosed:

    1. A copy of a government issued ID

    2. A copy of my police report

    3. A utility statement with my address

    4. A copy of the completed Affidavit from the Federal Trade Commission.

Please send this information to me at **no charge**, by no later than 30 days from your receipt of this letter. Please also send this information to my fraud investigator at the _____

Police Department at the following address: _____.

Please send me whatever forms are necessary for me to sign so that this account may be removed from my credit report. I am told by various agencies that I should not have to pay for notary fees for any such forms. Please note that the fraud perpetrator used the following fraudulent address:

_____ .

My current address is _____ .

Enclosed are a utility statement and a copy of my government issued identification. I have also included a completed copy of the Federal Trade Commission's Uniform Affidavit.

Please immediately remove this collection account from my credit report. Do not send any further threatening letters. Do not call me, my employer, or anyone else to harass me. Pursuant to federal law, please immediately notify the original credit grantor, and send me a copy of any correspondence. I look forward to receiving the above evidence of fraud.

Yours truly,

Enclosed:

1. Government issued ID

2. Utility bill

3. Police report

4. Federal Trade Commission Affidavit

LETTER 2 - C: Dealing With Credit Grantors – Non-Fraud
(For Creditors, Banks, Department Stores, Phone Card, Cell Phone, Etc.)

Your Name

Address

Phone

Cell Phone

Fax (your own or local office store)

E-mail (if you have it)

Date:

CERTIFIED MAIL
RETURN RECEIPT REQUESTED

Supervisor of Fraud Department / Customer Service
Banks, Credit Cards, Department stores

Re: Account No. _____
Fraud Alert
Change of mother's maiden name

Dear _____:

Pursuant to my conversation with _____ of your office on **[date]**, I notified you that I have been victimized by Identity Theft. I have filed a report with the _____ Police Department, Report No. _____. You may speak with _____ at _____ **[telephone number of investigator]** if you have files.

In reviewing my current statements from your company (or bank), it does not appear that the fraud perpetrator has invaded this account. However, I need to have you flag this account with a fraud alert and provide me a new PIN number and/or password (**other** than my mother's maiden name) so that this account will be protected. Please provide me with a form to change my password, or speak to me so I may change my mother's maiden name to a secret password instead.

Please contact me at **[office phone] [home phone]** or **[cell phone],** to verify all applications or requests for change of address. Do **not** notify the credit reporting agencies that my card has been stolen, since this card has **not** been affected. I only wish to obtain a new password and place a fraud alert on my account, so that an impostor cannot invade this account.

(For ATM cards – suggested, but optional) Please send me a new ATM card that does **not** have the Visa/Mastercard logo on it. I do **not** want changes made to my ATM account or checking account numbers; I only want an ATM card with the Visa/Mastercard logo removed. I want to use an ATM **only** for deposits and cash withdrawals. I don't want to use it as a credit card where money is automatically removed from my account.

Do **not** change my address without verifying with me by phone or fax that the address is to be changed. Do no make any other changes to my account without my password. I will provide you required documentation if I request changes to my account.

Please remove my name from **all** promotional lists. Do not sell or share my name and personal information to other companies or your affiliates without my prior permission. I've included a copy of my Driver's License and my current utility bill.

Please call me immediately or fax me any form to institute a new password.

_____

_____

Yours truly,

Enclosures:

1. Copy of state issued ID

2. Utility bill

LETTER 2-D: Dealing With Stolen Checks, Etc.

Your Name
Address
Phone
Cell Phone
Fax (your own or local office store)
E-mail (if you have it)

Date:

TO: CHECK VERIFICATION/CHECK-GUARANTEE COMPANIES

Certegy Check Services, Inc.
   P. O. Box 30046, Tampa, FL 33630
   (800) 437-5120   Fax: (727) 570-4936   www.certegy.com

Chexsystems, Consumer Relations,
   7805 Hudson Rd, Suite 100, Woodbury, MN 55125
   (800) 428-9623   Fax: (602) 659-2197   www.chexhelp.com

Cross Check (Check Center Inquiry)
   P.O. Box 6008, Petaluma, CA 94955
   (800) 843-0760

Global Payments, Inc.
   Attn: Fraud Dept. 6215 W. Howard, Niles, IL 60714
   (800) 766-2748   Fax: (847) 647-8023   www.globalpaymentsinc.com

Shared Check Authorization Network (SCAN), Electronic Transaction Corp.
   7805 Hudson Road, Suite 100, Woodbury, MN 55125
   (877) 382-7226   Fax: (800) 358-4506   www.scanassist.com

TeleCheck, Consumer Affairs
   P. O. Box 4451, Houston, TX 77210-4451
   (800) 710-9898   Fax: (713) 332-9300   www.telecheckcom

Dear Gentleperson:

   I called your office on _____ (date) to report the fraudulent use of checks in my name. My checks from _____ (bank name) checking account #_____ numbers _____ through _____ were stolen on _____ (date). I have stopped payment on these checks and ask that you place a fraud alert in your computer for use by companies requesting verification. I have closed that bank account and have obtained a new account number and now have a password on that account. I have enclosed a copy of the police report # _____ from _____Police Department, which details the fraudulent check situation. The detective's name and phone number are _____ at _____.

(*Optional*)

I found out that a checking account or credit line was opened using my name and identifying information without my consent. This identity theft has been reported to the police and I have enclosed the first page of the report. (**Or**, I have reported this to the _____ Police department fraud unit Investigator _____ telephone number _____.

(*Optional*)

I have learned that an impostor created new checks using my bank account number and my name. I have closed this account.

Please send me any forms I need to complete. I am aware that legally I am not required to pay for notarized affidavits. I have enclosed a bank signature from my own bank at the end of this letter. I have also enclosed a copy of my completed Identity Theft Affidavit form from the Federal Trade Commission. I have enclosed copies of forged checks as well (*if available*).

I have also included a copy of my driver's license (or state issued identity) and a utility bill for identity verification. Please note that the above is my true mailing address and phone number. Please contact me immediately to let me know what else is necessary for you to assist me.

Note: When notifying merchants, please let them know that this is fraudulent account and forgery has taken place so that my ability to have my checks accepted is not negatively affected. Your company and your merchant clients should report the use of these fraud checks to the Police Department listed above and assist in the investigation and prosecution of this case. In accordance with Federal Law, within four (4) days of receipt of notification of this fraud, you are to refrain from reporting any further negative information in my name regarding this fraud to the credit reporting agencies or other services.

Thank you for your prompt attention to this matter and your expedited reply.

Yours truly,

Bank Verification of Customer Signature:

_____

Bank Signature

Bank Branch

Address   Bank Stamp

Enclosures:
1. Police Report
2. FTC Affidavit
3. Driver's License
4. Utility bill
5. Copies of forged checks (if available)

LETTER 2 - E: Dealing With Credit Grantors — Other Non-Fraud
(For Bank Accounts, Investment Accounts, and Utility Companies)

Your Name
Address
Phone
Cell Phone
Fax (your own or local office store)
E-mail (if you have it)

Date:

CERTIFIED MAIL
RETURN RECEIPT REQUESTED

Re: Name:
       Social Security No.:
       Account No ./Investment No.:
       Identity Fraud Alert – Password / Change of Mother's maiden name

Dear _____:

I recently found out that I am the victim of identity fraud. I have reported this crime to the _____ Police Department with Police Report No. _____ and the Fraud Investigator's name and telephone is _____ if you need further information. **[Enclose a copy of the Police Report *if possible*.]**

The impersonator opened new fraud accounts and had documents sent to the following address: _____.

At this point, it does not appear that the fraud impersonator has invaded this true account. However, I wish to put a **fraud alert** on this account and issue a secret password instead of my mother's maiden name that must be used in every transaction. Please call me or send me a form to set up a new secret password. Do **not** change my present mailing address without verification from me by phone or fax. Do **not** make any other changes without verification from me by phone at _____ or in writing to my address above.

Do **not** open any new accounts in my name without verification from me at the above number.

Thank you for your assistance and prompt attention to this matter. I look forward to receiving the forms necessary to set up a password.

Yours truly,

Enclosed:
1. Police Report
2. Copy of Driver's License

LETTER 3 - A: Dealing With Law Enforcement (Police Report)

Your Name
Address
Phone
Cell Phone
Fax (your own or local office store)
E-mail (if you have it)

Date:

CERTIFIED MAIL
RETURN RECEIPT REQUESTED

— Supervisor - Fraud Division of Your Local Police Department
— Fraud Division of the Police Department in the City (or cities) in which the fraud occurred.
— Fraud Division of Secret Service, FBI, Postal Inspector, or the Social Security Inspector, etc. (if applicable).

Dear _____:

Pursuant to my telephone conversation with **[name]** in your Fraud Department, I have reported to you the fraudulent use of my identity. At this point in time, I do not know the full extent to which my identity has been used for financial gain, except for the following fraud account(s): (list these) _____.

The person who committed the crime had the credit cards (products) sent to **[address]**. My current address since _____ is: _____.

I am happy to help you investigate this as thoroughly as possible. The Investigative Report Number you gave me by phone (or *in person*) is _____.

Please immediately send me a copy of the police report and the name, address, and telephone number of whom I should continue to correspond to with regard to this police report. I have enclosed a check in the amount of **$_____** to cover the cost of the copy of the police report. Once I ascertain further fraud; I will contact you with the information and evidence. I would be grateful if an investigation would be initiated, but the most important concern is for me to have a complete report.

I am informed that I must carry a copy of the first page of the police report in my wallet. This will provide evidence of the fraud to credit grantors and banks that have my fraud alert on file since they may be suspicious of me. I must have this report as soon as possible to use it to have the fraud removed from my credit profiles with the *credit reporting agencies*.

I would be grateful if you would keep me informed as to the information you receive with regard to the fraud perpetrator, and if and when he/she is arrested. You may contact me by mail, e-mail, or phone. Once I obtain my Police Report, under federal law I can send that report to the credit grantors who issued the fraud accounts and request all evidence of the fraud to be sent to me and to you as well within 30 days of their having received my letter. So the sooner I get my Police Report, the sooner I can demand the documentation to help you.

If you make an arrest, please provide me a copy of the ***entire*** arrest report as well as a list and copy of all information received. Any information received or documents received with my name on it should be copied and sent to me so that I may utilize these documents to protect and clear up any question with regard to my credit. I will be happy to pay for the copying charges for any such documentation. Although I recognize the rights of the accused, it is **not** a privacy violation of the fraudster if documents have *my* name on them.

I understand there are confidentiality issues, but I understand they do **not** apply to documentation with **my** own confidential and personal information.

Please also inform me as to any other information I need. Please send me any pamphlets you have on this type of theft, and any other pertinent information. If you have a victim assistance department, please provide me the telephone number and the name of a contact there.

I have enclosed a copy of my completed universal affidavit form from the Federal Trade Commission with what I know has happened. I will be happy to cooperate in any way possible and provide you with updates as I learn more information.

I have contacted the three major Credit Reporting Agencies. When I receive my credit reports showing all of the credit fraud, I will provide further information to you to add to my police report. I will also ask that all creditors provide you evidence. Thank you in advance for your help and collaboration.

Please know that according to federal law, my police report *must list all the fraudulent information*, including account numbers and fraud addresses. With specific information listed on the report, I may regain my identity and credit worthiness. I will provide you a list of all fraud accounts as I learn more. I will show you copies of my credit reports, but to protect my finances I ask that you not include them with the report unless we block out my personal information and true credit history.

Thank you so much for your assistance in this matter. I look forward to your prompt response and a copy of the entire police report.

Yours truly,

Enclosed:

1. Check for copies of police report
2. Completed affidavit
3. Copy of Government issued ID – For identification purposes
4. Copy of my current utility bill – For identification purposes

LETTER 3 - B: Dealing With Law Enforcement
(Response to Refusal to Provide Police Report)

Your Name
Address
Phone
Cell Phone
Fax (your own or local office store)
E-mail (if you have it)

Date:

CERTIFIED MAIL
RETURN RECEIPT REQUESTED

Chief of Police
Your local Police Address

Dear Chief of Police:

On **[date]** I found out that I am the victim of identity fraud. I live in your jurisdiction. I have attached a completed Uniform Affidavit sanctioned by the Federal Trade Commission, which provides you a synopsis of what happened to me to date. I have enclosed a copy of my state issued identification and my current utility bill.

I immediately called your police department and spoke with **[name]** who refused to take a police report, indicating that the identity theft victim is the credit grantor, not me. Please know that I am far more victimized than the credit grantor. I am faced with the nightmare of cleaning up my credit. My credit is being ruined and I am being defrauded along with the credit grantors. There is a law in our state making Identity Theft a crime (*find your law at www.consumer.gov/idthef and click "State Laws"*). Also there is federal law (18 USC 1028), which makes Identity Theft a federal crime. New Federal Law under the Fair Credit Reporting Act <u>requires</u> that I submit a valid police report listing all fraud accounts and information. Please note that the perpetrator received the fraud accounts at **[address]**. My current address since _____ is: _____.
I live in your jurisdiction and must receive an informational report here to be able to remedy my situation. You are not required by law to investigate, but your department <u>is</u> required to provide me an appropriate report listing all of the fraud information. Please issue me a police report.

The following accounts were fraudulently opened: (list) **[company] [phone no.]** You may contact these companies for help in the investigation and prosecution. I have attached a specific listing of the fraud accounts, which you may use as an addendum to your informational reports.

Please understand, it is critical for me to have a police report in order to repair my credit. In the interest of my safety and that of the public at large, this crime should be investigated. If, however, you cannot investigate (due to lack of resources or the fraudster committed the crime in another jurisdiction), at least provide me an informational report to send to the *Credit Reporting Agencies* to restore my credit worthiness.

Please call me ***immediately*** with regard to whom I may speak with to write a police report. A police ***report listing all of the fraud accounts and other fraud information is*** necessary for the credit reporting agencies to block the fraud accounts from my report. As per federal law, (The

Fair Credit Reporting Act) the various credit grantors and credit reporting agencies will **not** remedy the situation without documentation that I have reported this crime to law enforcement.

I am also informed that I should carry a copy of the police report with me to show to my own credit grantors and banks since I have placed a fraud alert on my own true accounts. Once I receive a report, I would be grateful if you would contact the law enforcement agency in the city(s) where the fraud occurred.

I look forward to your prompt response.

Please call me at the above number by no later than _____ **[10 days].**

Yours truly,

Enclosed:

1. State issued identification

2. Current utility bill

3. Completed Uniform Affidavit

4. Addendum to Police Report form completed listing the fraud accounts

LETTER 3 - C: Follow-up With Law Enforcement Police Report
(After Credit Reports Received)

Your Name
Address
Home Phone
Cell Phone
Fax (your own or local office store)
E-mail (if you have it)

Date:

CERTIFIED MAIL
RETURN RECEIPT REQUESTED

[Fraud Investigator or Police Officer taking initial report]
[Address]

Police Report Case # _____

Dear (Investigator, Sergeant, etc.) _____:

Thank you for your assistance with my Identity Theft case. In your file you have the original police report written by _____, # _____, dated _____. Thank you for preparing the original police report. I have now received my credit reports from the three major Credit Reporting Agencies: Experian, TransUnion, and Equifax. I have more detailed information regarding the Identity Theft accounts and inquiries. I am willing to show you those credit reports; however, I prefer not to file copies of those reports because I know that those reports are accessible by the fraud perpetrator if he is apprehended and gets an attorney. I am also worried that my confidential financial information will then become **public** record if it is part of the police report. Therefore, instead, I have prepared an addendum to this police report, listing all of the fraudulent information on my three credit reports in an organized manner. It's attached to this letter.

Please let me know if you wish to have me meet with you to have you verify the fraud that's on my credit reports, and compare it with this addendum. Many states, as well as a new Federal law, require that I obtain a police report listing all fraudulent credit information and fraud debts appearing on my credit report in order to rectify my profile. The Credit Reporting Agencies will **only** block the fraudulent information, if the accounts appear **completely and specifically** on my police report (or as an addendum to my police report). Therefore, please stamp and sign this addendum to the Police Report, attach it to my original Police Report, and provide me a copy of the stamped document with your signature at your earliest convenience.

(*Optional*) Although the fraud did not occur in our jurisdiction (the fraudster had the fraudulent accounts issued to an address at _____ **[city, state]**), I am advised by the Federal Trade Commission to file my Police Report with the local law enforcement authorities, since I am not able to obtain help from law enforcement in the other jurisdiction. I am also aware that it is customary for my local law enforcement agency to contact the law enforcement agency of the jurisdiction(s) where the fraud occurred and, if possible, to notify an Identity Theft Task Force in the city where the fraud occurred. If you can do this, I would be grateful.

I'm also asking that your department search the Federal Trade Commission's Consumer Sentinel Database for other complaints affected in this community, which may relate to this case. Please go to www.consumer.gov/idtheft and access the Law Enforcement database.

I'm in the process of contacting the various creditors with whom my impostor opened accounts, and I am requesting them, pursuant to new federal legislation, to provide documentation of the fraud to both you and to me (within 30 days of receiving a copy of my police report), to help in the investigation and possible prosecution of this case.

I am mindful that you have many cases to deal with, and, although you may not be able to investigate my case, due to lack of resources, please immediately stamp, sign, file, and send me a copy of this Addendum to my police report at your earliest convenience. As I explained to you, under Federal Law, the credit reporting agencies will **only** block the fraud if they receive a valid Police Report listing the fraud information and accounts. Thank you for your understanding.

Pursuant to my discussion with your office, I am also enclosing a check for $_____ for copies of the stamped addendum to this police report so that I may send it to the credit reporting agencies and creditors, to regain my identity and credit worthiness, and receive evidence of the fraud. If you have any questions, concerns, or need for further information, please call me. I look forward to receiving the report by mail by **[date]** (10 days). Thank you very much for your kind assistance.

Yours truly,

Enclosed:

1. Completed Addendum to police report
2. Updated affidavit

DOCUMENT 3 – C (1): Addendum to Police Report

_____ Law Enforcement Signature

_____ Law Enforcement Stamp

Attachment #1 to Police Report #_____

ADDENDUM TO POLICE REPORT # _____

NAME OF VICTIM: _____

POLICE OFFICER WHO TOOK REPORT or FRAUD INVESTIGATOR: _____

The following items were fraudulently listed on the credit reports for the above victim:

EXPERIAN

1. Fraudulent or misrepresented personal information: (i.e.: name misspell, ss# incorrect, etc)

    a.   _____

    b.   _____

    c.   _____

    d.   _____

2. Fraudulent accounts or loans:

Fraudulent Institution	Account No.	Amount

3. Fraud Inquiries made: (These companies accessed victim's credit report fraudulently.)

Company Name: _____

Company Name: _____

Company Name: _____

EQUIFAX

1. Fraudulent or misrepresented personal information (i.e. name/social security number):

a. _____

b. _____

c. _____

d. _____

2. Fraudulent accounts or loans:

Fraudulent Institution	Account No.	Amount

3. Fraud Inquiries made:

Company Name: _____

Company Name: _____

Company Name: _____

TRANSUNION

1. Fraudulent or misrepresented personal information:

a. _____

b. _____

c. _____

d. _____

2. Fraudulent accounts or loans:

Fraudulent Institution	Account No.	Amount

3. Fraud Inquiries made:

Company Name: _____

Company Name: _____

Company Name: _____

The above items were listed on the credit reporting agencies' reports to the victim and shall be attached to the enclosed Police Report.

Police Officer: _____

Date: _____

Stamp or signature of agency or police officer: _____

LETTER 3 - D: Dealing With Law Enforcement and Prosecutors Regarding Criminal Identity Theft
(Where Perpetrator Commits Other Crimes in the Victim's Name)

Your Name
Address
Phone
Cell Phone
Fax (your own or local office store)
E-mail (if you have it)

Date:

CERTIFIED MAIL
RETURN RECEIPT REQUESTED

Name and Address for local law enforcement

Name and Address for Attorney General's office
(find the address for the Attorney General in your state at http://www.naag.org)

RE: CITATION/ARREST/PROSECUTION IN THE NAME OF (*Victim of Identity Theft*)

Dear Detective/Investigator/Attorney General _____,

I recently learned that I have become a victim of criminal identity theft, in which an impostor used my name while committing a crime (other than identity theft). I found this out in the following manner:

(*i.e. The identity thief was cited for a crime, the thief was arrested for a crime, the thief was prosecuted in my name for a crime, the thief was convicted of a crime, or my name was mistakenly associated with a crime — i.e. I was informed of the felony when I was stopped for a broken headlight*)

I understand that in some states there is a registry application process with the department of justice (California Department of Justice – phone: (888) 880-0240 website: www.caag.state.ca.us/ idtheft/packet.htm) for information.

I wish to obtain a Certificate of Innocence and have my name cleared from this crime and the criminal database. I am concerned that a criminal record will be attached to a background check, which would, of course, prevent me from getting employment, obtaining a security clearance and, basically, ruin my life.

[To Law Enforcement]
Please provide me all documentation relevant to this crime. I have made a police report in my own local jurisdiction, which is _____. The law enforcement officer who took my report of the Identity Theft's name is _____, and his/her telephone number is _____. I have also asked them to provide documentation to you. They have taken my photo and fingerprints to compare with the impostor's prints and photo. I am attaching them.

Please provide, in writing, the steps I should take in order to clear my name off of all of the criminal databases. Please provide me the name and phone number of a contact person who can help me with this situation.

(*Optional*) I have recently found out that I am a victim of identity theft, and that this case has been prosecuted by your office. I need a citation number, an arrest number, the court filing number, and all documents regarding this case in the file. Please provide me the name, telephone number, time, date, and location of any court hearings. Please assist me in any processes that I can take to clear my name in that same courtroom, and have those court documents corrected. If I need to file a petition with the court clerk, please let me know what I need to do in order to do this, and provide me all forms. I hope that your office can assist me in this process, so I don't need to hire an attorney.

Enclosed you will find:

1. A statement of facts that demonstrates and explains the situation, and how it would be impossible for me to be the perpetrator of this crime (i.e. I was out of town, I was at work, I've never lived in that jurisdiction).

2. Declaration by a witness – I've also enclosed a statement of facts, made under oath by _____ (my employer, my professor, my bank representative), stating the witness's personal information about me and the situation.

3. My police report, driver's license, photo taken by the police department, and copies of my fingerprints.

4. My completed Affidavit, which was developed by the Federal Trade Commission.

Please know that there is no reasonable cause to believe that I committed the offense for which I've been cited/arrested/convicted/become subject of a criminal complaint.

Here is my basic personal identification information (*Driver's License or State ID attached*):

Full name: _____

Date of birth: _____

Gender: _____

Height: _____

Weight: _____

Natural hair color: _____

Natural eye color: _____

Race: _____

Please provide me with any and all information that I need to have in order to clear my name in this state, and in the jurisdiction in which the crime occurred. Please provide to me the names and phone numbers of any persons whom I should contact, in order to rectify this Identity Theft.

Yours truly,

Enclosed:

1. Driver's License

2. Utility bill

3. Affidavit

4. Police Report

5. Other documentation of the crime and copies of evidence

LETTER 4: Dealing With Postal Authorities
(For Local Postmasters Where Fraudulent Cards Were Sent)

Your Name
Address
Phone
Cell Phone
Fax (your own or local office store)
E-mail (if you have it)

Date:

CERTIFIED MAIL
RETURN RECEIPT REQUESTED

Postmaster
Fraud and Claims Division
(*Local Post Office*)

U.S. Postmaster
U.S. Postal Inspection Service
475 L'Enfant Plaza West, SW
Room 3100
Washington, D.C. 20260-1000

        Re: Name:
               (*Address where fraudulent credit cards were sent*)

Dear Postmaster:

        Pursuant to my conversation with your office, I have informed you of the fact that an impersonator has committed identity theft against me and has diverted mail to the following address:

_____.

        Immediately stop delivery of any mail with my name on it to that address and forward it to me at my address _____. Please do not even deliver any "junk mail" to that address. This is **not** a change of address – **it is fraud**. I have enclosed a copy of my government issued ID and a utility bill to show my identity and correct address.

        Please provide me the name and telephone number of the postal carrier who delivers mail to the fraud address at _____. I have been advised that I should contact the carrier to notify him/her of the fraud so that he/she can check any future mail. It is critical to stop the new credit offers and other documents from being delivered to the impersonator.

        I have contacted my local police in _____city (county) and the police report number is _____. The fraud investigator is _____. I have attached the first page of the report to this letter. (*If possible.*)

        I am also enclosing my completed affidavit from the Federal Trade Commission.

I am hereby asking for a formal Postal Inspector criminal investigation for mail fraud and will be happy to provide you any necessary information in my possession. Please collaborate with the local police in the jurisdiction where the fraud is perpetrated.

Please provide me with any necessary forms to complete. Also, please send me any brochures you have dealing with mail theft, using the mail for fraud, etc.

Do not change my mailing address without verification from me at my home or cell phone number(s) _____ and my current address from the first page of this letter.

Please notify me at *(phone number)*_____ immediately if anyone attempts to divert my mail or change my address.

Thank you for your prompt attention to the above.

Yours truly,

Enclosed:
  1. Police Report

  2. Driver's License

  3. Utility bill

  4. Affidavit from Federal Trade Commission

LETTER 5 - A: Dealing With the Social Security Administration

Your Name
Address
Phone
Cell Phone
Fax (your own or local office store)
E-mail (if you have it)

Date:

CERTIFIED MAIL
RETURN RECEIPT REQUESTED

Social Security Administration
Fraud Hotline
P. O. Box 17768
Baltimore, MD 21235
Fraud phone number: (800) 269-0271
Or e-mail: http://www.ssa.gov/guideline.html

    Re: Full Legal Name:
            Social Security No.:
            Age: _____

Dear Gentleperson:

I recently found out that I had been targeted for identity fraud by **[name of perpetrator if available],** who I do not know. Using my name, Social Security number, etc., this person obtained credit cards and credit lines, and may have committed crimes, etc., in my name. I filed a police report with the _____ Police Department located at **[address and phone number],** Police Report No. _____ Investigator **[Name]**. I respectfully request that the Social Security inspector begin an investigation and/or collaborate with the police department as to this fraud.

Please place a fraud alert on my Social Security number not to issue a replacement Social Security card or my number at a different address without my verification at the above address or by my home phone, **[home phone number]** or my cell phone, **[cell phone number]**.

Please provide me a copy of my Personal Earnings and Benefit Estimate Statement, Form SSA-7004-SM so that I may ascertain if there is any fraudulent income reported as well.

Please let me know what other measures I need to take with your agency. I have included a copy of my affidavit and identity information, and my police report.

Thank you for your prompt attention to these requests.

Yours truly,

Enclosed:

1. Driver's License (or other government issued ID)

2. Affidavit

3. Police Report

(Alternative)

My child **[name]'s** Social Security Number: **[xxx-xx-xxxx],** was used by an impersonator. We found this out in the following manner:

_____

_____

_____

Since my child is under 14 years of age, has never worked, and has never applied for credit, we are advised to change his/her Social Security Number. Please provide us all forms and information in order to do this.

I have attached my child's Social Security Card, birth certificate and copy of the police report. Please provide any documentation of the use of his/her Social Security Number for earnings reports or other fraudulent activity.

Thank you.

Yours truly,

Enclosed:

1. Police Report

2. Social Security Card

3. Birth certificate

LETTER 5 - B: Dealing With IRS/State Tax Board

Your Name
Address
Phone
Cell Phone
Fax (your own or local office store)
E-mail (if you have it)

Date:

CERTIFIED MAIL
RETURN RECEIPT REQUESTED

Internal Revenue Service (Office in your State or County) 1-800-829-0433
State Tax Board (Office in your State)

Re: Name:
        Tax ID No.

Dear Gentleperson:

I recently learned I am the victim of identity fraud. An imposter has used my name, Social Security number, and other identifying information to gain credit, open accounts, and **[insert information]** fraudulently. I do not know if this person has worked using my name, but I have written to Social Security to see my earnings statement.

I have enclosed a copy of a letter I sent to the Social Security Administration.

Please place a fraud alert on my tax profile. I am concerned that the impersonator will use my Social Security number and adversely affect my taxes. I have heard of such things with regard to wage earnings, gambling receipts, etc. Please note my address above and notify me if you receive tax information from a different address.

Please put this letter in my file and notify me of any other information you need. Also, please send me any brochures or information that may help me to protect myself from further problems with regard to your agency.

(Optional)

I believe that an impostor is using my identity for employment purposes (payroll tax, unemployment compensation, worker's compensation etc).

(Or)

I believe someone has filled a tax return using my identity, Please contact the Police Investigator **[Name]**, at **[telephone number]**; **[address]** I request a formal investigation. I have enclosed a copy of my police report, and my completed affidavit developed by the Federal Trade Commission.

(Further Explanation)

Please provide documentation of all evidence of the fraud to me and my fraud investigator by **[date]** (30 days).

Please do not change my address without verification from me at my home address or by phone at this number **[home phone number]**.

Thank you for your assistance.

Yours truly,

Enclosures:

1. Copies of letter to Social Security

2. Police Report

3. Affidavit

LETTER 6 - A: Dealing With Department of Motor Vehicles

Your Name
Address
Phone
Cell Phone
Fax (Your own or local office store)
E-mail (if you have it)

Date:

CERTIFIED MAIL
RETURN RECEIPT REQUESTED

Department of Motor Vehicles
Your State Office – Fraud Office

Attention: [*person with whom you spoke*]

Re: Name as it appears on the License:
Driver's License No.:
Date of Birth:
Address as it appears on the valid Driver's License:

Dear _____:

Pursuant to my conversation with your department, I am writing to you to inform you that I am the victim of identity theft. An impersonator has obtained credit using my name, Social Security number, and other identifiers. I have reason to believe that the imposter has obtained a driver's license in my name or has a fraudulent license with her/his picture and my name with an address other then mine as above.

I have reported this fraud to the police. The report number is _____, the investigator is _____. Please see the attached Police Report (*if possible*), which I have enclosed (or please issue me an identity theft report.)

1. Please provide me information as to any and all driver's licenses issued in my name within the last ____ years. I have been living at this address since **[year]**.

2. Please also send me a copy of my driving record so I can see if the impersonator has committed any offense in my name. Let me know if there is any cost for this.

3. Also note on your computer that I have been victimized by fraud. Please do **not** issue any new driver's license in my name without first verifying it is me. You may contact me at the above address or call me at my home number, which is **[home number]** or my cell phone at **[cell phone number]** or my work number **[work phone number]**.

4. Please immediately place a fraud alert or protective status on my file. Let me know what inconvenience that will mean to me upon renewal or if I move.

5. If a new license has been issued to an imposter, please issue me a new driver's license number immediately, cancel my current number, and send me a new driver's license at my home address. I have included a utility bill and a copy of my current driver's license to verify my address.

6. I have attached a synopsis of the fraud with the enclosed complete affidavit, which was prepared by the Federal Trade Commission.

7. Please send me any forms to complete and any brochures explaining what I am to do in a case such as this. If you find that the impersonator has been issued a new driver's license using my name at a different address, please call or write me immediately.

8. Please contact my fraud investigator at the _____ Police. His/Her name is _____ and the phone number is _____.

I look forward to receiving a response at your earliest convenience, but by no later than **[two weeks]**.

Thank your for your prompt attention.

Yours truly,

Enclosed:

    1. Copy of current Driver's License

    2. Utility bill

    3. Police report

    4. Federal Trade Commission Affidavit

LETTER 6 - B: Dealing With Your Auto Insurer, Heath Care, or Other Insurance Policy if Necessary

Your Name
Address
Phone
Cell Phone
Fax (Your own or local office store)
E-mail (if you have it)

Date:

CERTIFIED MAIL
RETURN RECEIPT REQUESTED

Name of Your Agent
Your Insurance Company
Address

     Re: Name of Insured:
               Policy Number(s):

Dear _____:

As I explained in my telephone call, I just learned that I am the victim of identity fraud. The impersonator has used my name and Social Security number to obtain credit in my name. He/she may have a driver's license in my name as well. I have enclosed a copy of a letter that I sent to the Department of Motor Vehicles explaining the problem. He/she may be using my name and Social Security Number for other types of insurance as well.

Please keep this letter in my file and place a fraud alert on the computer for my account. If this person uses my name and violates the vehicle code or is involved in any accident, please inform me of any such situation at the telephone number above.

Enclosed is a copy of the police report I filed as to this fraud (*if possible.*)

Please do not change my address for my policy without first verifying with me by phone at my home number _____, work number _____ or my cell phone number, _____. Please also place an alert on my homeowner's insurance and all other insurance policies in my name.

I will give you a password to use for dealing with my profile. Please send me a form to do this.

Thank you for your assistance. Please let me know if you need anything else from me.

Yours truly,

Enclosed:

    1. Letter to Department of Motor Vehicles

    2. Police Report (if available)

    3. Other relevant information as necessary

(Alternative)

Life Insurance, Health Insurance or Disability, etc.

Dear Gentleperson:

I am the victim of identity theft. I am worried that someone may change or use my insurance with your company. Please place a fraud alert on my file and don't make any changes in my address or otherwise without verification from me by phone and/or in writing at the above address. My phone numbers are **[*home*], [*work*],** and **[*cell*].** I am attaching a copy of my police report.

I look forward to hearing from you. I wish to place a password on my policy with your office. Thank you.

Yours truly,

Enclosed:

1. Police Report

LETTER 7: Dealing With U.S. Passport

Your Name
Address
Phone
Cell Phone
Fax (your own or local office store)
E-mail (if you have it)

Date:

CERTIFIED MAIL
RETURN RECEIPT REQUESTED

[YOUR LOCAL AGENCY OFFICE] and
US Department of State
Passport Services

Consular, Lost/Stolen Passport Section
1111 19th Street, NW, Suite 500
Washington, DC 20036
(202) 955-0430

> Re: Name: [Full name as it appears on Passport]
> Passport No.: (*if you have one*)
> Social Security Number:

Dear Gentleperson:

I am writing to inform you that I have been the victim of identity fraud, which I found out about on **[date]**. The perpetrator of the fraud used a mailing address of _____. My mailing address is _____.

The police report number at the _____ Police Department is _____. The Fraud Investigator is **[name, telephone number, and address]**. I have enclosed the police report (*if possible*.)

I do not know if the perpetrator has applied for and/or obtained a fraudulent passport in my name.

I have enclosed a copy of the pertinent pages of my passport. (Or, I presently do not have a passport in my name. Please let me know if you have issued a passport on file in my name and, if so, send me a copy.) I have enclosed a copy of my driver's license and utility bill.

Please inform me of anything else that I need to do. I am very concerned that my impostor will leave the country and commit a crime using my name in a foreign country. I do not know if my letter could prevent this, however it should be noted in your file for future reference. Please place a fraud alert on my file, and let me know what else you suggest I do.

Please advise me as to what other precautions I must take with your office. I have enclosed a copy of my completed Universal Affidavit from the Federal Trade Commission, and other identifying information. Thank you for your assistance.

Yours truly,

Enclosed:

1. Police Report

2. Relevant Passport pages (if available)

3. Federal Trade Commission Uniform Affidavit

4. Driver's license (Government issued Identification)

5. Utility bill

LETTER 8 - A: Dealing With Civil Legal Actions Against You (Or Bankruptcy in Your Name)

Your Name
Address
Phone
Cell Phone
Fax (your own or local office store)
E-mail (if you have it)

Date:

CERTIFIED MAIL
RETURN RECEIPT REQUESTED

Clerk of the **[County]** Superior Court
[Address of the Superior Court]

[Name of opposing counsel]
[Address of opposing counsel]

    Re: Name: **[Your name]** Case #_____
               Identity Theft

Dear _____:

I spoke with your office upon learning that there is a case against me (or a judgment against me) which is filed in your court. I am a victim of identity theft. An impersonator has used my identity, Social Security number, and other identifying information to obtain credit (or an apartment or file bankruptcy).

I found out about this filed case by *(e.g.,* Internet search, through the credit reporting agencies which had a judgment listed on my report, a writ of attachment on my account, after being served with a lawsuit, etc.)

1. Pursuant to our conversation, please send a copy of the entire file to me at the above address. As per our conversation, I have enclosed a check in the amount of **$_____** to cover the cost of the copies.

2. Please let me know what I need to do to have the judgment expunged (or case dismissed) by your court. I wish to do this without an attorney, if possible.

3. I have enclosed a completed affidavit, which was developed by the Federal Trade Commission for victims of Identity Theft. It explains what has happened.

4. I have also included a copy of the police report (or other law enforcement report).

5. Also enclosed is my state issued identification and a utility bill showing my address.

6. Please also send me information to assist me, and a phone number for your Victim Assistance Program.

I would be grateful for any other suggestions or brochures explaining your court's rules and policies regarding rectifying identity fraud problems. If you have any further questions, please let me know. My work phone number is: _____, and my cell phone is: _____. I look forward to receiving my file as quickly as possible.

Thank you for your help.

Yours truly,

Enclosed:

1. Law Enforcement report

2. State issued identification (i.e. driver's license)

3. Completed Affidavit

4. Copy of lawsuit or other evidence

(Optional)

To Opposing Counsel.

Dear _____:

I recently found out that I am the victim of fraud. Your office has filed suit against me for _____ non-payment of _____. I am not the person you intended to sue. (other information)

I am enclosing a copy of my police report, my completed affidavit, and a copy of my government issued identification. Please send me any documentation you have of this fraud and let me know what steps I need to take so you can dismiss me from this case.

Yours truly,

Enclosed:

1. Police report

2. Affidavit

3. Identification

LETTER 8 - B: Dealing with a Judge
(After an Arrest of an Impersonator) – Victim Impact Statement

Your Name
Address
Phone
Cell Phone

Date:

The Honorable _____   (*Name of Case*)
(*Address*)   (*Case #*)
                                     (*Court*)

Dear Judge _____ (name):

Thank you for the opportunity to inform you of the impact of the crime of identity theft that was perpetrated upon me by the defendant, _____.

This person stole over $_____ from the credit grantors using my name. He has also **[add to this]**. Now I am spending hundreds of frustrating hours dealing by phone and letters with collection companies, banks, credit reporting agencies, governmental agencies, (IRS, Postal Authorities, Social Security, etc.) and various other companies and utilities to convince them of the fraud, and to clean up the disaster affecting my credit and other aspects of my finances and life.

The out-of-pocket costs are substantial (see attached logs of costs.) However, far more devastating is learning that someone has invaded every aspect of my life and taken my identity. My credit is ruined, my good reputation is stolen and tarnished, and my career and livelihood are impaired. (My family is harmed _____.)

I have enclosed a completed affidavit, which briefly outlines several aspects of this nightmare.

BURDEN ON THE VICTIM - CLEANING UP THE CREDIT (*EXAMPLE ONLY*)

(*For example only—insert your own facts here.*) I have spent over 500 hours calling, filling out documentation, writing over 90 letters *return receipt requested* to banks, credit reporting agencies, governmental agencies, companies, utilities, credit grantors, the State Bar, etc. to inform them of the fraud in an attempt to prove my own innocence. The burden is on the victim to prove fraud since there is great suspicion by the credit grantors. In fact, since I put fraud alerts and new passwords on all my accounts, I have experienced extensive questioning and delays in dealing with the various banks and agencies. I found out about the fraud almost ____ months ago and I am still writing letters to clear my name and stop the post office from delivering me new offers of credit at the fraud address. I am told by the Federal Trade Commission that my problems may go on for several years.

EMOTIONAL IMPACT

(*Example only—insert your own facts here—only two paragraphs.*) This has been a very frightening and invasive ordeal. I have had great difficulty sleeping and have awoken in cold sweats worrying about what else I will find out. For example, I was about to be sued by Thrifty Rental car after the defendant rented a car in my name using a false driver's license and a Capitol One credit card in my name. He/she had an accident and was unable to charge the final charges because I had canceled the card upon finding out about the fraud. Fortunately, I obtained the rental car contract from the police so I could address the situation and avoid a judgment against me.

I have had night terrors seeing the defendant invading my home and hurting my children. When the impersonator was arrested, a handgun was among his/her possessions. I am also informed that he/she claimed to be a private detective and received confidential information. I do not know what he/she has of mine or intends to do next.

VULNERABLE AND VIOLATED

(Example only—insert your own facts here.) Stealing my identity has made me feel very vulnerable and violated. It has been stressful and literally has made me ill. I have experienced fierce headaches, physical pain in my lower abdomen and back and have had to go for medical help. I do not like to think of myself as a victim. I thought at first that I could handle this stress without extra counseling. However, I found it so overwhelming that I had to see a therapist several times to stay conscious of my feelings. Even my children are fearful and anxious.

RESTITUTION REQUESTED

1. OUT OF POCKET EXPENSES $_____

See attached Log

2. LOST WAGES $_____

See attached Log

Enclosed please find logs of my out of pocket expenses and my time spent on these problems. I respectfully request that this court award me restitution in the amount of $_____ in out-of-pocket costs and $_____ in lost wages. Restitution should be paid to me by the perpetrator. Although the creditors have also lost money, they have the ability to write their losses off as the cost of doing business, so I respectfully request that I be awarded restitution prior to the banks who actually issued credit to my impostor without taking precautions to verify my identity.

CONCLUSION

(Example only—insert your own wording here.) I respectfully request that Your Honor consider the serious nature of this crime. I am hopeful that this defendant will be rehabilitated and find help for his/her problems. I believe he/she needs to learn that society will not tolerate this type of insidious crime. For that reason, I strongly urge that he/she experience at least two years of jail time, not just a couple months on probation.

I am concerned about what he/she will do to me in the future. I ask for a stay-away order from me, my family, and my property.

I hope that he/she will use her resources to change his/her life and become a respectful citizen. Please provide him/her with an opportunity to learn from his/her mistakes, obtain counseling, gainful employment, and a chance to receive positive opportunities to be a productive member of our society.

I trust you will take this crime seriously.

Thank you for your consideration.

Sincerely,

Enclosures:

   1. Completed affidavit/Historical chronology

   2. Log of Time Expended

   3. Log of Out-of-Pocket Expenses / Receipts (copies)

LETTER 9: Dealing With a Licensing Agency
(Such as State Accounting Board, Teacher's License, Contractor's Board, Medical Board, State Bar, etc.)

Your Name
Address
Phone
Cell Phone
Fax (your own or local office store)
E-mail (if you have it)

Date:

CERTIFIED MAIL
RETURN RECEIPT REQUESTED

Membership Records
Name of Licensing Board

    Re: **[Your Name and License No. _____]**

Dear _____:

This will confirm our telephone conversation on **[date]** *regarding* the fact that an impersonator has been assuming my identity and fraudulently obtained credit cards, and lines of credit using my name, Social Security number, date of birth, etc. This person may be also disseminating business cards using my profession to abuse consumers. The person may also be committing crimes in my name.

Please be informed of this fraud in case this person tries to use my license number to fraudulently take money from unsuspecting clients and customers. I am concerned that this person may injure the public. I have attached a copy of the police report (*if possible*), a copy of my driver's license, and a utility bill to prove my address.

Please do not change my address, or send out new licensing material without verification of my present address above and phone number by calling me at my home phone at _____ or my cell phone at _____.

Please flag my record with a fraud alert in your computers and place this letter in my file. Please also provide me a form to provide you with a verifying password. If you need further information, please call my home or cell phone at the above numbers.

Thank you.

Yours truly,

    Enclosed:

      1. Driver's license

      2. Utility bill

      3. Police Report (*if possible*)

DOCUMENT 10 — Federal Trade Commission's Uniform Affidavit

This document was developed for the Federal Trade Commission in Washington, D.C. by law enforcement, members of the financial industry, privacy advocates and others to provide a uniform reporting mechanism for Identity Theft victims. Mari Frank assisted in the development of this form and, although companies are not required to accept this specific affidavit, it is hoped that the new Federal regulations will recommend this specific affidavit to be accepted by all companies in all states.

Please use this form and update it frequently with additional information. Keep hard copies and a copy on your computer for easy amending.

ID Theft Affidavit

Victim Information

(1) My full legal name is _____

            (First)   (Middle)   (Last)   (Jr., Sr., III)

(2) (If different from above) When the events described in this affidavit took place, I was known as

_____
            (First)   (Middle)   (Last)   (Jr., Sr., III)

(3) My date of birth is _____
            (day/month/year)

(4) My Social Security number is _____

(5) My driver's license or identification card state and number are _____

(6) My current address is _____
           City   State   Zip Code

(7) I have lived at this address since _____
            (month/year)

(8) (If different from above) When the events described in this affidavit took place, my address was

_____
           City   State   Zip Code

(9) I lived at the address in Item 8 from _____ until _____
          (month/year)   (month/year)

(10) My daytime telephone number is ( ) _____

My evening telephone number is ( ) _____

How the Fraud Occurred

Check all that apply for items 11 - 17:

(11) ☐ I did not authorize anyone to use my name or personal information to seek the money, credit, loans, goods or services described in this report.

(12) ☐ I did not receive any benefit, money, goods or services as a result of the events described in this report.

(13) ☐ My identification documents (for example, credit cards; birth certificate; driver's license; Social Security card; etc.) were ☐ **stolen** ☐ **lost** on or about _____.
(day/month/year)

(14) ☐ To the best of my knowledge and belief, the following person(s) used my information (for example, my name, address, date of birth, existing account numbers, Social Security number, mother's maiden name, etc.) or identification documents to get money, credit, loans, goods or services without my knowledge or authorization:

_____	_____
Name (if known	Name (if known)
_____	_____
Address (if known)	Address (if known)
_____	_____
Phone number(s) (if known)	Phone number(s) (if known)
_____	_____
Additional information (if known)	Additional information (if known)

(15) ☐ I do NOT know who used my information or identification documents to get money, credit, loans, goods or services without my knowledge or authorization.

(16) ☐ Additional comments: (For example, description of the fraud, which documents or information were used or how the identity thief gained access to your information.)

_____

_____

_____

_____

_____

_____

(Attach additional pages as necessary.)

Victim's Law Enforcement Actions

(17) (check one) I ☐ **am** ☐ **am not** willing to assist in the prosecution of the person(s) who committed this fraud.

(18) (check one) I ☐ **am** ☐ **am not** authorizing the release of this information to law enforcement for the purpose of assisting them in the investigation and prosecution of the person(s) who committed this fraud.

(19) (check all that apply) I ☐ **have** ☐ **have not** reported the events described in this affidavit to the police or other law enforcement agency. The police ☐ **did** ☐ **did not** write a report. *In the event you have contacted the police or other law enforcement agency, please complete the following:*

(Agency #1)	(Officer/Agency personnel taking report)
(Date of report)	(Report number, if any)
(Phone number)	(email address, if any)
(Agency #2)	(Officer/Agency personnel taking report)
(Date of report)	(Report number, if any)
(Phone number)	(email address, if any)

Documentation Checklist

Please indicate the supporting documentation you are able to provide to the companies you plan to notify. Attach copies (NOT originals) to the affidavit before sending it to the companies.

(20) ☐ A copy of a valid government-issued photo-identification card (for example, your driver's license, state-issued ID card or your passport). If you are under 16 and don't have a photo-ID, you may submit a copy of your birth certificate or a copy of your official school records showing your enrollment and place of residence.

(21) ☐ Proof of residency during the time the disputed bill occurred, the loan was made or the other event took place (for example, a rental/lease agreement in your name, a copy of a utility bill or a copy of an insurance bill).

(22) ☐ A copy of the report you filed with the police or sheriff's department. If you are unable to obtain a report or report number from the police, please indicate that in Item 19. Some companies only need the report number, not a copy of the report. You may want to check with each company.

Signature

I declare under penalty of perjury that the information I have provided in this affidavit is true and correct to the best of my knowledge.

_____   _____
(signature)   (date signed)

Knowingly submitting false information on this form could subject you to criminal prosecution for perjury.

_____
(Notary)

[Check with each company. Creditors sometimes require notarization. If they do not, please have one witness (non-relative) sign below that you completed and signed this affidavit.]

Witness:

_____   _____
(signature)   (printed name)

_____   _____
(date)   (telephone number)

DOCUMENT 10 — MASTER LOG FOR IDENTITY FRAUD CORRESPONDENCE

Date	Company Agency Contact	Name of Person/Title	Phone / Fax E-mail	TimeSpent	Expenses Incurred	Certified Mail Date	Response Date	Call Back Date

Keep copies of all correspondence in a file labeled by company. Keep Master Log copies in a separate file for easy access.

DOCUMENT 11 — LOG FOR IDENTITY THEFT EXPENSES

(Copies of Receipts Attached)

Date	Postage Certified Mail/ Fed Ex	Phone Bills Local/ Long Distance	Photo- copies	Office Supplies	Travel Mileage	Medical Bills	Attorney's Fees	Contract Labor Secretary	Time Off Work/ Lost Earn- ings	Misc.

Keep copies of this log along with copies of receipts in a separate file.

Fraudulent Account Statement

Completing this Statement

- Make as many copies of this page as you need. **Complete a separate page for each company you're notifying and only send it to that company.** Include a copy of your signed affidavit.

- List only the account(s) you're disputing with the company receiving this form. **See the example below.**

- If a collection agency sent you a statement, letter or notice about the fraudulent account, attach a copy of that document (**NOT** the original).

I declare (check all that apply):

☐ As a result of the event(s) described in the ID Theft Affidavit, the following account(s) was/were opened at your company in my name without my knowledge, permission or authorization using my personal information or identifying documents:

Creditor Name/Address (the company that opened the account or provided the goods or services)	Account Number	Type of unauthorized credit/goods/ services provided by creditor	Date issued or opened (if known)	Amount/Value Provided (the amount charged or the cost of the goods/services)
Example Example National Bank 22 Main Street Columbus, Ohio 22722	01234567-89	auto loan	01/05/2002	$25,500.00

☐ During the time of the accounts described above, I had the following account open with your company:

Billing name: _____

Billing address: _____

Account number: _____

Appendix B

Resources to Assist You

Identity Theft and Privacy Protection

- **CALPIRG**

(California Public Interest Research Group)

Research and lobbying consumer group that addresses issues of identity theft and consumer issues.

Address:	1107 9th St., Suite 601
	Sacramento, CA 95814
Phone:	(916) 448-4516
E-mail:	info@calpirg.org
Web:	www.calpirg.org

- **Center for Democracy and Technology**

The goal of this organization is to bring democracy to the Internet.

Address:	1634 "I" Street NW, Suite 1100
	Washington, D.C. 20006
Phone:	(202) 637-9800
Fax:	(202) 637-0968
E-mail:	feedback@cdt.org
Web:	www.cdt.org

- **Computer Professionals for Social Responsibility**

Provides policy makers with realistic assessments of power, promise and problems of information technology.

Address:	P. O. Box 717
	Palo Alto, CA 94302
Phone:	(650) 322-3778
E-mail:	cpsr@cpsr.org
Web:	www.cpsr.org

- **Consumer Action Credit and Finance Project**

Provides publications on secured credit.

Address:	717 Market Street Suite 310
	San Francisco, CA 94103

Phone:	(415) 777-9635
	complaint hot line
Phone:	(415) 255-3879
	publication orders
Web:	www.consumeraction.org

- **Consumer Federation of America**

Association of 240 pro-consumer groups whose aim is to advance consumer interest through advocacy and education.

Address:	1424 16th St. NW, Suite 604
	Washington, D.C. 20036
Phone:	(202) 387-6121
Web:	www.consumerfed.org

- **Consumers Union**

Publishes Consumer Reports magazine and also acts as an advocacy office for consumer legislation.

Address:	1666 Connecticut Ave. NW,
	Suite 310
	Washington, D.C. 20009-1039
Phone:	(202) 462-6262
Fax:	(202) 265-9548
Web:	www.consumersunion.org

- **Electronic Privacy Information Center**

Monitors federal legislation and encryption policy pertaining to freedom of expression issues on the Internet.

Address:	1718 Connecticut Ave. NW
	Washington, D.C. 20009
Phone:	(202) 483-1140
Fax:	(202) 483-1248
E-mail:	info@epic.org
Web:	www.epic.org

- **Federal Citizen Information Center**

Referral to appropriate agency

(800) 688-9889 or (800) 333-4636

- ## Federal Communications Commission (FCC)

For cellular phone and long distance fraud. Consumer Information Bureau.

Address: 445 12th Street SW,
Room 5A863
Washington, DC 20554
Phone: (888) 225-5322
E-mail: fccinfo@fcc.gov
Web: www.fcc.gov

- ## Federal Deposit Insurance Corporation (FDIC)

The FDIC supervises state-chartered banks that are not members of the Federal Reserve System and insures deposits at banks and savings and loans.

Division of Compliance and Consumer Affairs
Address: 550 17th Street NW
Washington, DC 20429
Phone: (800) 934-3342 or
(202) 736-0000
Web: www.fdic.gov

- ## Federal Reserve System

The Fed supervises state-chartered banks that are members of the Federal Reserve System.

Division of Consumer and Community Affairs
Address: Mail Stop 801
20th St. and Constitution NW
Federal Reserve Board
Washington, DC 20551
Phone: (202) 452-3693
Web: www.federalreserve.gov

- ## The Federal Trade Commission Identity Theft Clearinghouse

The Consumer Protection Mission of the FTC is to protect consumers from companies that misinform or overreach with regard to our economy.

Identity Theft Clearinghouse
Address: 600 Pennsylvania Ave. NW
Washington, DC 20580
Phone: (877) IDTHEFT (438-4338)
Web: www.consumer.gov/idtheft

- ## The Foundation For Taxpayer and Consumer Rights

Non-profit organization to support consumer rights.

Address: 1750 Ocean Park Blvd.,
Suite 200
Santa Monica, CA 90405
Phone: (310) 392-0522
Fax: (310) 392-8874
E-mail: consumerwatchdog
@consumerwatchdog.org
Web: www.consumerwatchdog.org

- ## Identity Theft Prevention and Survival

Provides assistance to consumers and identity theft victims with resources, books, and legal assistance. Attorney: Mari Frank

Mari J. Frank, Esq.
Address: 28202 Cabot Road #300
Laguna Niguel, CA 92677
Phone: (800) 725-0807 or
(949) 364-1511
Fax: (949) 363-7561
E-mail: contact@identitytheft.org
Web: www.identitytheft.org

- ## Identity Theft Resource Center

Provides support and assistance to victims of identity theft.

Co-Directors: Linda Goldman-Foley, Jay Foley
Address: P.O. Box 26833,
San Diego, Ca. 92196
Phone: (858) 693-7935
E-mail: itrc@idtheftcenter.org
Web: idtheftcenter.org

- ## Internal Revenue Service

Office of the Privacy Advocate
Address: Room 7050 OS:PA
1111 Constitution Ave. NW
Washington, D.C. 20224
Fraud: (800) 829-0433
Taxpayer Advocates Office:
Phone: (877) 777-4778
Web: www.treas.gov/irs/ci
www.irs.gov

- ## Junkbusters Corp.

Provides self-defense against privacy-invading marketing.

Address: P.O. Box 7034,
Green Brook, NJ 08812
Phone: (908) 753 7861
Web: Junkbusters.com

Please do not send requests to be removed from marketing lists to this address.

Junkbusters only operates online. Requests may be mailed to the Direct Marketing Association.

• National Center for Victims of Crime

Refers victims of crime to local services. Provides counseling and victim services. Publishes bulletins on various criminal topics.

Address:	2000 M. St. NW, Suite 480
	Washington, D.C. 20036
Phone:	(800) FYI-CALL or
	(202) 467-8700
Web:	www.ncvc.org

• National Credit Union Administration (NCUA)

The NCUA charters and supervises federal credit unions and insures deposits at federal credit unions and many state credit unions.

Compliance Offer,
National Credit Union Administration

Address:	1175 Duke Street, Suite 4206
	Alexandria, VA 22314-3437
Phone:	(703) 518-6360
Web:	www.ncua.gov

• National Fraud Information Center

Consumer Assistance Service

Phone:	(800) 876-7060
	help line for victims of fraud
Web:	www.fraud.org

• National Organization for Victim Assistance (NOVA)

Refers victims of crime to local victim assistance programs.

Address:	1730 Park Rd., NW
	Washington, D.C. 20010
Phone:	(202) 232-6682
Hotline:	(800) 879-6682
Web:	www.trynova.org

• Office of Comptroller of the Currency (OCC)

The OCC charters and supervises national banks. If the word "national" appears in the name of a bank, or the initials "N.A" of its name, then the OCC oversees its operations.

Customer Assistance Group

Address:	1301 McKinney St., Suite 3450
	Houston, TX 77010
Phone:	(800) 613-6743
Fax:	(713) 336-4301
Web:	www.occ.treas.gov

• Office of Privacy Protection-California

Provides information for consumers and victims regarding California and Federal Law.

Address:	400 "R" Street, Suite 3080
	Sacramento, CA 95814
Phone:	(866)785-9663
	(916) 323-0637
Web:	www.privacy.ca.gov

• Office of Thrift Supervision (OTS)

The OTS is the primary regulator of all federal, and many state-chartered thrift institutions which include savings banks and savings and loan institutions.

Office of Thrift Supervision

Address:	1700 "G" Street NW
	Washington, DC 20552
Phone:	(202) 906-6000
E-mail:	publicinfo@ots.treas.gov
Web:	www.ots.treas.gov

• Privacy International

A public interest research group that deals with privacy issues at the national and international level.

Address:	1718 Connecticut Ave. NW,
	Suite 200
	Washington, DC 200009
Phone:	(202) 483-1217
E-mail:	privacyint@privacy.org
Web:	www.privacyinternational.org

• Privacy Rights Clearinghouse

A non-profit consumer information, privacy protection, and advocacy program.

Beth Givens, Director

Address:	3100 5th Ave. Suite B
	San Diego, CA 92103
Phone:	(619) 298-3396
Fax:	(619) 298-5681
Web:	www.privacyrights.org

- **Private Citizen, Inc**

Provides information and assistance on how to get rid of junk mailers and junk callers.

Address:	P. O. Box 233
	Naperville, IL 60566
Phone:	(800) CUT-JUNK (288-5865)
	(630) 393-2370
E-mail:	pci@private-citizen.com
Web:	www.privatecitizen.com

- **Social Security Administration**

Office of Inspector General
Social Security Administration
Office of Communications

Address:	Suite 300 Altmeyer Building
	6401 Security Blvd
	Baltimore, MD 21235

To report fraud
Phone:	(800) 269-0271
Address:	P.O. Box 17768
	Baltimore, MD 21235

To order Personal Earnings and Benefits Statement:
Phone:	(800) 772-1213

Office of Inspector General:
Phone:	(800) 269-0271
Web:	www.ssa.gov/org/publicfraud reporting/index.htm
	www.ssa.gov/org/guidelin.htm

- **US Department of State
Passport Services**

Consular Lost/Stolen Passport Section

Address:	1111 19th Street, NW, Suite 500
	Washington, DC 20036
Phone:	(202) 955-0430
Web:	www.travel.state.gov/passport/ lost.html

- **U.S. PIRG**

U.S. Public Interest Research Group, the national lobbying office for state PIRGs.

Edmund Mierzwinski, Director
Address:	218 "D" St., SE
	Washington, D.C. 20003
Phone:	(202) 546-9707
E-mail:	uspirg@pirg.org
Web:	www.pirg.org

- **U.S. Postal Inspection Service**

Address:	475 L'Enfant Plaza West SW
	Room 3100
	Washington, D.C. 20260-1000
Phone:	(202) 268-4396
Web:	www.usps.com/postal inspectors/

- **U.S. Securities and Exchange Commission (SEC)**

The SEC's Office of Investor Education and Assistance serves investors who complain to the SEC about investment fraud or the mishandling of their investments by securities professionals.

SEC Office of Investor Education and Assistance
Address:	450 Fifth Street NW
	Washington, DC 20549-0213
Phone:	(202) 942-7040
Web:	http://www.sec.gov/ complaints.html

- **U.S. Trustee (UST)**

Contact the Trustee in the region where fraudulent bankruptcy was filed.

Web:	http://www.usdoj.gov/ust/

Check-Verification/
Check-Guarantee Firms:

- **Certegy Check Services, Inc.**

Address:	P. O. Box 30046,
	Tampa, FL 33630
Phone:	(800) 437-5120
Fax:	(727) 570-4936
Web:	www.certegy.com

- **Chexsystems, Consumer Relations**

Address:	7805 Hudson Rd, Suite 100
	Woodbury, MN 55125
Phone:	(800) 428-9623
Fax:	(602) 659-2197
Web:	www.chexhelp.com

- **Cross Check (Check Center Inquiry)**

Address:	P.O. Box 6008,
	Petaluma, CA 94955
Phone:	(800) 843-0760

- **Global Payments, Inc.**

Address:	Attn: Fraud Dept.
	6215 W. Howard
	Niles, IL 60714
Phone:	(800) 766-2748
Fax:	(847) 647-8023
Web:	www.globalpaymentsinc.com

- **Shared Check Authorization Network (SCAN), Electronic Transaction Corp.**

Address:	7805 Hudson Road, Suite 100,
	Woodbury, MN 55125
Phone:	(877) 382-7226
Fax:	(800) 358-4506
Web:	www.scanassist.com

- **TeleCheck.**

  Consumer Affairs

Address:	P. O. Box 4451
	Houston, TX 77210-4451
Phone:	(800) 710-9898
Fax:	(713) 332-9300
Web:	www.telecheck.com

Credit Card Companies:

- **American Express**

Phone:	(800) 528-2122
Web:	www.americanexpress.com

- **MasterCard Global Service Center**

Phone:	(800) 307-7309
Web:	http://www.mastercard.com

- **Visa Assistance Center**

Phone:	(800) VISA911 (Hotline)
Web:	http://www.visa.com

Crediting-reporting Bureaus:

To order one free annual credit report from each of the three credit reporting agencies call 877-322-8228 or visit www.annualcreditreport.com. When you call to report fraud, you will get a voice mail and must provide your Social Security number. Use your cell phone number or home number as the number to call if creditors wish to check if you requested credit.

To opt out of pre-approved offers of credit for all three credit bureaus call:

Phone:	(888) 5 OPTOUT
	[(888) 567-8688]

- **Equifax**

  To report fraud:

Phone:	(800) 525-6285
Address:	P.O. Box 740241
	Atlanta, GA 30374-0241

  To order copy of report:

Phone:	(800) 685-1111
Address:	P.O. Box 740241
	Atlanta, GA 30374-0241
Web:	www.equifax.com

- **Experian (formerly TRW)**

  To report fraud:

Phone:	(888) 397-3742

  Experian Consumer Fraud Assistance

Address:	P.O. Box 9532
	Allen, TX 75013

  To order copy of report:

Phone:	(888) 397-3742
Address:	P.O. Box 9532
	Allen, TX 75013
Web:	www.experian.com

- **TransUnion**

  To report fraud:

Phone:	(800) 680-7289

  Fraud Victim Assistance Division

Address:	P.O. Box 6790
	Fullerton, CA 92834-6790

  To order copy of report:

Phone:	(800) 888-4213
Address:	P.O. Box 6790
	Fullerton, CA 92834-6790
Web:	www.transunion.com

Data Compilers:

To remove your name from lists that companies rent and sell, write or call the following companies:

- ## Mail Preference Service
  ### Direct Marketing Association

  Address: P.O. Box 643
                   Carmel, NY 10512-0643
  Web: www.dmaconsumers.org

- ## Federal Trade Commission

  Do Not Call Registry
  Phone: 1-888-382-1222
      (Must call from the phone number that you wish to register)
  Web: www.donotcall.gov

- ## First Data Info-Source Donnelley
  ### Marketing, Inc.

  Data Base Operations
  Address: 416 S. Bell
                   Aims, IA 50010
  Phone: (888) 633-4402

Legal Resources:

- ## Center for Law in the Public Interest

  Non profit law firm that specializes in public interest litigation and counseling on public policy.

  Address: 3250 Ocean Park Blvd.,
                   Suite 300
                   Santa Monica, CA 90405
  Phone: (310) 314-1947
  Fax: (310) 314-1957
  E-mail: information@clipi.org
  Web: http://www.clipi.org/

- ## FBI

  Criminal Justice Information Services Division
  J. Edgar Hoover Building

  Address: 935 Pennsylvania Avenue NW
                   Washington, DC 20535-0001
  Phone: (202) 324-3000
  Web: http://www.fbi.gov/

  National Fraud Info Hotline:
  Phone: (800) 876-7060

  If someone has committed a crime using your identity, write to the FBI and ask for your criminal history — include your fingerprints and a check for $18.00 — explain that you are a victim of identity theft.

  IFCC (Internet Fraud Complaint Center) FBI
  Web: www.ifccfbi.gov

- ## National Association of Consumer
  ### Advocates

  Address: 1730 Rhode Island NW, # 805
                   Washington, DC 20036
  Phone: (202) 452-1989
  Fax: (202) 452-0099
  E-mail: info@naca.net
  Web: www.naca.net

- ## National Consumer Law Center, Inc.

  Provides case assistance and legal research. Provides representation for low income and community based organizations.

  Address: 77 Summer St., 10th Floor
                   Boston, MA 02110-1006
  Phone: (617) 542-8010
  Fax: (617) 542-8028
  E-mail: consumerlaw@nclc.org

- ## National Association of
  ### Attorneys General

  Consumer Protection and Charities Counsel

  Address: 750 First Street, N.E. Suite 1100
                   Washington, D.C. 20002
  Phone: (202) 326-6000
  Fax: (202) 408-7014
  Web: http://www.naag.org

- ## U.S. Department of Justice,
  ### Identity Theft Information

  Web: www.usdoj.gov/criminal/
                   fraud/idtheft.html

- ## Attorney Assistance

  Contact your State Bar Association or your local Bar Association for the names of consumer-law attorneys in your area. You may also wish to contact and interview one or more of the attorneys below who are members of the National Consumer Law Center List Serve. These lawyers claim to have experience dealing with identity theft cases and are knowledgeable regarding the Fair Credit Reporting Act. Please know that any resources we provide to you including the name and contact information for these lawyers is not an endorsement but rather helpful information. You must make your own choices as to whether you need legal counsel and whom you believe would be most effective given your circumstances. Please review how to interview an attorney in Chapter Six of this book before you call for legal assistance. The following lawyers have provided their contact information for your review:

Alabama

Firm Name:	Alabama Injury Lawyers, P.C.
Attorney Name:	Penny Hays
Address:	401 Office Park Drive
	Birmingham, AL 35223
Phone:	(205) 870-9848;
	866-86-DEBTS
Fax:	(205) 871-8882
E-mail:	penny@lorantlaw.com
Website:	Lorantlaw.com
Contingency:	Yes
Hourly billing:	Yes

Arizona

Firm Name:	Floyd W. Bybee, PLLC
Attorney Name:	Floyd W. Bybee
Address:	2173 E. Warner Road, Suite 101
	Tempe, AZ 85284
Phone:	(480) 756-8822
Fax:	(480) 756-8882
E-mail:	floyd@bybeelaw.com
Contingency:	Yes

California

Firm Name:	Brennan, Wiener & Simon
Attorney Name:	Robert F. Brennan
Address:	3150 Montrose Ave.
	La Crescenta, CA 91214
Phone:	(818) 249-5291
Fax:	(818) 249-4329
E-mail:	rbrennan@brennanlaw.com
Website:	www.brennanlaw.com
Contingency:	Yes

California

Firm Name:	Mari J. Frank, Esq. & Associates (negotiation, mediation, expert witness testimony)
Attorney Name:	Mari Frank
Address:	28202 Cabot Road, Suite 300
	Laguna Niguel, CA 92677
Phone:	(949) 364-1511
Fax:	(949) 363-7561
E-mail:	contact@identitytheft.org
Website:	www.identitytheft.org
	www.marifrank.com
Hourly billing:	Yes

California

Firm Name:	Kemnitzer, Anderson, Barron & Ogilvie
Attorney Name:	Mark F. Anderson
Address:	445 Bush St. 6th Floor
	San Francisco, CA 94108
Phone:	(415) 623-3784 X101
Fax:	(415) 861-3151
E-mail:	mark@kabolaw.com
Website:	www.kabolaw.com
Contingency:	Yes

California

Attorney Name:	Paul E. Smith
Address:	16776 Bernardo Ctr. Dr. #203
	San Diego, CA 92128
Phone:	(858) 451-3655
E-mail:	psmith@paulsmithlaw.com
Website:	www.paulsmithlaw.com

California

Firm Name:	Trueblood Law Firm
Attorney Name:	Alexander B. Trueblood
Address:	10940 Wilshire Blvd., Ste. 1600
	Los Angeles, CA 90024
Phone:	(310) 443-4139

Florida

Firm Name:	Law Offices of Donald E. Petersen
Attorney Name:	Donald E. Petersen
Address:	P.O. Box 1948
	Orlando, FL 32802-1948
Phone:	(407) 648-9050
E-mail:	petersen@gbronline.com
Contingency:	Yes
Hourly billing:	Yes

Georgia

Firm Name:	Law Office of Lisa D. Wright, LLC
Attorney Name:	Lisa D. Wright
Address:	235 Peachtree Street, NE, Suite 888
	Atlanta, GA 30303
Phone:	(404) 588-1181
Fax:	(404) 588-1182
E-mail:	attorneywright@prodigy.net
Website:	www.attorneylisadwright.com
Contingency:	Yes

Hawaii

Firm Name:	Norman K.K. Lau, A Law Corporation
Attorney Name:	Norman K.K. Lau
Address:	820 Mililani Street, Suite 401 Honolulu, HI 96813
Phone:	(808) 523-6767
Fax:	(808) 523-6769
E-mail:	norm.lau@verizon.net
Contingency:	Yes
Hourly basis:	Yes

Illinois

Firm Name:	Edelman, Combs, Laturner & Goodwin, LLC
Attorney Name:	Daniel A. Edelman
Address:	120 S. LaSalle Street Chicago, IL 60603
Phone:	(312) 739-4200
Fax:	(312) 419-0379
E-mail:	Edcombs@aol.com
Website:	www.edcombs.com
Contingency:	Yes

Illinois (State and Federal), Indiana (Federal), Wisconsin (Federal), Missouri (Federal)

Firm Name:	Krohn & Moss
Attorney Name:	Larry Smith
Address:	120 W. Madison St., 10th Floor Chicago, IL 60602
Phone:	(800) FAIR CREDIT (312) 578-9428 (ext 214)
Fax:	(866) 289-0895
E-mail:	lsmith@consumerlawcenter.com
Website:	www.krohnandmoss.com www.creditreportproblems.com www.800faircredit.com
Contingency:	Yes
Hourly billing:	Yes

Louisiana (in all federal courts), Texas, Arkansas, Michigan, Arizona.

Firm Name:	Bodenheimer, Jones, Szwak & Winchell, LLP
Attorney Name:	David A. Szwak and Mary E. Winchell
Address:	401 Market Street, Ste. 240 American Tower Shreveport, LA 71101
Phone:	(318) 424-1400
Fax:	(318) 424-1476
E-mail:	BJKS1507@aol.com
Website:	www.bjswlaw.com
Contingency:	Yes
Hourly billing:	Yes

Louisiana

Firm Name:	Law Office of Steve R. Conley
Attorney Name:	Steve R. Conley
Address:	3350 Ridgelake Drive, Suite 200 Metairie, LA 70005
Phone:	(504) 734-9804
Fax:	(504) 733-1744
E-mail:	consumerlaw1@yahoo.com
Contingency:	Yes
Hourly billing:	Yes

Maryland, Washington, DC and New York

Firm Name:	Valentine Legal Group, LLC
Attorney Name:	Sonya A. Smith-Valentine
Address:	7319 Hanover Parkway, Suite C Greenbelt, MD 20770
Phone:	(301) 513-9500
Fax:	(301) 513-9565
E-mail:	sonya@valentinelegal.com
Website:	www. valentinelegal.com
Contingency:	Yes
Hourly billing:	Yes

Michigan

Firm Name:	Lyngklip & Taub Consumer Law Group, PLC
Attorney Name:	Adam G. Taub & Ian B. Lyngklip
Address:	24500 Northwestern Hwy. #206 Southfield, MI 48075
Phone:	(248) 746-3790
E-mail:	adamlaw@pop.net and ianlaw@pop.net
Contingency:	Yes

Michigan

Firm Name:	Law Office of Phillip C. Rogers
Attorney Name:	Phillip C. Rogers
Address:	40 Pearl Street, NW, Suite 336 Grand Rapids, MI 49503-3026
Phone:	(616) 776-1176
Fax:	(616) 776-0037
E-mail:	ConsumerLawyer@aol.com
Contingency:	Yes
Hourly billing:	Yes

Minnesota

Firm Name:	Consumer Justice Center
Attorney Name:	John H. Goolsby
Address:	342 East County Road D
	Little Canada, MN 55117
Phone:	(651) 770-9707
Fax:	(651) 770-5830
E-mail:	goolsbycjc@hotmail.com
Website:	www.consumerjusticecenter.com
Contingency:	Yes
Hourly billing:	Yes

Minnesota and Wisconsin

Firm Name:	Thomas J. Lyons & Associates
Attorney Name:	Thomas J. Lyons, Sr
Address:	342 East County Road D
	Little Canada, MN 55117
Phone:	(651) 770-9707
Fax:	(651) 770-5830
E-mail:	tlyons@lyonslawfirm.com
Website:	www. lyonslawfirm.com
Contingency:	Yes
Hourly billing:	Yes

Minnesota

Firm Name:	Thomas J. Lyons & Associates
Attorney Name:	Sue Wolsfeld
Address:	342 East County Road D
	Little Canada, MN 55117
Phone:	(651) 770-9707
Fax:	(651) 770-5830
E-mail:	swolsfeld@lynslawfirm.com
Website:	www.lyonslawfirm.com
Contingency:	Yes
Hourly billing:	Yes

Mississippi

Firm Name:	Webster Gresham & Kittell
Attorney Name:	Christopher E. Kittell
Address:	P.O. Drawer 760
	144 Sunflower Avenue
	Clarksdale, MS 38614
Phone:	(662) 624-5408
E-mail:	cekittell@wgklawyers.com

Missouri, Illinois, Kansas and Oklahoma

Firm Name:	Gateway Legal Services, Inc.
Attorney Name:	Debra Lumpkins
Address:	200 N. Broadway, Ste. 950
	St. Louis, MO 63102
Phone:	(314) 534-0404
Fax:	(314) 652-8308
E-mail:	dlumpkins@gatewaylegal.org
Website:	www.gatewaylegal.org
Contingency:	Yes (with hourly fee requested of defendant)

Nevada

Firm Name:	Law Office of Craig B. Friedberg
Attorney Name:	Craig Friedberg
Address:	3745 Edison Avenue
	Las Vegas, NV 89121
Phone:	(702) 435-7968
Fax:	(702) 435-6659
E-mail:	cbfriedberg@justice.com
Website:	www.firms.findlaw.com/attcbf/
Contingency:	Yes
Hourly billing:	Yes

Nevada, New York, Connecticut

Firm Name:	Law Offices of Mitch Gliner
Attorney Name:	Mitch Gliner
Address:	3017 West Charelston Blvd., Suite 95
	Las Vegas, NV 89119
Phone:	(702) 870-8700
E-mail:	gliner_mitchell@msn.com
Contingency:	Yes
Hourly billing:	No

New Mexico

Firm Name:	Feferman & Warren
Attorneys:	Richard Feferman, Susan Warren, Rob Treinen
Address:	300 Central Ave, SW, Suite 2000 East
	Albuquerque, NM 87102
Phone:	(505) 243 7773
Fax:	(505) 243 6663
E-mail:	consumer@nmconsumer warriors.com
Website:	www.nmconsumer warriors.com
Contingency:	Yes
Hourly billing:	Yes

New York

Firm Name:	Fishman & Neil, LLP
Attorney Name:	James B. Fishman
Address:	305 Broadway Suite 900
	New York, NY 10007
Phone:	(212) 897 5840
Fax:	(212) 897 5841
E-mail:	JamesR626@aol.com

Website: www.consumeratty.net
Contingency: Yes
Hourly billing: Yes

New York and California

Firm Name: Fishman & Neil, LLP
Attorney Name: Kevin Mallon
Address: 305 Broadway, Suite 900
                 New York, NY 11102
Phone: (212) 822-1474
Fax: (212) 897-5841
E-mail: kmallon@lawsuites.net
Website: consumeratty.net
Contingency: Yes
Hourly billing: Yes

Ohio

Firm Name: Murray & Murray Co., L.P.A.
Attorney Name: Sylvia A. Goldsmith
Address: 111 East Shoreline Drive
                 Sandusky, OH 44870
Phone: (419) 624-3000
Fax: (419) 624-0707
E-mail: sylvia@murrayandmurray.com

Oregon

Firm Name: Robert S. Sola P.C.
Attorney Name: Robert S. Sola
Address: 8835 SW Canyon Lane,
                 Suite 130
                 Portland, OR 97225
Phone: (503) 295-6880
Fax: (503) 291-9172
E-mail: rssola@msn.com
Contingency: Yes

Pennsylvania

Attorney Name: Clayton S. Morrow,
Address: 304 Ross Street, 7th Floor
                 Pittsburgh, PA 15219
Phone: (412) 281-1250
Fax: (412) 209-0658
E-mail: cmorrow@allconsumerlaw.com
Website: www.allconsumerlaw.com
Contingency: Yes
Hourly billing: Yes

Texas

Firm Name: Mark L. Aschermann,
                 Attorney at Law
Attorney Name: Mark L. Aschermann

Address: 3730 Kirby Drive, Suite 520
                 Houston, TX 77098
Phone: (713) 942-0808
Fax: (713) 942-0449
E-mail: aschermann.law@swbell.net
Website: www.divorceyourcredit.com
Contingency: Yes

Texas

Firm Name: Law Office of Jerry Jarzombek
Attorney Name: Jerry Jarzombek
Address: 714 W. Magnolia
                 Fort Worth, TX 76104
E-mail: jerryjj@airmail.net
Contingency: Yes
Hourly billing: Yes

Texas

Firm Name: Law Office of Craig Jordan
Attorney Name: Craig Jordan
Address: 1845 Woodall Rodgers Freeway,
                 Suite 1750
                 Dallas, TX 75201
Phone: (214) 855-9355
Fax: (214) 855-9389
E-mail: craig@warybuyer.com
Website: www.warybuyer.com
Contingency: Yes
Hourly billing: Yes

Texas and Tennessee

Firm Name: Law Office of James T. McMillen
Attorney Name: Jim McMillen
Address: 6318 St. Denis
                 Corpus Christi, TX 78414
E-mail: Jim@jamesmcmillen.com
Website: www.consumerlawoffice.com
Contingency: Yes
Hourly billing: Yes

Texas

Firm Name: Law Office of Russell
                 Van Beustring, P.C.
Attorney Name: Russell Van Beustring
Address: 9525 Katy Freeway, Suite 415
                 Houston, TX 77024
Phone: (713) 973-6650
Fax: (713) 973-7811
E-mail: russell@beustring.com
Website: http://www.beustring.com
Contingency: Yes

Virginia and North Carolina

Firm Name: Consumer Litigation Associates
Attorney Name: Leonard A. Bennett
Address: 12515 Warwick Blvd
                        Newport News, VA 23606
Phone: (757) 930 3660
Fax: (757) 930 3660
E-mail: lenbennett@cox.net
Contingency: Yes

Wisconsin

Firm Name: Consumer Justice Law Center
Attorney Name: DeVonna Joy
Address: P.O. Box 51
                        Big Bend, WI 53150
Phone: (262) 662-3982
Fax: (262) 662-0504
E-mail: djlaw@wi.rr.com
Contingency: Yes
Hourly billing: Yes

Privacy Newsletters

• Privacy Journal

P.O. Box 28577
Providence, RI 02908
Phone: (401) 274-7861
Web: www.privacyjournal.net
E-mail: orders@privacyjournal.net

• Privacy Newsletter

P.O. Box 8206
Philadelphia, PA 19101-8206
E-mail: privacy@mindspring.com

• Privacy Times

P.O. Box 302
Cabin John, MD 20818
Phone: (301) 229-7002
Web: www.privacytimes.com

Privacy Resources and Organizations

• Center for Media Education.

A national non-profit organization dedicated to improving the quality of electronic media, especially on the behalf of children and families. Provides guides, reports, and other information on children's and consumer privacy.

E-mail: cme@cme.org

• Coalition Against Unsolicited Commercial Email.

CAUCE is an all-volunteer, entirely Web-based organization, created by Netizens to advocate for a legislative solution to the problem of UCE (spam). CAUCE began as a discussion group called SPAM-LAW, formed of members who felt that legislation was necessary to stop spam from choking the life out of the Internet.

President: Edward Cherlin
E-mail: comments@cauce.org
Web: www.cauce

• Computer Professionals for Social Responsibility.

A national membership organization of people concerned about the impact of technology on society. CPSR sponsors working groups on civil liberties, working in the computer industry and others.

Address: PO Box 717
                   Palo Alto, CA 94302
Phone: (650) 322-3778
Fax: (650) 322-4748
E-mail: cpsr@cpsr.org or
                   cpsr-info@cpsr.org
Web: www.cpsr.org

• Consumer Project on Technology.

The CPT is currently focusing on intellectual property rights, healthcare, electronic commerce and competition policy.

Director: James Love
Address: Box 19367
                   Washington, DC 20036
Phone: (202) 387-8030
Fax: (202) 234-5176

• Consumers Against Supermarket Privacy Invasion and Numbering.

CASPIAN is a national Web-based organization opposing the current trends of supermarkets to require customer information in order to receive discounts.

Founder: Katherine Albrecht
E-mail   kma@nocards.org
Web: www.nocards.org

- **Electronic Frontier Foundation.**

Publishes newsletters, Internet Guidebooks and other documents, provides mailing lists and other online forums, and hosts a large electronic document archive.

Address:	1550 Bryant Street, Ste 725, San Francisco, CA 94103-4832
Phone:	(415) 436-9333
Fax:	(415) 436-9993
E-mail:	info@eff.org
	ask@eff.org

- **Electronic Privacy Information Center.**

EPIC conducts litigation, sponsors conferences, produces reports, publishes the EPIC Alert, and leads campaigns on privacy issues.

EPIC Executive Director:	Marc Rotenberg
Address:	1718 Connecticut Avenue, NW, Suite 200 Washington, DC 20009
Phone:	(202) 483-1140
E-mail:	info@epic.org
Web:	www.epic.org

- **Privacy Coalition.**

A nonpartisan coalition of consumer, civil liberties, educational, family, library, labor, and technology organizations in support of legislation that effectively protects personal privacy.

E-mail:	coalition@privacy.org

Appendix C

Techniques for Handling the Stress of Identity Theft

Dealing with stress, as you may have already learned, is a major problem for victims of identity theft. No matter what's happening right now, you'll be much calmer and happier if you keep reminding yourself *attitude is everything*. In short, it's not what life does to you; it's your perception and reaction that determines the outcome. You don't need to think of yourself as a victim even if you are victimized.

Making a commitment to stay calm and centered is not always easy to do. But it is do-able. If you already engage in de-stressing activities such as running, meditating, yoga, or prayer work, continue to do what works for you. Make sure you take care of yourself — exercise, eat healthy foods, take vitamins, and practice mental relaxation.

The stress of identity theft may cause post-traumatic stress disorder. If you can't eat or find yourself compulsively eating, have trouble sleeping, feel paranoid, or suffer vast mood swings, you're not going crazy — you're just experiencing a normal reaction to an abnormal situation. Consider seeing a psychological counselor for short-term therapy and/or seeking support through a local victim-assistance program, through your church, or the Identity Theft Resource Center www.idtheftcenter.org, which is listed among the resources in Appendix B. And, of course, ask for the help and support of your friends and family.

In addition, this appendix will offer several other ways you can seek to reduce stress. Included are: **(1)** Meditative Exercise **(2)** Suggestions For De-Escalating Conflict **(3)** Positive Thoughts on Serenity.

1. Meditative exercise

Sitting down in a quiet place to renew a few times during the day, especially in the morning and early evening, can be very helpful. Here is one method you might try:

How to use this exercise

- Read the following guided meditation to yourself and change or add any words that would be more comfortable for you.

- Get a cassette tape recorder and find a very quiet place to gently and softly read this exercise onto the tape. If you wish, you can play soft music in the background.

- Listen to your recorded exercise in a quiet and undisturbed place. You may take it with you in the car, but do *not* listen to it while driving. Use it at the office or wherever you can where you won't be disturbed.

A guided calming exercise

Close your eyes now, and sit very comfortably. Relax your body now, and feel each muscle let go of all tenseness. All stress is gently dissolving, as you just melt into your chair.

- You feel your toes getting heavier. Your feet are heavy and warm. Your legs are heavy and warm. The trunk of your body is heavy and warm, you're just resting peacefully in the chair. Your right arm is heavy and warm. Your left arm is heavy and warm. Your head is light and cool.

- You now direct your attention to your breathing, deeply, slowly — inhaling light and serenity. Take another deep breath — breathing in healing, soothing energy, and breathing out all negativity and discord. Take a moment now by yourself to just listen to your breathing… (Pause for a moment.)

- Feel yourself slowing down and centering within. You feel in perfect balance, totally within yourself. Release all concerns.

- Now turn your attention, in your mind's eye, to the area of your solar plexus. Visualize a dime-sized, golden light beginning to grow in that part of your body. It enlarges now, and it's filling the center of your body, moving up all the way to your chest — down to your legs — all the way down to your feet — up to your neck — outward to your arms. This golden light is expanding, as now it fills your head as well. Any discomfort in your body is soothed, and healed, and cured by this light — this healing light.

- As this gentle energy grows and fills beyond your body, it brightens. Your entire body is filled with a warm, pulsating, soothing energy. Your entire being is brilliantly lit with this calming light. As you see this light fill you and move around you, and go beyond the limits of your body, you may feel a gentle tingling, you may see changing colors: soft pink, and white, and gentle blue — any color that feels right for you. Take a moment to feel vibrations and see those soothing colors, as they heal and calm and bring peace to your mind and body.

- You are glowing, and at complete peace. You feel content, tranquil, calm and peaceful. There is a higher purpose to all challenging experiences in life.

- You are calm and confident. You have experienced challenges, but you are not a victim. As you breathe easily and slowly, you visualize harmony and understanding in all of your communications. You are in perfect balance, as you receive clear guidance. You are aligned and in harmony with body, mind, and spirit in all that you do.

- You feel and see a loving brilliance in and around you. You sense a peaceful energy permeate every cell of your substance. There is serenity all around you. Visualize a current of calmness enfold you. Take a moment now to just bathe in this radiance. Take a deep breath, breathing in that radiance, and breathing out only peace and tranquility.

- Now, gently return to the present time and place. Gently allow sensations of awareness and awakeness to permeate your body, from the tip of your toes, gently upward to the top of your head. Slowly move your toes, your fingers, and any other part of your body that will help you to awaken. Keeping your eyes closed, enjoy a sense of renewal, balance, centeredness, and increased energy. You feel alive and awakened. You feel a new confidence to deal with all of the challenges you need to address. You know that everything happens for a greater good.

- As you delicately open your eyes, you feel a flow of synergy all around you. You are renewed and revitalized to take all actions necessary to resolve any difficulty or discord in your life.

- As you return now to the present reality, you are assured of who you are and feel confident to face your day knowing that all is well.

2. Suggestions for de-escalating conflict when dealing with identity theft and various agencies

(The following is adapted from the article *De-Escalating Conflict* by Mari J. Frank in *Sharing Ideas Magazine* July, 1997. Copyright Mari J. Frank, 1997.)

We all occasionally deal with hostile or insensitive people. Such negativity causes us stress and escalates conflict — unless we have strategies to deflect anger appropriately. The key is to separate the people and our emotions from the problem. Instinctively, human beings react to conflict by fighting, fleeing, submitting, or freezing — none of which resolves anything. Meeting hostility with anger just fuels the flame, especially when dealing with bureaucracies.

Our goal in intense situations should be to respond proactively in a way that doesn't hook us into the whirlwind of another's anger or fear. As karate teaches: *"If someone gets you mad, (s)he CONTROLS you."*

When anger overtakes reason, our ability to think clearly is greatly impaired. Our conscious self is overridden, and we lose control. That's when we make *"the greatest speeches we will ever regret!"*

The following approach can be used any time someone attacks you, your concerns, or your actions. To help remember this 10-step strategy, the mnemonic **HARD LOVING** may be helpful.

H - HALT

Stop yourself immediately from saying anything in response to an offensive remark. Don't display any emotions, just breathe slowly and LISTEN. If you react to hostility in a like manner, you lose credibility. Any defensive posture will invite attacks, and you won't get your needs met.

A - ANGER CONTROL

Immediately direct your mind to what's happening to you physically. The physical reaction for negative emotions is very strong. Some typical reactions are: dryness in the throat, pain in the solar plexus, cold or sweaty hands, rigid shoulders, tightness in the neck, etc. Take a moment right now and close your eyes (this will allow you to focus). Imagine someone reprimanding you or yelling at you. What is happening in your body? When you identify your own physical reaction to verbal battle, you become conscious of your auto-reaction. The first time you analyze this it may be difficult to decipher what's happening to you. But once you know how you react physically, you have valuable information because you can work on overriding the response.

R - REVERSE REACTION

Your physical reaction can be reversed by a conscious decision. Knowing this frees you from being a victim of your emotions. For example: If you feel stabbing in the solar plexus, "remove the knife." Reverse cold hands by "placing" them in warmed gloves. "Feel" refreshing water in your dry throat. Do whatever is appropriate for you. Deliberately take slow, deep breaths until you are calm and centered.

Because we physically react to hostility similarly each time, your remedy will become increasingly more effective. With practice, this calming stage will take only a split second, and you will be able to detach physically.

D - DISENGAGE

Only when you have detached physically first, are you ready to disengage mentally. Once you are calm, focus on the *issue*, not the person's behavior. Remember, his/her or your perceptions are not truth, but interpretations of the facts. You'll never be able to convince him/her to see your way through argument or by acting defensively when he/she is in this angry state. Release any need to be right. If you disengage from opposition, you will not be engulfed in hostility and lose control or credibility.

L - LISTEN EFFECTIVELY

Listen actively to every word. Focus only on hearing, *not* on your response. Look at your antagonist directly or listen carefully if you are on the phone. Don't resist in *mind* or *body* anything they say. (This does **not** mean you agree. You are just recognizing he/she has a different perspective.)

This approach is the opposite of what the angry person expects. Your courteous, non contentious listening will diffuse the hostility automatically. Your listening demonstrates that you're receptive to understanding. This, in turn, promotes a reciprocal receptivity. You *both* gain information, which gives you power to resolve the real issues.

O - OPENLY MIRROR

No matter how abrasive the other person is, you must restate what was said to you *without* a nasty tone of voice. Your neutral response may be *"You stated that you believe I owe this bill and that I am using fraud as a way of not paying this bill. I understand that you are distrustful. If I were in your position, I would also be suspicious. It is most frustrating for me as a victim, and I am distrustful as well."*

(This way you're legitimizing — but not agreeing with — his accusation.)

V - VOICE OPEN ENDED QUESTIONS

Follow up a restated hostile remark by voicing an *open-ended* question to refocus on the issue at hand. For example: *"It is understandable that you are distrustful. How can we quickly resolve this so that you will have what you need and I can get my problem handled?"* This opens the door for you to explain your side of the issue.

Information questions are simple but formidable: What? When? Where? How? *Non*-intimidating phrases such as, *"allow us to understand the basis for your position,"* or *"clarify for me what you believe would be fair,"* or *"tell me more about your concerns in assisting me."*

These greatly empower the questioner and listener. This is *not* psychological counseling but a skill to transform hostility effectively. The answers you get will provide you with powerful de-escalation remedies.

I - IMAGINE SOLUTIONS

Jointly brainstorm options for solutions. Engage your counterpart in creative problem solving. All parties need to share:

(1) What they believe would be fair under the circumstances;

(2) What the parties really need (the basis for their position); and

(3) What would resolve the issue for all concerned.

N - NON-AGGRESSION

Talk calmly, slowly, and in a non-aggressive tone. No matter how aggressive the other party is, stay conscious and do *not* react to the anger. Stay focused.

G - GO AWAY

Remove yourself with dignity from the conversation before you lose your respectability. If all else fails, get off the phone or leave the business with finesse, giving the other party a chance to return to discussions without groveling.

If you don't have to deal with the person again, you have the choice of not resuming the conversation. Find a supervisor to deal with. If you must deal with this same person again, put the past behind you and renew with Step 8: *Imagine Solutions.*

Remember you can prevent conflict from escalating by staying conscious and turning adversity into powerful solutions. It's not easy, but the rewards are empowering.

3. Thoughts on Serenity

We all have the power to shift our attitudes about any situation. We need to recognize that every hardship is a growth opportunity in disguise. We must trust that a greater good will come later (sometimes *much* later!) and that we can recover from the initial devastation, and refocus with a problem-solving approach. In short, we can choose faith instead of despair. We can let go of what we can't control, and take action to change what is within our power.

I wrote the simple poem on page 160 to express these truths. I share it with you as a gift of my hope for your serenity.

With hopeful thoughts for your peace,
Mari J. Frank

About The Author

Mari Frank, an attorney, professor, expert witness, and professional trainer in private practice in Laguna Niguel, California, has worked in the district attorney's office, practiced law in insurance defense, and has had a general civil law practice. As a mediator, she has successfully resolved thousands of disputes. Ms. Frank is a Certified Continuing Education Trainer for the State Bar of California, has been a law professor, and currently teaches courses at the University of California. She received her bachelor's degree from the University of Wisconsin (Madison), her master's degree from Hofstra University, and her law degree from Western State University College of Law. She received her post law school negotiation and mediation training from McGeorge School of Law, and Harvard Law School.

As a privacy expert, Ms. Frank has authored the *Identity Theft Survival Kit, From Victim to Victor: A Step-By-Step Guide For Ending The Nightmare Of Identity Theft (First and Second Edition with CD)*, and *Safeguard Your Identity: Protect Yourself With A Personal Privacy Audit,* and Co-Authored *Privacy Piracy* with Beth Givens, the Director of the Privacy Rights Clearinghouse. Ms. Frank's own identity was assumed by an impostor who stole thousands of dollars, and even assumed her profession as a lawyer. But Mari refused to be defeated as a victim; instead she chose to help thousands of victims with her web site, books, legislative work, and privacy advocacy.

She has appeared on *Dateline, 48 Hours, NBC,* and *ABC Nightly News, Investigative Reports, The O'Reilly Factor, Connie Chung Tonight,* dozens of other national television programs, and almost 200 radio shows. She has been featured in the *New York Times, The Los Angeles Times, U.S. News and World Report, Your Money Magazine, The Wall Street Journal, The Washington Post, The Chicago Tribune, The*

American Bar Journal, and many other national publications.

Ms. Frank testified several times before the U.S. Senate, the California Legislature, the Federal Trade Commission, the Social Security Administration, and other agencies. She presented a televised C-Span speech at the White House for members of the legislature and former President Bill Clinton in 1999 regarding financial privacy. She is a sheriff reserve on the High Tech Crime Unit, in Orange County, California. She serves on the Advisory Board of the State of California Office of Privacy Protection, the Identity Theft Resource Center, and she is a consultant for the governmental Office of Victims of Crimes. Ms. Frank provides expert testimony, consulting, and training programs on privacy and identity theft for law enforcement, lawyers, governmental agencies, and national corporations.

Ms. Frank recently presented a live seminar for PBS Television entitled "Identity Theft: Protecting Yourself in the Information Age." This nationally aired program included a pledge drive for public television. Two of her books, *Safeguard Your Identity: Protect Yourself With A Personal Privacy Audit,* and *From Victim To Victor: A Step-By-Step Guide For Ending The Nightmare Of Identity Theft,* Second Edition with CD, and the video of her live presentation, served as pledge gifts when the viewing audience called in donations to support Public Television. For more information about privacy and identity theft, Ms. Frank's background, services and other publications, please visit:

www.identitytheft.org
and
www.MariFrank.com.

You may also contact her at:

Mari J. Frank, Esq. and Associates
28202 Cabot Road, Suite 300
Laguna Niguel, California 92677

Phone: 949-364-1511
Fax: 949-363-7561

To order books from Porpoise Press, Inc; call 800-725-0807; or visit Identity Theft Prevention and Survival at www.identitytheft.org.

SERENITY ON THE SEA OF LIFE

by Mari J. Frank

As I sail upon the uncertain sea of Life
An inner voice says that I am free to *choose* happiness or strife.
Though gusty winds and crashing waves are not within my powers—
I faithfully accept that threatening storms may last for many hours.

With my attitude, tiller, and mind within my control,
I trust the inner guidance to gently lead my soul.
I release flapping sails, turn the tillers with might—
Staying vigilant, and flexible through the dark night.

Believing that challenge brings Spirit's divine gift,
I focus on non-resistance and give my heart a lift.
Keeping my attention on the truth and the bright,
I'm assured that the outcome will bring peace, serenity and light.

When the turbulence of life's sea brings you fear or pain
Be still, and let God's love dissolve your stress and strain.
May all your adversity be transformed into great opportunity—
To give you harmony, happiness, prosperity, and global unity.